THE CAMBRIDGE COMPANION TO CARYL CHURCHILL

Caryl Churchill's plays are internationally performed, studied and acclaimed by practitioners, theatre scholars, critics and audiences alike. With fierce imagination the plays dramatize the anxieties and terrors of contemporary life. This *Companion* presents new scholorship on Churchill's extraordinary and groundbreaking work. Chapters explore a cluster of major plays in relation to pressing social topics – ecological crisis, sexual politics, revolution, terror and selfhood – providing close readings of texts in their theatrical, theoretical and historical contexts. These topic-based essays are intercalated with other essays that delve into Churchill's major collaborations, her performance innovations and her influences on a new generation of playwrights. Contributors explore Churchill's career-long experimentation – her risk-taking that has reinvigorated the stage, both formally and politically. Providing a new critical platform for the study of a theatrical career that spans almost fifty years, the *Companion* pays fresh attention to Churchill's poetic precision, dark wit and inexhaustible creativity.

ELAINE ASTON is Professor of Contemporary Performance at Lancaster University.
ELIN DIAMOND is Professor of English and Comparative Literature at Rutgers University.

A complete list of books in the series is at the back of this book

THE CAMBRIDGE COMPANION TO
CARYL CHURCHILL

EDITED BY
ELAINE ASTON AND ELIN DIAMOND

CAMBRIDGE UNIVERSITY PRESS
Cambridge, New York, Melbourne, Madrid, Cape Town, Singapore, São Paulo, Delhi

Cambridge University Press
The Edinburgh Building, Cambridge CB2 8RU, UK

Published in the United States of America by Cambridge University Press, New York

www.cambridge.org
Information on this title: www.cambridge.org/9780521728942

First published 2009

Printed in the United Kingdom at the University Press, Cambridge

A catalogue record for this publication is available from the British Library

ISBN 978-0-521-49322-2 Hardback
ISBN 978-0-521-72894-2 Paperback

CONTENTS

NOTES ON CONTRIBUTORS

ELAINE ASTON is Professor of Contemporary Performance at Lancaster University. Her authored studies include *Sarah Bernhardt: A French Actress on the English Stage* (1989); *Theatre as Sign-System* (1991, with George Savona); *An Introduction to Feminism and Theatre* (1995); *Caryl Churchill* (1997/2001); *Feminist Theatre Practice* (1999) and *Feminist Views on the English Stage* (2003). Her edited work includes four volumes of plays by women; *The Cambridge Companion to Modern British Women Playwrights* (2000, with Janelle Reinelt); *Feminist Futures: Theatre, Performance, Theory* (2006, with Geraldine Harris), and *Staging International Feminisms* (2007, with Sue-Ellen Case). Her most recent monograph is *Performance Practice and Process: Contemporary [Women] Practitioners* (2008, with Geraldine Harris). She currently serves as associate editor of *Theatre Research International.*

ELIN DIAMOND is Professor of English and Comparative Literature at Rutgers University. She is the author of *Unmaking Mimesis: Essays On Feminism And Theater* (1997) and *Pinter's Comic Play* (1985), and editor of *Performance And Cultural Politics* (1996). Her essays on performance and feminist theory have appeared in *Theatre Journal, ELH, Discourse, TDR, Modern Drama, Kenyon Review, Cahiers Renaud-Barrault, Art And Cinema, Maska,* and in anthologies in the USA, UK, France, South Korea and India. She is currently at work on a new book on Modernism and performance.

R. DARREN GOBERT is Associate Professor of English and Theatre Studies at York University, Toronto, where he specializes in comparative Western drama (especially modern and contemporary), and dramatic and performance theory. He has published articles on Bertolt Brecht, Michel Marc Bouchard, the classicist Jacob Bernays and Molière. He is on the Editorial Advisory Board, and is Book Review Editor, of *Modern Drama*. His special issue of that journal, on contemporary playwriting from the UK, appeared in fall 2007. Also a theatre practitioner, he has directed plays by, among others, Albee, Beckett and Chekhov.

JEAN E. HOWARD is George Delacorte Professor in the Humanities at Columbia University and Chair of the Department of English and Comparative Literature. At

Columbia she has also served as Chair of the Institute for Research on Women and Gender and as Vice Provost for Diversity. She is one of the four editors of *The Norton Shakespeare*. Her books include *Shakespeare's Art of Orchestration: Stagecraft and Audience Response*, *The Stage and Social Struggle in Early Modern England*, *Engendering a Nation: A Feminist Account of Shakespeare's English Histories* (with Phyllis Rackin), and *Theater of a City: The Places of London Comedy 1599–1642*. In November of 2008 the latter won the Bernard Hewitt Award for the Year's Outstanding Book of Theater History.

MARY LUCKHURST is Chair of Modern Drama and the co-founder of the new Department of Theatre, Film and TV at the University of York. Her published works include *Theatre and Celebrity in Britain, 1660–2000* (2005), *Dramaturgy: A Revolution in Theatre* (2006), *A Companion to Modern British and Irish Drama* (2006), and *A Concise Companion to Contemporary British and Irish Drama* (2007). She has published many essays on contemporary dramatists such as Crimp, Kane, McDonagh and Pinter, and is currently working on a monograph entitled 'Death and Terror on the Modern Stage'. She is also a director and most recently staged Churchill 's *Far Away* and *Mad Forest* at the York Theatre Royal. In 2006 she was made a National Teaching Fellow by the Higher Education Academy for her outstanding contributions to teaching and scholarship in the fields of drama and of actor and director training.

SHEILA RABILLARD is Associate Professor of English, University of Victoria, Canada. She has edited a collection of essays on Churchill and published articles on modern drama and performance in a number of scholarly journals including *Theatre Journal*, *Modern Drama*, *Theater*, *Essays in Theatre*, *Criticism*, *Journal of American Drama and Theatre*, *Cycnos* and *Australasian Drama Studies*.

DAN REBELLATO is Professor of Contemporary Theatre at Royal Holloway, University of London. He has published widely on British theatre including *1956 and All That* (1999), and essays on Mark Ravenhill, Sarah Kane, David Greig, Caryl Churchill, David Hare, theatrical violence, the state of the nation play, Terence Rattigan and Noel Coward. *Theatre & Globalization* (2009) appears in the 'Theatre&' series that he is co-editing with Jen Harvie. He is a contributing editor to *New Theatre Quarterly* and an associate editor of *Contemporary Theatre Review*, for whom he has edited two special issues, on Theatre and Globalization and on the Broadway Musical. He is also a playwright whose plays have been performed in Britain, Europe and America and include *Showstopper, Erskine May, Here's What I Did With My Body One Day, Outright Terror Bold and Brilliant, A Modest Adjustment* and *Futurology*.

JANELLE REINELT is Professor of Theatre and Performance at University of Warwick in the UK. She was President of the International Federation for Theatre Research (2004–2007) and former Vice President for Research and Publications of the Association for Theatre in Higher Education (ATHE). She is also a former editor of *Theatre Journal*. Her books include *After Brecht: British Epic Theater* (1994), *Crucibles of Crisis: Performing Social Change* (1996), *Critical Theory and Performance* with Joseph Roach (1992), *The Performance of Power* with Sue-Ellen Case (1994), and *The Cambridge Companion to Modern British Women Playwrights* with Elaine Aston (2000).

LIBBY WORTH is a Senior Lecturer in Theatre Practice at Royal Holloway, University of London. She trained in dance with San Francisco-based artist Anna Halprin and co-authored a book with Helen Poynor on Halprin's work for the Routledge Performance Practitioner series. She has published articles in *Contemporary Theatre Review* on Halprin and Australian writer/director Jenny Kemp and for Arts Based Educational Research on the making of a physical theatre performance concerning young male suicide. Her current research focuses on stage directions for movement in work by Peter Handke, Caryl Churchill, David Lan and Jenny Kemp.

NOTE ON EDITIONS

The majority of Caryl Churchill's plays have been anthologized either by Methuen or Nick Hern Books. For ease of reference, chapters in the *Companion* cite the collected editions of Churchill's work. Exceptions are where a single play edition is used to refer to notes or illustrations that do not appear in the main published collections. Full details of all editions can be found in the Select bibliography.

CHRONOLOGY

1938	Caryl Churchill born in London.
1948	Family move out to Montreal, Canada. Educated at Trafalgar School for Girls in Montreal.
1957–60	Studies English Language and Literature at Lady Margaret Hall, University of Oxford. Student production of *Downstairs*, a one-act play (1958) which went on to the Sunday Times / National Union of Students Drama Festival (1959).
1960	*Having a Wonderful Time* performed at the amateur Questors Theatre, London.
1961	Student radio production of *You've No Need to Be Frightened.* Marriage to barrister David Harter.
1962	*Easy Death*, Oxford Experimental Theatre Club, Oxford Playhouse. *The Ants*, first professional radio broadcast on BBC Radio 3, produced by Michael Bakewell.
1963–9	Birth of three sons.
1967	*Lovesick* broadcast on BBC Radio 3, directed by John Tydeman.
1968	*Identical Twins* broadcast on BBC Radio 3, directed by John Tydeman.
1971	*Abortive* and *Not Not Not Not Not Enough Oxygen* broadcast on BBC Radio3, both directed by John Tydeman.
1972	Writes *The Hospital at the Time of the Revolution* – unperformed stage play.

	Schreber's Nervous Illness and *Henry's Past* broadcast on BBC Radio 3, both directed by John Tydeman. *Schreber's Nervous Illness* performed at King's Head Theatre, London (one-man show). *The Judge's Wife* broadcast on BBC 2 television, directed by James Fearman. First professional stage production, *Owners*, Royal Court Theatre Upstairs, London, directed by Nicolas Wright.
1973	*Perfect Happiness* broadcast on BBC Radio 3, directed by John Tydeman. *Owners* performed in Mercer-Shaw Theatre, New York.
1974	*Turkish Delight* broadcast on BBC 2 television, directed by Herbert Wise.
1974–5	Writer in Residence, Royal Court Theatre.
1975	*Objections to Sex and Violence*, Royal Court Theatre Downstairs, directed by John Tydeman. *Moving Clocks Go Slow*, Royal Court Theatre Upstairs, directed by John Ashford. *Perfect Happiness*, stage performance at Soho Poly, London, directed by Suzanna Capon. *Save it for the Minister*, with Mary O'Malley and Cherry Potter, broadcast on BBC 2 television.
1976	*Light Shining in Buckinghamshire*, Joint Stock, Traverse Theatre, Edinburgh; on tour, and Royal Court Theatre Upstairs, directed by Max Stafford-Clark. *Vinegar Tom*, Monstrous Regiment, Humberside Theatre, Hull; on tour and ICA and Half Moon theatres, London, directed by Pam Brighton.
1977	*Traps*, Royal Court Theatre Upstairs, directed by John Ashford.
1977–8	*Floorshow*, Monstrous Regiment, cabaret, on tour, scripted with Bryony Lavery, Michelene Wandor and David Bradford.
1978	*The After-Dinner Joke* broadcast on BBC 1 television, directed by Colin Bucksey. *The Legion Hall Bombing* broadcast on BBC 1 television in censored version, directed by Roland Joffé. Writes unperformed stage play *Seagulls*.

1979 *Cloud Nine*, Joint Stock, Dartington College of Arts; on tour and Royal Court Theatre, directed by Max Stafford-Clark.

1980 *Three More Sleepless Nights*, Soho Poly and Royal Court Theatre Upstairs, directed by Les Waters.
Cloud Nine revival at Royal Court, co-directed by Max Stafford-Clark and Les Waters.

1981 *Cloud Nine*, American premiere at Lucille Lortel Theatre, New York, directed by Tommy Tune.

1982 *Crimes* broadcast on BBC 1 television, directed by Stuart Burge.
Top Girls, Royal Court Theatre Downstairs, directed by Max Stafford-Clark. Transfers to the Joseph Papp Public Theater, New York.
Cloud Nine wins Obie award.

1983 *Fen*, Joint Stock, University of Essex, Colchester; Almeida and Royal Court Theatres, London, directed by Les Waters. New York transfer to Public Theater.
Top Girls wins Obie Award.

1984 *Softcops* (written in 1978) staged by the RSC at the Barbican Pit, London, directed by Howard Davies.
Midday Sun (with Geraldine Pilgrim and Peter Brooks) ICA, London, directed by John Ashford.
Fen wins Susan Smith Blackburn Award.

1985 First collection of plays published by Methuen.

1986 *A Mouthful of Birds*, with David Lan, Joint Stock, Birmingham Repertory Theatre; on tour, and Royal Court Theatre, directed by Ian Spink (choreography) and Les Waters.

1987 *Serious Money*, Royal Court Theatre, directed by Max Stafford-Clark. London West End transfer to Wyndham's and New York transfer to Public Theater.
Serious Money wins several awards including an Obie Award, Susan Smith Blackburn Award, Olivier Award for Best Play of 1987, Evening Standard Award for Best Comedy and Best Play Award from Plays and Players.

1988 *Fugue*, play with dance, broadcast on Channel 4 television, choreography and direction by Ian Spink.
Omnibus on Caryl Churchill broadcast on BBC 1 television.

	Serious Money, Broadway premiere at Royale Theatre, New York.
1989	*Icecream,* Royal Court Theatre Downstairs, directed by Max Stafford-Clark. *Hot Fudge,* Royal Court Theatre Upstairs, performance reading.
1990	*Mad Forest*, project with Central School of Speech and Drama, directed by Mark Wing-Davey, staged at Central; National Theatre of Romania, Bucharest, and Royal Court Theatre. *Icecream* and *Hot Fudge* in New York production at the Public Theatre, directed by Les Waters. Second collection of plays published by Methuen. Collection of *Churchill: Shorts* published by Nick Hern.
1991	*Lives of the Great Poisoners*, in collaboration with Orlando Gough (composer) and Ian Spink (choreography/director) at the Arnolfini, Bristol; on tour, and Riverside Studios, London, directed by James Macdonald. *Top Girls* broadcast on BBC television.
1994	*The Skriker,* Cottesloe, Royal National Theatre, London, movement by Ian Spink and direction by Les Waters. *Thyestes* (translation), Royal Court Theatre Upstairs, directed by James Macdonald.
1996	*The Skriker,* American premiere at the Public Theater, movement by Sara Rudner and direction by Mark Wing-Davey.
1997	*Hotel*, Second Stride, Schauspielhaus, Hanover, Germany; on tour, including to The Place, London, with music by Orlando Gough and direction/choreography by Ian Spink. *This is a Chair*, Royal Court Theatre at the Duke of York's, London, directed by Stephen Daldry. *Blue Heart*, Out of Joint and the Royal Court Theatre at the Theatre Royal, Bury St Edmunds; Traverse Theatre, Edinburgh, and Royal Court at the Duke of York's, directed by Max Stafford-Clark.
1998	Third collection of plays published by Nick Hern.
1999	New York premiere of *Blue Heart* at Brooklyn Academy of Music.
2000	*Far Away,* Royal Court Theatre Upstairs, directed by Stephen Daldry.

2001 West End transfer of *Far Away* to Albery Theatre, London.

2002 *A Number*, Royal Court Theatre Downstairs, directed by Stephen Daldry, accompanied by a season of 'Caryl Churchill Events': rehearsed readings of select early works – *Seagulls, Three More Sleepless Nights, Moving Clocks Go Slow* and *Owners* – and productions without décor of *This is a Chair, Not Not Not Not Not Enough Oxygen* and *Identical Twins. A Number* wins Evening Standard Award for Best New Play.
American premiere of *Far Away*, New York Theatre Workshop, directed by Stephen Daldry. 'She Bit her Tongue' (text) for *Plants and Ghosts*, Siobhan Davies Dance Company, premiered in USAF Air Force Base, Upper Heyford, Oxfordshire. Text recorded and spoken by Linda Bassett.

2003 'Iraqdoc', contribution to *War Correspondence*, Royal Court Theatre.
West End transfer of *A Number* to Albery Theatre.

2004 *A Number,* American premiere, New York Theatre Workshop, directed by James Macdonald.

2005 *A Dream Play* (a version), Cottesloe, Royal National Theatre, directed by Katie Mitchell.

2006 *Drunk Enough to Say I Love You?*, Royal Court Theatre Downstairs, directed by James Macdonald. *We Turned on the Light* (text), composer Orlando Gough, The Shout (choir), BBC proms.

2008 Translates *Bliss* (*Félicité*) by Olivier Choinière, performed at the Royal Court Theatre Upstairs.
Top Girls, Broadway premiere, Manhattan Theater Club at the Biltmore Theater, directed by James Macdonald.
A series of one-off readings at the Royal Court Theatre, London, directed by ten playwrights to celebrate Caryl Churchill's seventieth birthday: *Owners* (directed by April de Angelis); *Light Shining* (directed by Mark Ravenhill); *Vinegar Tom* (directed by Winsome Pinnock); *Top Girls* (directed by Nicholas Wright); *Three More Sleepless Nights* (directed by debbie tucker green); *Icecream* (directed by Wallace Shawn); *The Skriker* (directed by Zinnie Harris); *Blue Heart* (directed by Marius von

	Mayenburg); *Far Away* (directed by Martin Crimp) and *A Number* (directed by Joe Penhall). *Drunk Enough to Say I Love You?*, American premiere at The Public Theater, New York, directed by James Macdonald. Fourth collection of plays published by Nick Hern. *A Number* filmed for television by HBO and BBC, directed by James Macdonald.
2009	*Seven Jewish Children – A Play for Gaza*, Royal Court Theatre Downstairs, directed by Dominic Cooke.

I

ELAINE ASTON AND ELIN DIAMOND

Introduction: on Caryl Churchill

The scene is set for intimacy. Two men occupy a sofa on an otherwise empty stage. They talk – one with an American accent, the other English. Their conversation is elliptical. Half-formed sentences leave the spectators to fill in blanks and gaps, but offer enough to suggest a state of renewed sexual attraction, a power game that leads one man (English), to declare his intention to leave his family and join the other (American) on a grotesque spree of global domination. This is how *Drunk Enough to Say I Love You?*, Caryl Churchill's most recent, full-length play (at the time of writing this introduction) opened at London's Royal Court Theatre Downstairs in 2006, the theatre with which Churchill has forged a close and enduring relationship, dating back to 1972 when she made her professional playwriting debut with *Owners*.

Characteristically, *Drunk Enough* is a politically charged play which evidences Churchill's unsurpassed ability to dramatize the anxieties and concerns of the contemporary moment. In this particular instance, it is the nightmare realities created by the wholesale, worldwide exportation of materialist values in which the lives of others are devalued, damaged and destroyed by a 'turbo' capitalist creed of greed. This is not, however, a new topic for Churchill. Rather, the painful realities of a world divided by those who 'own' and those who are 'owned' and the havoc this wreaks on the lives and communities of men and especially women is a subject that frequently haunts her playwriting. Hers is an oppositional, political theatre voice for contemporary times. 'Most plays', Churchill argues 'can be looked at from a political perspective' whether this was or was not what a playwright intended: '[w]hatever you do your point of view is going to show somewhere. It usually only gets noticed and called "political" if it's against the status quo.'[1] Over the years, Churchill's theatre has repeatedly argued 'against the status quo' by exploring social worlds scarred by an inability to democratize and to revolutionize, both nationally and internationally.

Hence, wherever one looks the Churchillian landscape is 'frightening'. At the same time, it is also highly original. For equally unsurpassed among contemporary playwrights is Churchill's capacity for dramaturgical invention and innovation. Each time she interrogates the realities of dystopia created under capitalism she experiments with the dramaturgical form such questioning might take. For Churchill, dramatizing the political is not just a question of content, but also of form. With the renewal of form comes the renewal of the political: new forms *and* new socially and politically relevant questions. Consider, for a moment, how in *Fen*, a self-congratulatory monologue about transnational capital investment in the soil-rich fens is juxtaposed with an iconic image of peasant labour – women '*potato picking down a field*'.[2] Or how in *Serious Money*, the seventeenth-century origins of modern market speculation emerges in the bouncy iambics of sexually aroused traders: 'I thought we'd never manage to make a date. / You're more of a thrill than a changing interest rate'.[3] In *Drunk Enough* Churchill's critique of American imperialism takes the surprising form of a personal, romantic attachment. As the Englishman Guy[4] embarks on his love affair with Sam/America the aggression and 'back killings'[5] of decades of American foreign policy become the sweet nothings each whispers in the other's ear.

At this point in time, it is arguably significant that the personal–political landscape of *Drunk Enough* is one which takes us back over a period of twentieth- and twenty-first-century history, as it overlaps to a large extent with the years of Churchill's playwriting career. Over this period, her commitment, through theatre, to the realization of more fully democratic futures has been unerring, while at the same time the attainability of her vision for society which she described back in 1982 as 'decentralized, non-authoritarian, communist, non-sexist – a society in which people can be in touch with their feelings, and in control of their lives'[6] has slipped further and further away. As *Drunk Enough*, like so much of Churchill's recent work, shows the risks inherent in not being able to see the implications of how personal lives are woven into a bigger, political fabric, it also interrogates what role theatre as a public art form and forum plays on the political stage. As the two-man sofa rises into darkness, it is also edged by a frame of theatre dressing room light bulbs. A metaphor for the theatre in politics, perhaps, but also a framing-up and questioning of theatre's role in the political. All in all, we might suggest, this is a moment in which Churchill, from the perspective of *Drunk Enough*, looks quizzically and self-reflexively back on the art form to which she has committed her creative labour. Similarly, from this retrospective vantage point, we can now look back at the years of Churchill's theatre work and set the scene and contexts (social, cultural, political and theatrical) for the essays on Caryl Churchill brought together in this *Companion*.

Looking back: politics and plays

Oxford-educated in the late 1950s, Churchill's first playwriting experiences were for student and amateur productions. Throughout the 1960s, however, her professionally produced work was mainly for radio, plays which in her own words Churchill has described as treatments of 'bourgeois middle-class life and the destruction of it'[7] (see Chronology for early career details).[8] While writing for radio may have had lasting effects on her theatrical imagination (see Elin Diamond, Chapter 8), it was also something she was able to manage in combination with raising three small children. At the time, Churchill explains, there were few opportunities available to playwrights. 'When I began it was quite hard for any playwrights to get started in London.'[9] During the 1970s, and due in part to a relatively benign period of state sponsorship from the Arts Council, things slowly improved for emergent playwrights as new fringe theatre companies and studio spaces were created. A beneficiary of such openings, Churchill had her first professionally produced play, *Owners*, staged at the Royal Court Theatre's Upstairs studio space, which opened in 1969 as a response to the growing trend in new theatre writing. By 1975 Churchill had graduated to the Court's main house, Downstairs Theatre, with *Objections to Sex and Violence*, directed by John Tydeman, who had produced the majority of her earlier, professionally broadcast radio plays. She was also appointed as the Court's first woman writer in residence (1974–5).

To be labelled a first woman or woman anything can be both an honour and a dubious privilege – dubious when praise for a writer is used pejoratively with 'woman' to propose a '*lesser* category'.[10] Yet it is important to understand that the feminist climate of the 1970s gave Churchill 'a context for thinking of' herself 'as a woman writer'.[11] Like many women in Britain and the US at that time, Churchill's gender awareness was raised through personal experience, specifically a growing discontent with the isolated conditions of her domestic life (see Janelle Reinelt, Chapter 2). Discovering feminism meant identifying the social and sexual inequalities of women's lives and seeking ways to change them. For Churchill it was 'exciting' to discover that personal 'development' was not just a question of self, but was conditioned by the historical moment.[12] Talking of this, she referred to Tillie Olsen's *Silences*[13] – a seminal feminist text that looked at how writers, especially women writers from earlier generations, were silenced by circumstances of gender, race or class, and how transformation of those circumstances could open up new creative horizons. In the 1970s, in a climate of feminist change, theatre horizons presented the 'woman writer' with more opportunities than before. As Churchill observed: 'For a while, a lot of writers were getting produced for the first time, though far fewer women than men. Gradually during the seventies the number of women increased, coming partly through fringe theatres and partly through women's theatre groups.'[14] In 1976, Churchill worked with the then newly formed, women's theatre company, Monstrous Regiment, one of the UK's most influential feminist theatre groups.[15] Working in a feminist theatre context with Monstrous Regiment on *Vinegar Tom* and again on the cabaret *Floorshow*, brought Churchill 'both artistic and intellectual stimulation and also a recognition that she belonged to a [women's] movement' (see Reinelt, Chapter 2).

Given the feminist and leftist climate of the 1970s it is not then surprising to find sexual politics surfacing in several of Churchill's major plays from the 1970s through to the early 1980s, including *Vinegar Tom*, *Cloud Nine*, *Top Girls* and *Fen*. Acknowledging that 'socialism and feminism aren't synonymous', Churchill was clear that she felt 'strongly about both and wouldn't be interested in a form of one that didn't include the other'.[16] Where socialist analysis frequently failed to recognize gender in its critique of class and labour hierarchies, the material conditions of class, history and *gender* are all determinants in the socialist–feminist analysis of women's oppression. Taking up a distinctly anti-capitalist position in her plays, Churchill, therefore, also brought gender concerns to bear on her topics. Her dramatizations of economic and social conditions in seventeenth-century England in *Vinegar Tom* and *Light Shining in Buckinghamshire*, for instance, demonstrate that poor women, punished as witches (*Vinegar Tom*), are doubly disenfranchized on account of their class and gender (*Light Shining*).

Light Shining was the first of four productions Churchill undertook with the new writing company Joint Stock.[17] Just as her production with *Vinegar Tom* for Monstrous Regiment brought her into a feminist theatre community, beginning work with Joint Stock was also to prove a seminal, politicizing experience. She learned methods of making work collaboratively, of experiencing theatre-making as 'joint', democratized labour informing all aspects of process, practice and production. Even when she did the actual playwriting in private, her ideas and images were viscerally inspired by the labour of the actors and director in rehearsal. The experience of working with both of these companies in the mid-1970s had an important impact and influence on Churchill's evolving dramaturgy (see Elaine Aston, Chapter 9).

How to challenge the 'status quo' of capitalism and/or gender oppression remains an enduring question for Churchill and it surfaces in a number of dramatizations where critical attention is paid to the material conditions that have underpinned Britain's organization of labour, family and capital (see Jean E. Howard, Chapter 3). In one of her lesser-known plays, *The After-Dinner Joke*, written for television, Selby, a naïve do-gooder, attempts to eschew capitalism by working for charities to solve the problem of world poverty. In due course, Selby learns that every charitable act turns out to be a political and economic transaction. As a lone woman challenging the inequities of capitalism, Selby fails to do any good. Individual acts of female kindness are not enough to save the world, as Churchill would later illustrate in her major play, *The Skriker*. In contrast to this individual act of resistance, Churchill also explored collective acts of resistance where the democratization of capital and/or social organization is the goal. In our collection, Mary Luckhurst (Chapter 4), for example, examines Churchill's staging of three revolutionary histories in *The Hospital*, *Light Shining*, and in a later play, *Mad Forest*, where each play rehearses the possibilities of egalitarian futures which fail to materialize. The failure to revolutionize can be linked to the geopolitical operations of global capital, brilliantly dramatized by Churchill in her award-winning satire *Serious Money*.

Serious Money is a play, as Jean E. Howard describes in Chapter 3, that captures the 1980s ethos of capitalist greed enshrined in the policies and values of the Conservative government under the leadership of Margaret Thatcher. Elected in 1979 and remaining in power until 1990, Thatcher engineered a Britain divided by wealth and class, promoted private ownership of nationalized industries, and reduced public subsidy – especially for the arts. In theatre this meant harsh economic times: cuts rather than expansion and an active pursuit of corporate sponsorship. In short, Thatcher's Britain shored up the economic divide of rich and poor, the 'us and them' that Churchill wittily and incisively critiqued in *Top Girls*. 'Top girl' Marlene represents an individualistic style of 'feminism' (called, at the time, 'bourgeois feminism'), eager to assert her right to compete as ruthlessly as her fellow male capitalists. If the 1980s were to be a 'stupendous' decade, as Marlene predicts,[18] this would obtain only for those in positions of economic privilege – male or female. Moreover, this would be at the cost of less privileged others, female others in particular, as prophesied in the play's final word/line, spoken by the disadvantaged adolescent, Angie: 'Frightening'.[19]

Britain would have to wait eighteen years before the Conservatives were voted out of power. Labour's return in 1997 with Tony Blair as prime minister, however, re-branded left-wing politics so that Labour 'could shed its reputation for being stuck with postwar socialist dogma and be seen instead as a youthful and forward-thinking alternative to a beleaguered, fractious and increasingly weary-looking Conservative Party'.[20]

New Labour, with its 'cool Britannia' hype, distanced itself from the 'old' ideologies of socialism and feminism. By now these had lost their political bite: the former in the wake of the end of the Cold War, the collapse of Soviet Russia (1991) and its Eastern European outposts; the latter as a consequence of the transatlantic backlash against feminism and feminism's internal struggles over identity politics (see Reinelt, Chapter 2).

In consequence, in the 1990s Churchill's vision of a society founded on socialist and feminist principles seemed increasingly 'far away'. Questions of identity and of self-knowledge, which are mapped throughout Churchill's plays, as R. Darren Gobert explores in Chapter 7, are acutely in flux. Philosophical and psychological questions of selfhood are at sea, unanchored in a world that increasingly seems to offer no personal or political means of self-knowing. So, for Churchill, an urgent political theatre question has become how to further our 'selves' democratically in the absence of any ideological base from which to challenge the status quo. Given the sustained erosion of a credible, counter-political strategy, Churchill has moved towards what might best be described as strategies of dis-identification with life under intensifying regimes of transnational capitalism. In plays such as *The Skriker*, *This is a Chair*, *Far Away* or *Drunk Enough to Say I Love You?* she insists on re-viewings of the 'frightening', terrifying and damaging consequences of our contemporary world, hurtling towards economic and ecological warfare (see Sheila Rabillard, Chapter 6) and a constant state of global terror (see Diamond, Chapter 8). Core to Churchill's re-viewing strategies is her resolve that we re-evaluate what claims our attention – often underscoring the need to redress a blind or blinkered view of the bigger political picture, distanced by personal considerations. This is not a new consideration for Churchill, as this observation dating back to 1973 illustrates:

> I'm often very conscious of the absurd things people take for granted, and the whole different systems people have for judging whether things are important or not. If I cut my finger now, for example, it would be an awful thing, but obviously much worse things are happening far away and one can't relate to them. That kind of discrepancy, in lots of different ways, is something I've thought about for a long time. In fact my first radio play [*The Ants*] was really about that.[21]

That Churchill draws a through-line from 1962 when *The Ants* was first produced to 1973, and referred to it again in an interview in 1982,[22] attests to a foundational conjuncture represented by that short radio play. Like all great writers, Churchill has, as we have noted, abiding concerns, and surely, weaving its way through most if not all of her plays, is the affective gap between violence and harm 'out there' versus a protected, if anxious, 'here' (see Diamond's discussion of *The Ants,* Chapter 8). *This is A Chair* and *Far Away* explore the theme explicitly. In biting contrast, *Drunk Enough to Say I Love You?*, with the sofa on which the global schemers sit rising into the ether, offers a satiric primer on how to *widen* the gap between what 'we' do here and the awful consequences out there.

Churchill's attention to the affective gap between here and there is registered in another way – by her methods of research and writing, by her insistence that politics is both out there and within her characters. In her 'Afterword' to the anthologized printing of *Objections to Sex and Violence,* composed ten years after the play was first produced, Churchill reveals the organic relationship of composition to research:

> I've looked through the notebooks in which I wrote [the play] to see where I started from and how the situations of the play gradually emerge ... Among the *notes groping towards characters and events are notes on what I was reading*, Reich on Aggression, Hannah Arendt on Violence, with quotes from Marx, Fanon, Sartre; Eric's [the play's would-be terrorist] quote about 'the power to act shrinks every day' is by Pareto at the turn of the century, via Arendt. Most of the IRA bombings in England hadn't happened when I wrote the play, and it's hard to unthink them and see the play without them. [Our emphasis] [23]

While reticent about her intentions or about specific meanings in the plays, Churchill is revelatory about her writing practice. Her research notebooks are her plays in embryo. Facts are not impediments to theatrical invention but a stimulant. The commentary above follows productions of *Vinegar Tom* and *Light Shining in Buckinghamshire* in which Churchill's use of the *Malleus Maleficarum* for the former, and of Leveller and Digger pamphlets for the latter have been well documented. In other words, the historical record has not only informed Churchill's writing, it has helped to produce the writing.

As Churchill suggests above, readings of political theorists and philosophers are equally suggestive to her writing practice and the chapters in this volume variously chart her creative engagement with political ideas: Mary Luckhurst describes Churchill's particular dialogue with Fanon's *Wretched of the Earth*; Elin Diamond examines Churchill's inventive engagement with Foucault's 'docile bodies' and technologies of discipline; and Janelle Reinelt shows how the community of feminist historiography has informed Churchill's writing. One might say that Churchill's use of historical texts and political critique suggests a deep interest in intervening in the historical record, not through dogma or preaching but by engaging the imagination and curiosity of her audience.

Theatrical invention

As we noted earlier, in Churchill's work politics and formal invention go hand in hand, and if there are strong thematic tendencies in her work, her ability to reinvent theatrical technique and language from play to play seems inexhaustible. Let us begin with her torquing of time. Churchill's plays can be aggressively nonlinear, and none more so than her theatrical puzzle *Traps*, which was constructed, Churchill writes in a prefatory note, around the figure of a Mobius strip. In *Traps*, scenes are internally coherent but without logical sequence, so that while characters and discrete situations are recognizable, what *happens* is impossible to explain. The characters of *Traps*, Churchill writes, 'can be thought of as living many of the possibilities at once', occupying, in other words, multiple dimensions, multiple spatial realities, giving rise to a 'skewed ontology', as R. Darren Gobert puts it in Chapter 7. *Traps*, Churchill explains, 'is like an impossible object'; what occurs on stage 'cannot be reconciled'[24] with our expectations of reality – and those expectations, Churchill teaches us, are enmeshed in dramatic conventions of temporal and causal sequence. Churchill's famous *Cloud Nine,* in which, between Acts I and II, historical time leaps forward 100 years while characters are only 25 years older, offers no problems of comprehension and, suitable to comedy, carries hope for increasing human connection. But like *Traps, Cloud Nine* makes the larger point that if the past is never settled, the present becomes temporally unstable and indeed the play demonstrates both startling rupture and depressing continuities in sexual politics. *The Skriker* is Churchill's *tour de force* contribution to the shocks of time travel, for her eponymous goblin's 'fairy' time annihilates space by compressing linear time to an instant or by making what feels like an instant actually a passage of hundreds of years. Long before theorists of the postmodern identified 'time–space compression'[25] and 'radically discontinuous realities'[26] as the distinctive features of our 'postmodern condition', Caryl Churchill was developing a dramaturgy that translated this 'condition' into a palpable experience in the theatre.

Equally palpable, and the means by which temporal disturbances are conveyed, are Churchill's unforgettable characters – or rather the unforgettable and surprising voicings that register psychic and social disturbance. In her satiric plays, Churchill's characters have a kind of hyper-recognizability, their gender, class and historical moment telegraphed instantly through styles of speech that collide for comic and political effect. Formally unique as each Churchill production is, one may hear verbal and stylistic echoes from play to play. The disordered speech patterns of Miss Forbes, the flustered older woman who gives voice to the inertia that afflicts all the characters in *Objections,* might be traced back to Vivian's stuttering in the radio play *Not Not Not Not Not Enough Oxygen* and are heard again in Betty's speeches in *Cloud Nine*, and Maisie's in *Blue Heart*. The neurotic materialism of Marion in *Owners* morphs into the unembarrassed greed of Marlene, Nell and Win in *Top Girls* and of Scilla, Mary Lou and Jacinta in *Serious Money*. Churchill's wonderful ear for self-deluding verbal tics generates comic effects (Clive and Martin in *Cloud Nine;* Selby in *The After-Dinner Joke;* Pierre in *Softcops*; Crippen in *Lives of the Great Poisoners*) or points to darker zones of incomprehension (Vera and Lance in *Icecream;* Flavia in *Mad Forest*; Salter in *A Number*). But perhaps the most prominent figure – and language – on the Churchill stage is that of the isolated woman, sometimes a daughter or wife, often a mother, whose words are an unsentimental register of longing, confusion, fear and rage. Here are a just few representative voices:

> FRANÇOISE The dress looked very pretty but underneath I was rotting away. Bit by bit I was disappearing.
>
> (*The Hospital at the Time of the Revolution*)[27]

> IVY Sometimes I think I was never there. You can remember a thing because someone told you. (*Fen*)[28]

> LILY I know everyone's born. I can't help it. Everything's shifted round so she's in the middle. I never minded things. But everything dangerous seems it might get her. (*The Skriker*)[29]

> ALICE I'm not a witch. But I wish I was. If I could live I'd be a witch now after what they've done. I'd make wax men and melt them on a slow fire. I'd kill their animals and blast their crops and make such storms ... (*Vinegar Tom*)[30]

Like all stage characters Churchill's are made of words, and while her words, especially in the speeches above, are redolent of emotion, they never reveal motives or present a coherent personal narrative. Indeed, Churchill stamps out continuities of personality before they can be expressed. From the writing of *Three More Sleepless Nights* to the present, she has undermined the informational and confessional nature of dialogue by having characters speak over each other's lines, creating intermittent verbal cacophonies that subvert the convention of individualized dramatic character. Double casting also undermines identity, throwing our focus not on individual agents but on the form and patterns of the whole. (See Gobert, Chapter 7, for a full discussion of identity.) And finally, as though merely human characters could no longer convey the historical resonances she seeks, Churchill has, since *Fen,* added the nonhuman: angels, ghosts, goblins, vampires, figures out of a shared cultural past that deliberately unsettle the present.

Which brings us back to the question of time and the part played by Churchill's audiences. 'Playwrights don't give answers; they ask questions', Churchill wrote at the beginning of her career.[31] Her characters are incarnations of the restless questioning that informs her plays, and that questioning is not in spite of her politics but an aesthetic strategy *of* her politics. Perhaps the most startling and direct example of this occurs in the exquisitely written first scene of *Far Away* when the child Joan questions her aunt about the horrific brutality she has witnessed. The aunt deflects her questions through manipulation and intimidation, but the larger question – why, despite endless critique, despite all that we know, do we continue to tolerate unspeakable brutality all around us?– hangs in the air and in our minds long after the curtain comes down. The child Joan learns to stop asking questions; we, responding to Churchill provocations, can choose to do otherwise.

Churchill in theatre contexts

The Royal Court

While the political landscape has shifted dramatically over the decades in which Churchill has been writing and in consequence influenced the subjects of her plays, one constant for Churchill has been her association with The Royal Court Theatre. The Court's commitment to writers and its support of *new* writers has been warmly endorsed by Churchill, whose own work has, since the 1972 production of *Owners,* found a home there. As a home, the Court has provided Churchill with many important theatre 'relations'. Significant in this respect is her association with Max Stafford-Clark, who managed the Court throughout the 1980s. Churchill's first encounters with Stafford-Clark were on the Joint Stock productions, *Light Shining in Buckinghamshire* and *Cloud Nine*. Thereafter, their creative partnership flourished at the Court as, under his term of office (which lasted until 1993), Stafford-Clark directed premieres of *Top Girls, Serious Money* and *Icecream*, making Churchill the theatre's 'archetypal [playwright] figure' in the 1980s.[32] Churchill's continued association with the Royal Court has seen her working with directors James Macdonald, Ian Rickson, Dominic Cooke and Stephen Daldry, Stafford-Clark's successor who directed three Churchill productions: *This is a Chair*, *Far Away* and *A Number.* Although her prominence among contemporary British playwrights now guarantees Churchill a main house production, 'the focus of

Downstairs' is something which, on occasion and in keeping with her preference to be out of rather than in the limelight, she shies away from.[33] On the other hand, her stature is such that her work has appeared simultaneously in both the studio and main house spaces: coinciding with *A Number* in 2002 was a series of 'Caryl Churchill Events' which included rehearsed readings and productions without the décor of earlier plays, including some of her unperformed works. Churchill's special relationship with the Court was also celebrated in 2008 on the occasion of her seventieth birthday, for which the theatre hosted a series of 'Caryl Churchill Readings' (see Chronology for details of both of these events). Early in 2009, when Churchill wanted to respond quickly to the war in Gaza, the Court was willing to stage her short, politically outspoken play, *Seven Jewish Children*.[34]

Churchill's enduring allegiance to the Court is significant for the way in which it evidences her commitment to subsidized, state-funded arts. She tends to avoid the more lucrative, commercial opportunities of theatre, film or television that have tempted other of her contemporaries away from the public arts sector. As proof of her anti-capitalist stance, some of Churchill's toughest moments at the Court have been those when her principles on state subsidy have clashed with the theatre's (reluctant) endorsement of private sponsorship in the interests of economic survival. In 1989, for example, the Court's decision to go with the sponsorship offered by Barclays Bank for a 'New Stages' festival of work resulted in Churchill's resignation from the theatre's Council: 'I can understand and respect the view that what matters is to keep the work going and so the theatre should take whatever money it can get. But I can't share it. I feel that my plays are saying one thing and the theatre something else.'[35]

This is not to say that the productions of Churchill's major plays have not made money. As she herself commented in the mid-1990s: 'In the last 10 years since *Cloud Nine* [her biggest earner] went to America, I've been making more than a living.'[36] *Cloud Nine* was one of several major-play transfers to New York which earned her work transatlantic recognition, in turn generating a truly international interest in staging productions of her theatre. At the same time, 'capitalizing' on successes at the Court in the form of London West End transfers and transfers to New York's Off-Broadway, have also helped to keep the Court financially afloat. *Serious Money*, 'the most commercially successful play' in Stafford-Clark's regime,[37] made £14,000 a week for the Court and facilitated the play's transfer into the West End. All things considered, it might be a fair summing up to suggest that the Royal Court and Churchill, theatre and writer, have had a 'sustaining' influence and effect on each other.

Interdisciplinary performance contexts

With its reputation as a writers' theatre and for new plays which represent unrepresented communities and give expression to the experiences, issues or questions pertinent to the contemporary moment, the Royal Court is an obvious choice for Churchill's plays. At the same time, Churchill's commitment 'to use the theatre medium more fully', to realize the possibilities of 'new forms' in theatre, as Libby Worth explains in Chapter 5, means that her work has also been staged in contexts and venues which profile performance work from a range of (mixed) arts media: ICA, Arnolfini, Riverside Studios or The Place.

A defining moment for Churchill in realizing the possibilities of working across art forms came in 1979 when she saw *The Seven Deadly Sins*, a dance-music collaboration between dancer/choreographer Siobhan Davies and performer/singer Julie Covington. This fuelled Churchill's aspiration to make work fusing all three arts – theatre, dance and music. The group she found to collaborate with in this way was the dance/multi-media company Second Stride, formed in 1982 by Richard Alston, Siobhan Davies and Ian Spink. Churchill made significant interdisciplinary 'strides' in 1986, working with Spink on *A Mouthful of Birds*. Several dance-theatre collaborations with Spink were to follow (detailed by Worth in Chapter 5), including the 1991 production *Lives of the Great Poisoners*, in which, for the first time, Churchill was able to realize a collaboration which fused all three art forms, as Spink and Churchill were joined by composer Orlando Gough. Churchill's interest in and willingness to experiment in this way has recently involved her in writing a monologue, 'She Bit her Tongue', for *Plants and Ghosts* by the Siobhan Davies Dance company which premiered at an abandoned US Air Force Base in Oxfordshire, and words for Orlando Gough's ecological choral composition, *We Turned on the Light* performed at the BBC proms (see Rabillard, Chapter 6).

To separate out the theatre contexts and strands of Churchill's plays and performance texts as we have done here is useful for orientation purposes. However, we also need to signal that Churchill's scripts and texts are not neatly positioned either side of a theatre/performance binary. Dividing lines, marking out the territories of, for example, what is dance or what is theatre do not apply. It is the hyphen, a sign of joining things together (dance-theatre or dance-theatre-music) which is important. Hyphenated, performance yields the possibility of thinking, 'writing', making 'new forms'; it should also call to mind Churchill's special working process. We should remember that Churchill has been quite explicit about the fact that formal breakthroughs have evolved from her daily contact with theatres, actors and the problem-solving that is part of mounting a production. Always present at rehearsals, Churchill thrives on the collaborative environment of theatre (see Aston, Chapter 9). Her openness to the possibilities of new hyphenated connections derives from long-standing practice.

Reception and influences

Given Churchill's stature among contemporary British playwrights, the production of a new Churchill play is an eagerly anticipated event. This is now so much the case that it is easy to forget that individual, major plays by Churchill have not always enjoyed instant success. *Top Girls*, for example, is now constantly revived (including the Court's major revival in 1991, also broadcast for BBC television, and a highly praised revival in New York City in May 2008); several editions of the play are in print; it has been adopted on to the theatre syllabus for A-level examinations in the English secondary school system, and a monograph-length study of the play for a student readership has been published.[38] However, as director Max Stafford-Clark recollects, *Top Girls* was not an immediate success either at the box office or with the critics, who at the time of the original 1982 production viewed the play 'as one of a number of plays that were more or less achieved and promising, along with a range of other new work that year'.[39]

Rehearsing this observation, Stafford-Clark also touches on a difficulty endemic to theatre reviewing: a tendency to 'trivialize' and not see 'an important work' on a first viewing.[40] When a work is new, it can be its very newness that confounds. This is especially the case when critics and audiences have simply not known what to make of a new Churchill play; when their horizons of Churchillian expectation have been completely undone. Audiences for *A Mouthful of Birds*, for example, which opened in the main house of Birmingham's Repertory Theatre, were challenged by the dance-theatre composition of the piece. They came with the expectation of the next *Top Girls* play by Churchill and/or an idea of Joint Stock as a company profiling new writing, often political new writing, and left (many of them at the interval) feeling confused and bewildered on all counts by a production which ticked none of these boxes. Both from a critic's perspective and from a performer's point of view, seeing or being involved in one Churchill play is not a way of being prepared for the next. This is quite simply because, as critic David Benedict states, with Churchill 'there are no repeats'.[41]

Churchill's capacity for theatrical inventiveness enlivens political landscapes that speak to the contemporary moment. This is a significant factor when it comes to accounting for the esteem in which Churchill is held by her playwriting peers (see Dan Rebellato, Chapter 10). Interviewed at the time of *Drunk Enough to Say I Love You?*, Royal Court playwrights April de Angelis, Stella Feehily and Laura Wade paid tribute to the innovative qualities of Churchill's theatre that have so enriched the contemporary British theatre scene: '[s]he's still consistently challenging us and challenging herself' (Feehily); '[s]he's a great playwright because she doesn't fit into any one era, she's forever' (de Angelis); and '[t]here's something really compelling about a body of work that is so diverse' (Wade).[42] It is an originality that has been important especially to younger generations of women dramatists, for whom the 'incredible things' Churchill has been able to do 'with structure' have helped to dispel the erstwhile, commonly held view in theatre that structure is what 'women can't do'.[43] What playwrights of either gender are able to imagine they can 'do' in the theatre has been keenly influenced, as Rebellato explains, by 'Churchill's continual engagement with form' (Chapter 10). Summing up her importance and influence, playwright Mark Ravenhill credits Churchill with having 'created some of the most iconic moments in contemporary British theatre: the cross-dressing colonials of *Cloud Nine*; the meal shared by a collection of female historical figures in *Top Girls*; the swaggering, foul-mouthed yuppies of *Serious Money*; the grotesque parade of designer-hatted prisoners in *Far Away*, and the cloned brothers of *A Number*'.[44]

The Companion

These and other 'iconic [Churchill] moments' are brought together in this *Companion* in a collection of essays which pay their own scholarly tributes to Churchill's theatre. The nonlinear structuring which characterizes Churchill's plays applies to the composition of this volume where we have refused a linear, chronological charting of Churchill's career. Instead contributors were invited to explore a set of ideas, topics or issues that Churchill revisits in different plays, at different times: feminism and sexual politics (Reinelt, Chapter 2); the politics of owning (Howard, Chapter 3); revolutionary histories (Luckhurst, Chapter 4); questions of ecology (Rabillard, Chapter 6), identity (Gobert, Chapter 7), and terror (Diamond, Chapter 8). Selecting plays for discussion in individual chapters on this basis makes visible the ways in which Churchill renews her engagement with questions she perceives as urgent to and for our contemporary times. It also allows for some 'iconic moments' to be revisited across chapters: to offer different slants on a major play – the terror and ecological concerns represented in *Far Away*; revolutionary history and the politics of ownership in *Light*

Shining, or the complex weave of the ecological, capitalist or gender damage figured by the Skriker.

While theatrical, cultural and social contexts are important to all of the chapters in different ways and to varying degrees, three *Companion* chapters have more explicit contextualizing work to do in respect of detailing Churchill's projects on text and dance with Ian Spink (Worth, Chapter 5); looking at the artists and artistic communities with whom and in which Churchill has collaborated (Aston, Chapter 9), and examining Churchill's influences in the context of contemporary British theatre (Rebellato, Chapter 10). This provides a mapping of key influences on Churchill and her work as a source of inspiration to and influence on others.

Ultimately, our joint endeavours in this *Companion* work towards an 'ensemble' collection that illuminates the enduring ideas and questions in Churchill's work and details the innovative strategies and the collaborative processes that underpin her unforgettable theatre writing.

NOTES

1. Caryl Churchill, interview in Kathleen Betsko and Rachel Koenig (eds.), *Interviews with Contemporary Women Playwrights* (New York: Beech Tree Books, 1987), pp. 75–84, p. 79.
2. Churchill, *Fen*, in *Plays: Two* (London: Methuen, 1990), p. 148.
3. Churchill, *Serious Money*, in *Plays: Two*, p. 300.
4. In the original performance the English man was named Jack but Churchill subsequently changed this to Guy in order to avoid the association that theatre reviewers understandably made between Sam/Uncle Sam/America and Jack/Union Jack/Britain and the 'special relationship' between Bush and Blair. Uncharacteristically (given her tendency to refrain from commenting on interpretations of her work) Churchill corrects this reading in the introduction to *Plays: Four* (London: Nick Hern Books, 2008), pp. ix–x.
5. Caryl Churchill, *Drunk Enough to Say I Love You?* in *Plays: Four*, p. 284.
6. Caryl Churchill, quoted in Judith Thurman, 'The Playwright Who Makes You Laugh about Orgasm, Racism, Class Struggle, Homophobia, Woman-Hating, the British Empire, and the Irrepressible Strangeness of the Human Heart', *Ms.* (May 1982), 51–7, 54.
7. Caryl Churchill quoted in Catherine Itzin, *Stages in the Revolution: Political Theatre in Britain Since 1968* (London: Methuen, 1980), p. 281.
8. Production dates and details for the plays discussed in the Introduction and throughout the *Companion* can all be found in the Chronology.
9. Churchill, interview in Kathleen Betsko and Rachel Koenig (eds.), *Interviews with Contemporary Women Playwrights*, p. 77.
10. Caryl Churchill, 'The Common Imagination and the Individual Voice', *New Theatre Quarterly*, 13 (February 1988), 3–16, 5.
11. *Ibid.*
12. Churchill, interview in Kathleen Betsko and Rachel Koenig (eds.), *Interviews with Contemporary Women Playwrights*, p. 77.

13. Tillie Olsen, *Silences* (London: Virago, 1980 [1965]).
14. Churchill, interview in Kathleen Betsko and Rachel Koenig (eds.), *Interviews with Contemporary Women Playwrights*, p. 77.
15. For an account of Monstrous Regiment see Gillian Hanna (ed.), *Monstrous Regiment: A Collective Celebration* (London: Nick Hern Books, 1991), and Janelle Reinelt, 'Resisting Thatcherism: The Monstrous Regiment and the School of Hard Knox' in Lynda Hart and Peggy Phelan (eds.), *Acting Out: Feminist Performances* (Ann Arbor: University of Michigan Press), pp. 161–79.
16. Churchill, interview in Kathleen Betsko and Rachel Koenig (eds.), *Interviews with Contemporary Women Playwrights*, p. 78.
17. For a history of the Joint Stock company see Robe Ritchie (ed.), *The Joint Stock Book: The Making of a Theatre Collective* (London: Methuen, 1987).
18. Churchill, *Top Girls*, in *Plays: Two*, p. 137.
19. *Ibid.*, p. 141.
20. Graham Saunders, introduction, in Rebecca d'Monté and Graham Saunders (eds.), *Cool Britannia?: British Political Drama in the 1990s* (Basingstoke: Palgrave-Macmillan, 2008), pp. 1–15, p. 11.
21. Churchill, Interview, in *Plays and Players*, January 1973. Interview published on p. 40 of the magazine and p. 1 of inserted script publication of *Owners*, quotation from p. 1 of insert.
22. See Churchill in Thurman, 'The Playwright Who Makes You Laugh', p. 54.
23. Caryl Churchill, 'Afterword' to *Objections to Sex and Violence* in Michelene Wandor (ed.), *Plays By Women: Volume* IV (London: Methuen, 1985), p. 52.
24. Churchill, *Traps*, in *Plays: One* (London: Methuen, 1985), p. 71.
25. David Harvey, *The Condition of Postmodernity* (Cambridge, MA and London: Blackwell, 1990), pp. 284–307.
26. Fredric Jameson, *Postmodernism, or, The Cultural Logic of Late Capitalism* (Durham, NC: Duke University Press, 1991), p. 413.
27. Churchill, *The Hospital at the Time of the Revolution* in *Churchill: Shorts* (London: Nick Hern Books, 1990), p. 146.
28. Churchill, *Fen*, in *Plays: Two*, p. 177.
29. Churchill, *The Skriker*, in *Plays: Three* (London: Nick Hern Books, 1998), p. 277.
30. Churchill, *Vinegar Tom*, in *Plays: One*, p. 175.
31. Caryl Churchill, 'Not Ordinary, Not Safe: A Direction for Drama?', *The Twentieth Century*, 168.1005 (November 1960), 443–51, 446.
32. Max Stafford-Clark, Interview, in M. Aragay, H. Klein, E. Monforte and P. Zozaya (eds.), *British Theatre of the 1990s; Interviews with Directors, Playwrights, Critics and Academics* (Basingstoke: Palgrave Macmillan, 2007), p. 33.
33. Stafford-Clark in Philip Roberts and Stafford-Clark, *Taking Stock: the Theatre of Max Stafford-Clark* (London: Nick Hern Books, 2007), p. 178. The observation is made in the context of a Royal Court script meeting about the decision as to whether *Far Away* should play in the studio or on the main house stage. 'Apparently, Caryl doesn't want the focus of Downstairs', writes Stafford-Clark, 'I understand, but she's evading her own significance' (p. 178).
34. Directed by Dominic Cooke, *Seven Jewish Children – A Play for Gaza* was performed Downstairs as a companion piece to Marius von Mayenburg's *The Stone* (February 2009). Performances were free of charge with a collection for Medical Aid for Palestinians (MAP). The play has proved controversial,

provoking accusations of anti-Semitism, publicly refuted by Churchill. See Churchill 'My Play is not anti-Semitic', letter to the *Independent*, 21 February 2009.

35. Churchill, quoted in Philip Roberts, *The Royal Court Theatre and the Modern Stage* (Cambridge: Cambridge University Press, 1999), p. 208. More recently, after the Royal Court went through a major refurbishment programme under Stephen Daldry's Artistic Directorship (1993–8) and sponsorship came from the Jerwood Foundation to make up the shortfall of monies required to complete the project, Churchill was among those who objected to the implications this might have for the integrity of the Court as a writers' led theatre.
36. Churchill, quoted in Claire Armitstead, 'Tale of the Unexpected', *Guardian*, Arts section, 12 January 1994, 4–5, 5.
37. Stafford-Clark in *Taking Stock*, p. 124.
38. Alicia Tycer, *Churchill's Top Girls* (London: Continuum, 2008).
39. Stafford-Clark quoted in Lizbeth Goodman, 'Overlapping Dialogue in Overlapping Media: Behind the Scenes of *Top Girls*', in Sheila Rabillard (ed.) *Essays on Caryl Churchill: Contemporary Representations* (Winnipeg, Canada: Blizzard Publishing, 1998), pp. 69–101, p. 76.
40. *Ibid.*
41. David Benedict, speaking in 'Reputations: Caryl Churchill', *Theatre Voice*, 8 April 2005, www.theatrevoice.com/the_archive/, discussion chaired by Benedict, with Linda Bassett, Graham Cowley, Deborah Findlay and Rick Fisher.
42. All quotes from Jane Edwardes 'Celebrating Caryl Churchill', *Time Out*, 14 November 2006 (www.timeout.com/london/theatre/features/2259.html).
43. De Angelis quoted in Mark Ravenhill, 'She made us Raise Our Game', *Guardian*, 3 September 2008, Arts Section, p. 23.
44. *Ibid.*

2

JANELLE REINELT

On feminist and sexual politics

In the summer of 1975, eight of my women friends and I began dreaming and planning. In March 1976, we opened the Stockton Women's Center in space rented from a local church with $275 we raised at a garage sale. We had two programmes initially: a rape crisis line and a 'non-sexist' day-care centre in one of the two rented rooms. Of the eight initial women, all were Caucasian, although one had Native American ancestors. We were mostly college-educated (I was a doctoral student), all married at the time; later three of us divorced – including me. We were all straight; later one of us came out as lesbian. Stockton was a middle-sized Californian city with a diverse population and a struggling economy. We were variously searching for community, stimulation, and service. When we started meeting, we split our time between personal sharing ('consciousness raising'),[1] discussing books and how to organize something larger than our small group meetings in our living rooms.

I start this chapter with personal reminiscence because my story details a set of experiences that capture the typicality of the early years of what has come to be called 'second-wave feminism'. In considering Churchill's work in the context of feminist theory and activism, it is important to stay close to personal experience, situated contexts and evolving ideas. My goal is to create for younger readers a more nuanced approach to Churchill as a feminist thinker and writer than can arise from the media's broad-stroke, often distorted, portrayal of second-wave feminism. In order to do that, some of the excitement and pleasure of that time needs to be balanced with the critique of the mistakes we made, the very real successes balanced with the failures. After all, it comprises a complex history.

Caryl Churchill has herself a typical personal story with regard to feminism. She came to it when she felt a need to work together with other women and when experiences of personal/professional sharing opened up important linkages between her ideas, her politics and her creative practice. Churchill was well educated (at Oxford) and embarked on a writing career in the 1960s as a stay-at-home barrister's wife raising small children. She has commented in a number of often-quoted interviews that she was absorbed with her situation in those years, trying to work out a balance between her work and the needs of her children, and feeling quite isolated from larger events. Out of those experiences came the need for something more. In her recent student guide to *Top Girls*, Alicia Tycer pulls together some of Churchill's disparate feelings and quotes her discontents and growing politicization:

> I didn't feel a part of what was happening in the sixties. During that time I felt isolated. I had small children and was having miscarriages. It was an extremely solitary life. What politicized me was being discontent with my own life of being a barrister's wife and just being at home ... it seemed claustrophobic ... By the mid-60s, I had this gloomy feeling that when the Revolution came I would be swept away.[2]

Trying to reconcile work and family, female health and isolation are the significant issues that drew women together in the 1970s. In Britain as well as the US, Women's Centres began cropping up across the country. One of the earliest, the Essex Road Women's Centre in Islington, described their genesis:

> The Women's Centre grew out of a need to meet and talk to other women about the particular problems we all face. Many of us feel anxious that we alone are responsible for the problems we have – like loneliness if we're stuck with our kids all day and can't get out, finding a decent place to live, worrying about our health and our kids' health, or worrying about work and keeping a home going as well.[3]

About the time I engaged with my eight friends in consciousness-raising and Center planning, Caryl Churchill was also emerging as a self-conscious feminist. She met the women of the feminist theatre company Monstrous Regiment on an abortion march in 1976. Newly constituted, the Monsters had a socialist–feminist viewpoint and wanted to create work free from male bias. After writing mainly for radio, Churchill had achieved a breakthrough in her own work with *Owners* in 1972 at the Royal Court, and by 1975 she was the first woman to have a residency at the Court, where she was tutor for the Young Writers Group. Her play was a critique of capitalist ideas of ownership and within its real estate subject matter she interwove a critique of possessiveness relative to other humans such as lovers and children. Exemplifying ownership as power and control, both financial and emotional, Churchill's real-estate entrepreneur Marion was also reacting to her prior experience as a mental patient:

> CLEGG When Marion was in hospital, they tried to tell her she'd be happier and more sane as a good wife... But she wouldn't listen. Three weeks later she came out of there with staring eyes and three weeks later she bought her first house.[4]

This reaction is equally a courageous act of rebellion against an assigned gender role and a distorted capitalist response equating ownership with self control and power (see Howard, Chapter 3, pp. 36–51). Early in her work, Churchill was already asking ethico-political questions about how to live life in an alienated world; showing the challenges and contradictions confronting women who want something more than the ordinary.

When Churchill began to achieve some success theatrically in the mid-1970s, she also began to find like-minded colleagues who helped her feel part of something communal and focused. Her two projects with Monstrous Regiment (*Vinegar Tom* and *Floorshow*) brought her both artistic and intellectual stimulation and also a recognition that she belonged to a movement: 'I've found that as I go out into the world and get into situations that involve women what I feel is quite strongly a feminist position and that inevitably comes into what I write.'[5] In her contribution for the *Companion*, Elaine Aston describes the other significant collaborative experience that began for Churchill at this time – working with Max Stafford-Clark and the Joint Stock Theatre Company (see Chapter 9). Recognizing that Churchill's major pieces for theatre in this period can be linked to the work of these collaboratively based companies, her feminism and socialism were clearly nourished by these encounters. For feminism, grasping the import of these experiences is dependent on perceiving the factors of discovery and pleasure in like-minded views and beliefs. Juxtaposing Gillian Hanna's comments on the historical moment (Hanna was one of the founders of Monstrous Regiment) with Churchill's account of her initial encounter with the company makes the impact of the historical moment quite palpable:

> Feminism was leaping in our heads... To be a woman in 1975 and not to have felt the excitement of things starting to change, possibilities in the air, would have meant that you were only half alive. (Hanna[6])

> I felt briefly shy and daunted, wondering if I would be acceptable, then immensely happy and stimulated by the discovery of shared ideas and the enormous energy and feeling of possibilities in the still new company. (Churchill[7])

It may be difficult now to imagine that initial burst of energy in the women's movement. But anyone who has had a collective experience that validates the thoughts and feelings they have previously only held in private can imagine a time of exponentially productive creativity and critique. In the rest of this chapter, I discuss Churchill's works in tandem with critical areas of feminist praxis that accompanied her artistic journey.

Recovering 'her-story'

Second-wave feminist scholars emerged in the UK and the US at several different sites, but one of the most important was historiography (the theory of historical methods and objects – how to do history). At Oxford, although Churchill was originally unaware of it, women formed a group and challenged male hegemony with regard to the production of history. The History Workshop at Ruskin College, Oxford sponsored the first British Women's Liberation Movement Conference in 1970. One of the buzz-words of the time, 'her-story', emphasized the exclusions from history of the agency of women and the importance of their roles, the neglect of research on ordinary women and the dearth of material about their everyday life, and the significance of sex and gender differences to the conceptualization of socio-political life in any era. As a corollary, feminist historians also insisted on the importance of personal, subjective experiences, domestic sphere activities and practices of reproduction and kinship systems as central to historical investigation. Women's Studies courses often began in history departments and women historians were one of the main scholarly influences on their development.[8]

Churchill's work engaged with every aspect of this feminist scholarship. In works such as *Light Shining in Buckinghamshire* and *Vinegar Tom* (both 1976), she asked about the construction of women's identity at turbulent historical moments in the seventeenth century. The renowned leftist historian Christopher Hill had published his revisionist history of the seventeenth century, *The World Turned Upside Down*, in 1975.[9] Going beyond his emphasis on class-inflected historiography, Churchill not only made ordinary people the fulcrum of history, she also dramatized how ordinary women were disciplined and punished for deviant behaviour and how they resisted. She portrayed the collusion of state power with religion in this oppression and also showed how women built fragile connections to each other in spite of their situations. In *Fen* (1983), she experimented with oral history – one of the important areas for women researching women – basing her play on Mary Chamberlain's important collection of interviews, *Fenwomen*,[10] and conducting her own interviews with the Joint Stock Company that produced the work. And in *Cloud Nine* (1979), she traced the legacy of colonial regimes' sexual and racial oppression in contemporary life. She even put the agency of remarkable women on stage in the dinner party scene of *Top Girls* (1982), featuring famous historical women such as Isabella Bird and Lady Nijo. Looking back over her oeuvre, we can see Churchill developing this historical strand of her creative interests in relation to the newly evolving approaches of feminist historians.

Women's health and the body

Perhaps no area was more central to second-wave feminism than the focus on health and the female body. In the 1960s, innovations in contraception and the right to legal abortion (1967 in Britain) led to the recognition that, as Juliet Mitchell put it in 1966, 'Once childbearing becomes totally voluntary ... its significance is fundamentally different. It need no longer be the sole or ultimate vocation of woman: it becomes an option among others.'[11] It may be a bit of a stretch for young women in 2009 to see this as 'new news' but it triggered a fundamental rethinking for many women concerning their ability to control their own bodies. Then, too, sharing examples of patronizing or oppressive treatment at the hands of medical authorities and doctors led many women to protest this treatment and to try to learn more about their bodies and health care in order to assert their rights and take better care of themselves. Concurrently, it became public knowledge that the development of new technologies such as the pill and other birth control measures were often carried out at the expense of Third World women utilized in drug trials in Puerto Rico, Mexico or Thailand. Worries about the safety of new technologies generally and the desire to learn more about bodily functions in order to take charge of one's own health soon led to self-help groups and women's health clinics, and an emphasis on women helping other women outside of or in augmentation to the state or private health systems. Midwifery suddenly gained new prominence in relation to this aspect of the movement, along with home birthing. Sex education, mental health practices and breaking the taboo of talking about breast cancer are only some of the topics women wanted to open to debate and reform. Criminalization and institutionalization of mentally ill women was also an important topic of the time, linked to an analysis of gender oppression under patriarchy as one root cause.

Our Bodies, Our Selves was the product of a group of women in Boston who, like my group in California, wanted to make a difference to a larger community. Their efforts began in a workshop where the women shared frustrations about treatment by doctors and agreed to put together a list of 'reasonable' doctors and gynaecologists in the Boston area, meaning 'doctors who listened to the patient, respected her opinions, and explained procedures and medications'.[12] When they realized there was no list, they decided to do their own research in order to produce a book that would be helpful to other women. The result was originally printed on newsprint by the New England Free Press and sold for seventy-five cents. It became a comprehensive book on women's health and sexuality, and by 2005 had sold over four million copies and been translated into eighteen different languages.[13] The book is a lasting reminder of how important this topic was at the time – it spread like wild fire.

Sheila Rowbotham, writing about British women's health issues, documents efforts by women's groups across Britain to establish health clinics, improve abortion services, increase education and choice around childbirth, and include child care at medical facilities. The Essex Road Women's Centre in Islington set up a health group in 1974 that exemplifies the extent of British concern in this area:

> [It] produced literature on women's health, did pregnancy testing, provided a woman doctor for advice sessions, learnt self-examination, took health classes with schoolchildren, collected information on doctors and their treatment of women, provided information on abortion facilities, and more generally, argued for the importance of preventive health care rather than simply curative medicine.[14]

Trying to capture the deep need women felt for this investigation into self-help in the area of health, I can think of no stronger representation than Caryl Churchill's *Vinegar Tom*. Although written about seventeenth-century women, contemporary songs break up the play's narrative; producing a kind of Brechtian cabaret, they were set to contemporary music and catapulted the historical references of the drama into the present. As do many of Churchill's works, this play juxtaposes the past with the present to enable spectators to see both change and continuities. Monster's Susan Todd has remarked concerning their intentions: 'We didn't want to allow the audience to ever get completely immersed in the stories of the women in the play. We wanted to make them continually aware of our presence, of our relationship to the material, which was combative, anguished.'[15]

I saw a recent London revival of the play by fringe theatre company Gilt and Grime (July 2008). Nine women and two men recreated the play on the Victorian music hall stage of the Cobden Club. A large group of women performing together recalled the early days of feminist theatre when the desire to expand creative opportunities for women on stage was a top priority. A new score by Harry Blake supported the deliberate breaks between historical narrative and contemporary life that first provoked audiences, and Churchill's lyrics continued to challenge our post-feminist culture.

Looking back on this text, the links to the Women's Health Movement are very clear. The play shows the interconnections between poverty, old age and deviance in targeting women for oppression and projection (seeing them as witches). One bourgeois farmer's wife oppresses an older unmarried woman (Joan) while her husband lusts after Joan's daughter, Alice, a sexually active single mother. Betty is a 'respectable' girl who doesn't want to marry, and finds herself perceived as ill, tied to a chair and bled into submission: the ancient treatment creates a theatrical image of draining away the girl's energy to resist, as well as showing her 'treatment' to be punishment. Susan, Alice's friend, has had a number of pregnancies and miscarriages and goes to the 'cunning woman', Ellen, who offers a herb that ends her current pregnancy. But Susan feels guilty about taking the potion and joins her neighbours in accusing Ellen of witchcraft. The most serious threats to the ruling social order are those who attempt to live outside it, so Ellen and Joan are hanged as witches while the younger women's fate remains uncertain and at risk. The play shows how class and fear divide the women and prevent them from supporting each other and how ruling institutions, such as medicine and the church, legitimated oppression.

About halfway through the play, there is a break in the action and two cross-dressed women in top hat and tails do a music hall routine impersonation of Kramer and Sprenger, delivering lines from *Malleus Maleficarum*. This treatise from the late fifteenth century was widely circulated throughout Europe and is thought to have been instrumental in the persecution of witches during the next two centuries (in English, *The Hammer of Witches*). This tool of the Inquisition is highly misogynistic, accusing women of being susceptible to witchcraft because they are weak and evil. Kramer and Sprenger share these lines: 'All witchcraft / comes from carnal lust / which is in woman / insatiable.'[16] As a theatrical strategy, this comic turn cools off the brutality of the scene's violence toward the women characters while linking it to historical beliefs and authority. The irony of the performance as music hall also suggests how this attack on women has been incorporated into common ideology and internalized by culture. Funny and horrific at the same time, this part of the performance is another instance of Churchill's support of a new version of women's history through her work. This play also dramatizes a variety of women's subject positions under patriarchy, helping to explain how women become interpellated into their prescribed roles. The final song, playing on the mythical but still present association of women with evil and lust, asks contemporary audiences:

> Evil women
> Is that what you want?
> Is that what you want to see?
> On the movie screen
> Of your own wet dream
> Evil women.[17]

Sex, race, class: theories of identity

Second-wave feminism began theorizing the oppression of women as a class – as constituting a 'we' with common experiences and oppressions. This very quickly became an inadequate conception of women in relation to each other. As Sara M. Evans writes, '[i]n the late 1970s and early 1980s, there was a growing recognition that theoretical frameworks available for analyzing race, class, and gender each reified particular identities in ways that obscured or even obliterated the others'.[18] Challenged first by women of colour and lesbians for what were often perceived as middle-class, white or heterosexist assumptions, the Women's Movement shifted gears and began to speak of 'feminisms'. While Britain had been more attuned to working-class women and poor women, the US was the site of strong articulations of the differences of race. In a ground-breaking anthology, Cherríe Moraga and Gloria Anzaldúa collected together a myriad group of women of colour who announced their own feminist agenda and criticized their treatment in the development of American second-wave feminism. In *This Bridge Called My Back*, the authors defined their goal:

> We want to express to all women – especially to white middle-class women – the experiences which divide us as feminists; we want to examine incidents of intolerance, prejudice and denial of differences within the feminist movement. We intend to explore the causes and sources of, and solutions to these divisions.[19]

Recent narratives of second-wave feminism typically indicate that various diverse constituencies could not work together and eventually caused feminism to fall apart, but that is too simple an account of what was going on. Substantial coalitions across differences also produced significant changes and many women were keenly attuned to the dangers of generalizing identity in an effort to claim solidarity.[20] Churchill herself is an example of a white, straight, middle-class artist whose work was nevertheless attentive to the need to represent a diverse range of class, race, sex and other particulars of female subjectivity. Moreover, Churchill frequently staged women who exhibited within themselves multiple identities in flux or in conflict. Staging these multiple and mobile identities in plays such as *Cloud Nine, A Mouthful of Birds* (1986) and *The Skriker* (1994) helped spectators imagine a complex range of subjects and offered many points of entry for identification or recognition.

As many women opened themselves to radical changes in their sexualities and other self-identificatory behaviours, feminist scholars were trying to form a theory that would account for the seismic shifts brought about during this era. There were several ways of understanding identity and subjectivity, depending on whether one emphasized continuity or change. One of the key arguments was the tension between essentialism and social construction. Essentialism perceived certain traits or characteristics to be part of women's nature from birth or else to be overdetermined by history as fixed attributes. Proponents of social construction emphasized that different historical conditions, different class backgrounds, racial groups, different experiences in childhood – all could result in various defining characteristics, and also that these were not fixed but infinitely modified in a flux of contradictory pressures and influences, creating selves that were multiple, fluid and shape-changing. In the most radical formulations of this view, scholars such as Judith Butler and Elizabeth Grosz argued that bodies themselves are altered and reconfigured depending on phenomenological experience and disciplinary regimes.[21] The significance of these arguments – what was at stake in them – was really the possibility of feminism itself:

> In denying women any shared features, anti-essentialism seemed to imply that there is nothing in virtue of which women can rightly be identified as forming a distinct social group... [I]f women share no common social location they cannot readily be expected to mobilise around any concern at their common predicament, or around any shared political identity or allegiance. Moreover, if essentialism is false then it becomes unclear how feminists can 'represent' women's interests, since women have no unitary set of interests for the putative representatives to articulate.[22]

The theatre proved to be a fruitful site for investigating some of these issues in the context of subjunctive imaginings (what if ... then ... but ... maybe). Through a rich combination of classical mimesis (based on likeness) and deconstructive anti-realist strategies such as Brechtian *Gestus*, myth, dreams and fragmented narrative structures, the stage could posit certain female experiences and yet stop short of claiming they were universal or unchanging. Churchill's experiments with creating characters that confront the reality of historical constraints while also revealing themselves as the product of artistic manipulation of the means of representation enabled her theatre pieces to capture the questions about difference that were critically engaging feminists in the 1980s and 1990s. As Elin Diamond, one of her most perceptive commentators, describes, this created 'a double strain in Churchill's work':

> ... on the one hand, a commitment to the apparatus of representation (actor as sign of character; character as sign of a recognizable human fiction) in order to say something *about* human oppression and pain ... on the other hand, a consistent though less obvious attention to the powers of theatrical illusion, to modalities within representation that subvert the 'aboutness' we normally call the work's 'content'.[23]

This balance on a knife's edge is perhaps most fully represented in her *Cloud Nine*, which I discuss in detail below, but it is also present in the 'raising of the dead' – what Diamond calls the death-space in *Fen*[24] – the spirit-possession of the 'undefended day' in *A Mouthful of Birds* (1986), or the shape-shifting of *The Skriker* (1994). It also manifests in the dinner party scene that opens *Top Girls*. Another important recent strategy Churchill employs is a deliberate suspension of the status of the real: *Far Away, A Number* and *Drunk Enough to Say I Love You?* create precisely calibrated suspended realities where temporal and spatial coordinates are impossible to secure and the action skirts the surreal.

Of all the plays that Churchill has written, *Cloud Nine* perfectly matched its content and form to the zeitgeist of the time – it captured the tumultuous project of sexual experiment in its utopian aspect while equally capturing the confusion and pain of rapid social change. It is the best example of the reasons why Churchill has been an inspiration to feminists in theatre and performance studies.

Cloud Nine

I first heard about Cloud Nine *from feminist theatre scholar Susan Mason, who had somehow obtained a copy of the playscript. It was 1979 and the play had not been published yet in the United States. It was photocopied and passed around from hand to hand, sent across the country along with the rumour that here was a 'totally radical' new play, at once funny and sad, provocative and shocking, and hugely political (which most often meant socialist in the context of the US). When it got to me, I remember trying to figure out the cross-gender casting. It was hard to visualize, as I hadn't seen anything like it before. I finally annotated my script with little male and female symbols to remember how the casting produced its effects (Betty played by a man and Edward by a woman in Act I, and Kathy by a man in Act II). The opening of the play set up these role strains with rhyming commentary: 'What father wants', says Edward, 'is what I'd dearly like to be. I find it rather hard as you can see.'*[25] *Still, when you are just reading and not seeing the body, you can forget. I found it essential to remember a female actress was playing Edward when in a later scene he is scolded and slapped for playing with dolls, or when he is humiliated in a ball game because he can't throw straight. My initial difficulty with the text graphically illustrates how bodies matter on stage.*[26]

The play was developed in a Joint Stock workshop, and marked Caryl Churchill's second collaboration with director Max Stafford-Clark. It was deliberately conceived as being about sexual diversity and the identity redefinition prevalent in those years, and according to Stafford-Clark, 'the idea for a workshop on sexual politics was hers'.[27] The interesting thing about the workshop was the deliberate distribution of roles: 'The ensemble collected for the workshop … included a straight married couple, a straight divorced couple, a gay male couple, a lesbian, a lesbian to be, at least two bisexual men and … the usual large number of heterosexuals.'[28] Similar to CR groups but including a variety of gender/sex identifications, the workshop for *Cloud Nine* included personal testimony, not only of the cast but also of others brought in to constitute 'the rich sexual experience of the other people we interviewed'.[29] This workshop makes it clear that Churchill was never a separatist – it was not that she wanted only to work with women and write about women; rather she wanted to write about the changing identities of all people at this time, with attention and privilege accorded to oppressed voices in an economy of social relations that was struggling with new interventions from gays and lesbians, men who were trying to adjust to change and offer themselves as 'feminist men', and eventually transsexuals who complicated the equation by seeming to reify gender categories while clearly being outside the norms of typical categories of sexual behaviour.

Cloud Nine is inclusive of identities to the point of making even the difficult contradictions and questions experienced by the characters seem valuable and acceptable. It was clearly utopian while at the same time it laid out the various conflicts and unresolved contradictions among radical people trying to rethink and live new kinship relations. A historical rupture sets Victorian colonial life in Africa against contemporary London life, while the characters' continuity challenges the 'realistic' historical frame: thus Betty, married to patriarch Clive in the first-act story, somehow catapults from Victorian Africa to 1970s London where she tries to find a way to live as a divorced, sexually active, mature woman and also to understand her children, gay Edward and lesbian-in-transition Victoria (who was played as a rag doll in the first act).

There are many examples of changing and conflicted gender identities in the play, but the most powerful for me are the scenes that have to do with child rearing. Kathy is a girl-child (played by a male) being raised by a lesbian single mother. At one point her mum Lin says 'I've bought her three new frocks. She won't wear jeans to school anymore because Tracy and Mandy called her a boy.'[30] Kathy is a tough little girl who won't be overly intimidated or otherwise imprisoned by feminine behaviour, even if she does beg her mother to wear a dress to a school meeting. She refuses to go to bed in order to be put aside so grown-ups can talk: 'I'm watching telly… I'm not going to bed now.'[31] Despite the comedy inherent in a large man playing a girl, Cathy commands sympathy as she tries to understand her lesbian mum and a peculiar group of friends and relatives that make up a new sort of primary family – not through biology but through affiliation.

The play's contemporary figures are trying to make new families – beyond heterosexual contracts and monogamous privileges there is an opportunity to bind together in one household a brother and sister and female friend who are polymorphously sexual, and who would raise Kathy in a new community of kinship and affection. Kathy likes guns and aggression, but at the end of the day, she just wants a kiss and a cuddle. She is touching and wonderfully monstrous (every performance I have seen with a male cast in the role features hairy legs and a masculine vocal register), creating a specific subjectivity for Kathy that transgresses dominant conceptions of normal childhood gender and sexual characteristics, while pulling heartstrings to affirm her legitimacy as a young child with a right to be loved and tutored into adulthood. The performance could open a space for both identification with Kathy and also for new understanding for those who would have ordinarily misrecognized Kathy as not normal or dangerous to normal family relations. Her characterization stretches identity categories, does not reify a stable sense of acceptable childhood gender behaviours, and ultimately persuades that children of many different types and behaviours deserve to be loved and nurtured and not forced into any univocal mode.

In every scene of *Cloud Nine*, Churchill challenges notions of fixed identity and normative sexual identifications, but in her juxtaposition of Victorian and contemporary moments, she is also vigilant to represent how the legacy of the past makes differentiation in the present complex and extremely difficult. Her 'take' on feminist debates about essentialism and social construction is to show how possible yet difficult it is for actual human beings to transform themselves into new, non-normative identities. As utopian as *Cloud Nine* is, it has also presented within it the pain and confusion of gender ambiguity and radical socio-sexual change across a range of subject positions, including class, sexual, racial and generational differences.

Women and work

Probably one of the most contested topics of second-wave feminism was the relationship between women and work. It was not about equality – feminists agreed that women should be treated fairly and equitably in the workplace – but about how that actually worked out for women in various positions (working-class women in factories, middle-class women in professions, and unemployed women as either rich stay-at-homers or poor unmarried mothers without jobs at all). The debates were often framed around the three categories of feminists called liberal or bourgeois, radical or cultural, and socialist or materialist. While liberal feminists were identified especially with the US and perceived to focus on equality with men and their potential for equal earnings and status, radical or cultural feminism was at the heart of essentialism insofar as it emphasized women's culture and women's communities and wanted to analyse how women as a class or group (or after the critique of women of colour and lesbians, as a coalition of diverse but similar women) could build a women-centred socio-political movement based on sisterhood and solidarity among women. Socialist feminists or materialist feminists were different from the other two types of feminists because they recognized hugely powerful socio-economic categories among women and men, making some lived realities more unequal than others, and they also criticized radical feminists for failing to understand how much difference class made in the lived experiences of women who did not really share values when divided by status and money. Nevertheless, looking back, we can see how these categories were often inter-related in terms of analysis and affiliation.

In Caryl Churchill's *Top Girls*, the tensions between the various types of feminism and the lived reality of life in the heyday of the Thatcher government were brilliantly portrayed. Over the years, this play has held its relevance to contemporary existence, although different communities of spectators have received the text differently. Churchill has said that in part she wrote *Top Girls* as a reaction to a visit to the US in 1979 where she heard women emphasize opportunities for women as top executives in business. Meanwhile, in the UK, Margaret Thatcher was a highly visible top girl, but as Alicia Tycer notes, she was far from being a 'sister':

> Britain's unemployment figures more than doubled between Thatcher's election and the play's premiere, reaching over three million, which represented more than 11 per cent of the population. Thatcherite policies affected low-income mothers in immediate ways, with cuts in maternity provisions and ending of free school meals. During the 1980s, working mothers had increasingly to fit their family responsibilities around multiple part-time jobs.[32]

Churchill, with her finger on the pulse of contemporary culture, wanted to address how material success for a few women did not build solidarity or foster change for the majority. She also began to imagine the personal costs paid by women who attained the status of 'high flyer' (a term Marlene uses in *Top Girls* to describe herself). The historical and fictional women in the stand-alone first scene intimate a high flyers' club of female friendship, but that impression is quickly countered as they self-obsess, talk over each other, and admit they are miserable. What price independence?

An important aspect of the play and one little commented on in reviews and even most scholarly commentary, is the depiction of the employment agency and the range of female types Churchill creates in the middle section of the play. The women earn pink-collar salaries while they interview other women for jobs. Nell and Win are friends, but also rivals within the agency, and Nell is jealous of Marlene and thinks of moving on for the prospect of more money. Coming to interview at the agency, Louise is from an older generation and instinctively resents the young and judgmental person who interviews her (Win). Describing her previous situation, she comments, 'I don't greatly care for working with women'.[33] Shona bluffs her way through most of her interview: she is young and brash and has imagined a life on the road. At first, Nell is taken in until Shona overplays her hand and gives herself away. The other woman who puts in an appearance is Mrs Kidd, wife of Howard, who has just been passed over for the head job secured by Marlene. She recalls women hostile to women's advances because they have predicated their life on putting their husbands first. Her resentment boils over when Marlene rebuffs her suggestion that she step aside in favour of Howard: 'You're one of these ballbreakers / that's what you are. You'll end up miserable and lonely. You're not natural.'[34] The short scenes in the employment agency do more than fill in the narrative background to Marlene's central progress as a top girl. They also chart the difficulty of women bonding with each other in a competitive economic climate of the zero-sum game, where any advance of one takes something away from another, and where mistrust and lack of understanding create rifts among women who have made different life choices in a rapidly changing environment.

The last part of the play, the extended argument between the working-class, single mother, Joyce (who has raised Marlene's daughter Angie), and the newly middle-class, ambitious career woman, Marlene, takes the play into Churchillian dialectics of socialism and feminism. While Joyce may present a bitter, unappealing figure, she has also been the dependable caretaker of both Angie, and Joyce and Marlene's elderly mother. The attractive and exciting 'Aunty Marlene' has been absent from both responsibilities. As the sisters fight about their lives, their politics also flare up. Marlene thinks the country is improving under Thatcher, who is 'a tough lady' and 'Aces' as the first woman prime minister. Joyce counters, 'What good's first woman if it's her? I suppose you'd have liked Hitler if he was a woman. Ms Hitler. Got a lot done, Hitlerina.'[35]

Arguably, Churchill balances the play's sympathies between the sisters, giving each of them credibility and critique while Angie, and her possible future, is the moral fulcrum of this weighing up. At the time, the play seemed a warning to feminists not to mistake material reward for real progress and liberation; however, when the backlash against feminism began to be felt, the balance of this scene could slip into a harsher criticism of Marlene (as I witnessed in some US productions in the early 1990s). Then again, the import of the play has changed more recently. In 2000, Lyn Gardner reviewed a revival, keenly spinning the play's last line: 'In 1982, Marlene seemed a Thatcherite monster. Twenty years on she is all around us and we hardly notice. Frightening.'[36] Most recently, film critic Charles Isherwood compared the recent New York production to *Sex and the City*:

> 'Top Girls' offers a bracing corrective to the gauzy visions of female accomplishment marketed by Sarah Jessica Parker and her colleagues in the movie, which is a disappointingly escapist addendum to the far more thoughtful and intelligent television series. Some of the women gathered in Ms. Churchill's opening scene could, in a sense, be seen as the historical equivalents of the Carries and Mirandas and Samanthas of today: smart, successful women who questioned or challenged the traditional notions of women's roles and their relationships to men in their cultures.[37]

Even if Isherwood has to water down the sophistication and politics of Churchill's work in order to make this connection with pop culture, he illustrates the way *Top Girls* continues to address topical issues about how women live their lives twenty-five years after its premiere.

Churchill after

I position my cursor to type 'Feminism' following 'Churchill after' as I move to close this chapter. I decide not to do it: not to produce a heading called 'Churchill after feminism'. As I worried in another essay, agreeing that we are now living in a post-feminist age involves participating in making it so – it is a performative act.[38] Yet intellectual honesty recommends what any fool can see – there is not now a strong, organized *movement* that has feminism as its central driving cause. So in a way, Churchill is now writing after feminism. Some very interesting and committed work has been done under the term 'third-wave feminism', and I am drawn to this scholarship which sees environmentalism, human rights and anti-corporate activism as sites for feminist responses to globalization and technology.[39] Indeed, it is exactly in this dimension that Caryl Churchill continues to creatively express her own political commitments, and what I have called the 'residue' of the second wave is clearly visible in her most recent work.[40] Concern for the welfare of children remains prominent in *A Number* and *Far Away*; the threat to meaningful global peace from neoliberal economics and categorical hatred finds expression in these plays and in *This is a Chair* where the headlines of contemporary situations such as 'The War in Bosnia' or 'The Labour Party's Slide to the Right' are set as titles to scenes which are concerned with domestic betrayals, cruelties and deceit.[41] At first glance, they have nothing in common, but upon reflection, spectators see that the patterns of human behaviour in cameo are versions of larger problems – they exist in metonymic relationship. Thus the scene labelled 'Pornography and Censorship' shows parents coercing their (girl) child to eat her food, threatening her with unmentioned consequences if she does not. The 'discipline and punish' scenario repeats later in the text under the label, 'The Northern Ireland Peace Process'. This time we might be seeing the US as the father, Tony Blair as the mum, and Northern Ireland as Muriel, in the feminized position of the child/fledgling/emergent entity. These readings are too literal of course – that is why the same scene is repeated twice with different titles: to make it clear how loose the associational links are while still making them. Is this Churchill after feminism? No, I prefer to think of it as feminism after Churchill.

NOTES

1. Consciousness raising (CR) was a term that referred to sharing personal life experiences with a goal of breaking down isolation. 'Consciousness-raising groups did not aim for total introspection, but advocated moving on from personal narratives to evolving strategies to deal with oppression.' This linked closely to the movement's slogan, 'The Personal is Political'. See Sarah Gamble (ed.), *The Routledge Critical Dictionary of Feminism and Postfeminism* (London and New York: Routledge, 1999–2000), p. 208.
2. Churchill quoted in Alicia Tycer, *Caryl Churchill's Top Girls* (London and New York: Continuum, 2008), p. 6. Originally cited in Mel Gussow, 'Caryl Churchill: Genteel Playwright, Angry Voice', *New York Times*, 22 November 1987, 1, 26.
3. Quoted in Lynne Segal, 'A Local Experience', in Sheila Rowbotham, Lynne Segal and Hilary Wainwright (eds.), *Beyond the Fragments; Feminism and the Making of Socialism* (Boston, MA: Alyson Publications, Inc., 1981), p. 168.
4. Caryl Churchill, *Owners* in *Plays: One* (London: Methuen, 1985), p. 10.
5. Quoted in Ann McFerran,'The Theatre's (Somewhat)Angry Young Women', *Time Out*, 28 October–3 November 1977, p. 13.
6. Gillian Hanna, 'Introduction', *Monstrous Regiment: A Collective Celebration* (London: Nick Hern Books, 1991), pp. xxvii–xxix.
7. Caryl Churchill, *Vinegar Tom*, in *Plays: One*, p. 129.
8. For an excellent discussion of the methods of feminist historiography as it developed during the second wave, see Chapter 1:'Women's History', in Joan Scott's *Gender and the Politics of History* (New York: Columbia University Press, 1988), pp. 15–27. Although Scott is an American historian, her narrative of feminist historiography is equally useful from a UK perspective.
9. Christopher Hill, *The World Turned Upside Down: Radical Ideas During the English Revolution*, 2nd edn (London: Penguin Books, Ltd, 1991).
10. Mary Chamberlain, *Fenwomen: A Portrait of Women in an English Village* ([1975] London: Routledge & Kegan Paul, 1983).
11. Quoted in Sheila Rowbotham, *The Past is Before Us* (London: Pandora Press, 1989), p. 62. This volume is especially good on these issues of health and the body. See Chapter 4, 'Not an Easy Choice', pp. 61–93.
12. Wendy Kline, 'The Making of *Our Bodies, Ourselves*: Rethinking Women's Health and Second-Wave Feminism', in Stephanie Gilmore (ed.), *Feminist*

Coalitions: Historical Perspectives on Second-Wave Feminism in the United States (Urbana and Chicago: University of Illinois Press, 2008), p. 65.

13. *Ibid.*
14. Quoted in Robowtham, *The Past is Before Us*, p. 79.
15. Quoted in Philip Roberts, *About Churchill: The Playwright and the Work* (London: Faber and Faber, Ltd., 2008), p. 186.
16. Churchill, *Vinegar Tom*, in *Plays: One*, p. 178.
17. *Ibid.*
18. 'Foreword' to Gilmore, *Feminist Coalitions*, p. viii.
19. Cherríe Moraga and Gloria Anzaldúa (eds.), 'Introduction', *This Bridge Called My Back* (Watertown, MA: Persephone Press, 1981), p. xxiii.
20. For a sustained argument about the efficacy of diverse coalitions during the second wave, see Gilmore, *Feminist Coalitions*.
21. For an excellent review of the shifting positions of feminist theorists from the 1970s to the present, see Alison Stone, 'On the Genealogy of Women: A Defense of Anti-Essentialism', in Stacy Gillis, Gillian Howie and Rebecca Munford (eds.), *Third Wave Feminism: A Critical Exploration* (Basingstoke and New York: Palgrave Macmillan, 2004), pp. 85–96.
22. Alison Stone, 'On the Genealogy of Women', p. 88.
23. Elin Diamond, *Unmaking Mimesis; Essays on Feminism and Theater* (London: Routledge, 1997), pp. 83–4.
24. *Ibid.*, p. 93.
25. Churchill, *Cloud Nine*, in *Plays: One*, p. 252.
26. Other feminist scholars record their own first encounters with *Cloud Nine*. Canadian Susan Bennett describes her experience with the play under different production conditions and historical moments by way of illustrating the play's mobile construction and reception. Susan Bennett, 'Growing Up on *Cloud Nine*: Gender, Sexuality and Farce', in Sheila Rabillard (ed.), *Essays on Caryl Churchill: Contemporary Representations* (Winnipeg and Buffalo: Blizzard Publishing, 1998), pp. 29–40.
27. Philip Roberts and Max Stafford-Clark, *Taking Stock: The Theatre of Max Stafford-Clark* (London: Nick Hern Books, 2007), p. 68.
28. *Ibid.*, p. 70.
29. *Ibid.*, p. 69.
30. Churchill, *Cloud Nine*, in *Plays: One*, p. 299.
31. *Ibid.*, pp. 305–6.
32. Tycer, *Caryl Churchill*, p. 21.
33. Churchill, *Top Girls*, in *Plays: Two* (London: Methuen, 1990), p. 106.
34. *Ibid.*, p. 113.
35. *Ibid.*, p. 138.
36. Quoted in Tycer, *Caryl Churchill*, p. 74.
37. Charles Isherwood, 'Glass Ceiling, Meet Sisterhood', *New York Times* (15 June 2008). www.nytimes.com/2008/06/15/theater/15ishe.html?partner=rssnyt&emc=rss.
38. See Janelle Reinelt, 'Navigating Postfeminism: Writing Out of the Box', in Elaine Aston and Geraldine Harris (eds.), *Feminist Futures?: Theatre, Performance, Theory* (Basingstoke: Palgrave Macmillan, 2006), pp. 17–33.
39. Especially helpful is the collection by Gillis, Howie and Mumford, *Third Wave Feminism*. With specific regard to Churchill's work, see Sheila Rabillard's essay

on ecology in this collection and also essays by Amelia Howe Kritzer and Robert Baker-White in Rabillard (ed.), *Essays on Caryl Churchill*, pp. 159–73 and 142–58.

40. Reinelt, 'Navigating Postfeminism', p. 20.
41. See Caryl Churchill, *This is a Chair*, in *Plays: Four* (London: Nick Hern Books, 2008), pp. 37–58.

3

JEAN E. HOWARD

On owning and owing: Caryl Churchill and the nightmare of capital

Pathologies of money-lust: *Owners*

In Caryl Churchill's first full-length professionally produced play, a woman named Marion deals with the aftermath of a nervous breakdown by becoming a real estate magnate and voraciously acquiring property. Constantly eating bananas and chocolate bars and anything else that comes to hand, Marion consumes and acquires, the avidity of her appetite for food mirroring the avidity of her pursuit of one more block of flats, one more townhouse. Her cure for mental illness is not therapy, but acquisition pure and simple, capitalism's all-purpose panacea. But this cure brings new pathologies in its wake. It does not matter to Marion whom she ousts from the buildings she acquires or what pain she causes by her deals. At one point, in a scenario Swiftian in its cruelty, she gets the bedraggled and impoverished wife of her former love, Alex, to sign over to her their newborn baby, a human being replacing a building in Marion's endless acquisition schemes.[1]

Marion's reasons for this transaction are multiple but ultimately somewhat mysterious. She wants a piece of her former lover for her own; she wants to spite the woman Alex had married; she wants to give her own husband the son she herself has not produced; and above all, she wants the baby because others do. When the birth mother pleads to get back her child, Marion insists: 'I will keep what's mine. The more you want it the more it's worth keeping.'[2] At no point does Marion herself show any interest in the actual baby or in its wellbeing. At a crucial point in the plot, she does not notice that the baby left in her care has gone missing.

Throughout her theatre career, Churchill returns to the pathologies induced by money-lust and to the suffering caused by the dreadful disparities capitalism creates between those who own and those who owe, between the titans of the earth and those whose lives and energies are drained away by poverty and debt. Often, though not always, the illnesses of acquisition are refracted through plots in which maternity goes awry. In this play a loving mother is driven to give up her child because she is bone-achingly weary of the struggle to support the family she already has, and Marion, the self-styled Genghis Khan of the play,[3] carelessly acquires and then thoughtlessly loses that same baby.[4]

The impulse to probe the conjunction of owning and owing springs in part from Churchill's unselfconscious commitment to socialist ideals.[5] She came of age as a playwright in the 1970s, a period when British society was still struggling to adjust to its reduced international status following the Second World War and the 1956 loss of the Suez Canal, an influx of new immigrants, the effects of aggressive inflation and labour unrest. The Labour Party, first under Harold Wilson (1964–70 and 1974–6) and then under James Callaghan (1976–9), attempted, with weak parliamentary majorities, to build a safety net for the working class and to deal with the economic turbulence of the period. Their political situation was precarious, however, and in 1979 Labour was pushed from power. It did not again win a national election until Tony Blair's New Labour victory in 1997. From 1979 to 1990, the Iron Lady, Margaret Thatcher, headed a powerful Tory government bent on replacing Labour's socialist vision with an aggressive commitment to free trade, private enterprise and individual home ownership.

Churchill wrote *Owners* in 1972 when the future Tory ascendancy was not yet a reality, though the Tory leader, Edward Heath, was in power. *Owners* is fuelled by the urgent sense that a lot is at stake in the then ongoing struggle over whether and how the beast of capitalism would be contained and its violence blunted by regulation, continued nationalization of key industries, and the creation of social welfare programmes. Churchill never turns plays into propaganda, but they often unfold in response to the urgent social issues of the day whether those be the relationship between Britain and the United States under the regimes of Bush and Blair (*Drunk Enough to Say I Love You?*), the consequences of Tory economic policies in the 1980s (*Serious Money*), or the struggles between Labour and Tories over the direction of the British economy in the 1970s (*Owners*).

In the character of Marion, *Owners* finds a focal point for its exploration of capitalist subjectivity, giving the lie to the essentialist fiction that women's maternal instincts provide protection from the penetration of market logic into domestic situations, and underscoring how the drive to consume and acquire destabilizes every kind of human connection. The play also presents in the figure of Alex, Marion's former lover and the father of the baby she acquires, one of Churchill's first attempts to imagine an escape from market logic. Alex also has undergone some kind of nervous breakdown, but in his case, recovery entails a Zen-like passivity that makes him immune to what is considered 'normal' desires. He does not hold a job, does not want the money that Marion offers him, does not want to own a house – in short, does not want. As his wife describes him: 'He just wants nothing. He seems to feel everything's all right.'[6] This strange figure is unsettling, however, in that Churchill uses his escape from the ethic of ownership to probe the limits of that 'freedom'. He does not, for example, contest his wife's contractual surrender of their baby to Marion and avers, at one point, that he does not necessarily love his own children more than anyone else's.[7] He seems to lack the 'natural' possessiveness that blood ties are typically taken to engender. When he visits his comatose mother in the hospital, he quietly disconnects the drip that is keeping her alive, saying: 'There. That saves a lot of bother.'[8] What, Churchill seems to be asking, is the proper antidote to atavistic ties of blood and the acquisitive drive of capitalist culture? Is an indifference to desire and blood ties a positive social good, and what are its limits? To make the question more complicated, at the end of the play, Churchill has Alex walk into a burning building to save the life of a child who is not his own, courting certain death. Is Alex a saint or a mutant whose suffering has made him no longer fully human?

'Borrowing' from history: *Light Shining in Buckinghamshire*

In 1976, just four years later, Churchill returned with an astonishing and astonishingly different play, *Light Shining in Buckinghamshire*, to some of the questions raised in *Owners*, but this time she set the action, not in contemporary Britain, but in the English Civil War of the 1640s when radical movements and sensibilities flourished and regimes of ownership were profoundly, if fleetingly, called in question.[9] Having first thought of a play on the Crusades, Churchill eventually found her way to the millenarian writings of the seventeenth century and to those historical voices, recorded in the texts of the period, that spoke of the dream of a common life: 'give give give give up, give up your houses, horses, goods, gold ... have all things common'.[10]

The play's title, *Light Shining in Buckinghamshire,* comes from the title of a Digger pamphlet of 1649, and, inspired by Digger writings, Churchill represents the events of the late 1640s as a watershed struggle over the meaning of property and the rights that accrue to ownership. Among the most radical groups to emerge in the Civil War, the Diggers argued for the communal ownership of land and the end of private property.[11] Their ideas served as the impetus for Churchill's exploration of the suffering of the propertyless and the search for alternatives to the social system that perpetuated their pain. This exploration was made urgent by the pressing economic problems in the England of the 1970s and, more locally, by Churchill's own newly formed collaboration with the experimental theatre company Joint Stock, which came into being in 1974. Their practices lastingly affected Churchill's relationship to her craft and were key to the striking dramaturgical originality of her re-animation of the Civil War period.[12]

Joint Stock practised a radically democratic approach to making theatre. Playwrights and actors typically worked together during an initial workshop period, pooling ideas, conducting research and using group improvisation exercises to develop ideas for a play. Then, most often, the playwright would use this material to create a text that would then be sculpted and shaped during the actual rehearsal process. Working closely with Joint Stock artistic director Max Stafford-Clark, Churchill followed this process in developing *Light Shining* with exhilarating results. As she wrote, 'I'd never seen an exercise or improvisation before and was as thrilled as a child at a pantomime.'[13] In one exercise, the actors took a bit of Biblical text and used it to improvise a sermon; in another, actors impersonating particular characters developed a storyline tracing their pre-war lives, what happened to them during the period of conflict, and where they ended up during the Restoration. Much of that work became part of the final script, as did an exercise involving an apple being passed around at a fictionalized prayer meeting.

In turning this collective work into a play, Churchill created a series of striking scenes that each crystallized the politics of an encounter or moment, the Brechtian *Gestus*.[14] Together they captured the arc of excitement and disillusionment that marked the participation of the common people in the events that included the execution of Charles I, the defeat of the Royalist forces by Cromwell's New Model Army, and the outpouring in the popular press of untold numbers of pamphlets, sermons and tracts advocating the radical re-alignment of social relations and exploring various forms of Republican and what we would now call Communist rule. In keeping with the Joint Stock ethos and a Brechtian theatre practice, the play did not focus on 'heroes' with whom the audience would identify, but on ordinary people – vagrant women, common soldiers, labourers – caught in a period of extraordinary flux and ferment. The script freely mixes historical figures such as two Ranters, Laurence Clarkson and Abiezer Coppe, and the Roundhead leader, Thomas Cromwell, with completely fictional figures such as a vagrant, Margaret Brotherton, and a nameless vicar. In thus mixing the real and the imagined in her staging of the revolutionary moment, Churchill was able to simulate the voices of those most often missing from the historical record.

In forging language for her characters, Churchill engaged in what could be called a daringly socialist literary practice. To create speech at once slightly archaic and distancing and yet also capable of powerful emotional effects, Churchill borrowed freely from texts *from* the period, such as the Digger pamphlets, and from texts important *to* the period, such as the Bible.

Gathering together textual fragments from many sources, Churchill then wove them into a new theatrical tapestry. The Biblically inflected yet often colloquial and deliberately antiquated language employed in *Light Shining* is strikingly different from the contemporary realism of *Owners*, and it is one of the many Brechtian devices used to create for the audience an awareness of historical distance and to invite reflection on the unfolding action. The play opens with the cast in unison singing from Isaiah 24: 'Fear, and the pit, and the snare are upon thee, O inhabitant of the earth.'[15] Here, appropriating the language of Biblical prophecy and warning, Churchill predicts the shudderings of the world's foundations that her play will explore, religious discourse providing the terms through which social catastrophe and utopian yearnings alike will be expressed. The intermingled terror and ecstasy that overtook many is captured elsewhere in the play in the words quoted from the visionary dream vision of Abiezer Coppe who saw a great light and heard the voice of God, 'whereupon with exceeding trembling and amazement on the flesh, and with joy unspeakable in the spirit, I clapped my hands, and cried out, Amen, Hallelujah, Hallelujah, Amen'.[16]

There is also extensive borrowing from the Putney Debates: the extraordinary three-day conversation between the common soldiers who had fought in Cromwell's army, a number of whom were Levellers, and the leaders of the New Model Army, including Oliver Cromwell and Henry Ireton, his son-in-law. The debates were fundamentally about what we would now call democracy, about who would be granted a stake in governing the country for whose future they had fought. Levellers argued that all men, and not only those with freeholds of forty shillings a year, should have the right of election. Ireton, and those on his side, argued that without property, people had 'no real or permanent interest in the kingdom',[17] but were 'here today, and gone tomorrow',[18] and should have no vote. Questions about the role of property in establishing personhood and the franchise eclipsed all other issues during this three-day conversation in which the Leveller position was eventually defeated.

Churchill embeds a redacted enactment of the Putney debates in the final scene of the first Act of her play, making those debates the conceptual pivot around which other incidents are clustered and given meaning (see also Luckhurst, Chapter 4, pp. 58–62). The consequences of owning or not owning property are played out in ever-varying forms. In one scene, for example, 'Margaret Brotherton is Tried', a vagrant woman, caught begging, is forced to undergo a legal interrogation before Justices of the Peace who level at her a series of questions she can hardly comprehend, let alone answer. Summarily, without hearing any opposing argument, the Justices condemn her to 'be stripped to the waist and beaten to the bounds of this parish and returned parish by parish to ... the parish where you were born'.[19] With extraordinary vividness, the scene shows that to be without the protection of property makes one powerless before institutions, here the legal system, that serve the interests of the rich and the landed.[20]

In another scene, 'Two Women Look in a Mirror', nameless women tell of having broken into the great house of a property owner who had fled or been killed in the fighting. They enumerate what wonderful objects they found there: a bed with white linen sheets and three wool blankets and pictures, in rows, of the landowner's ancestors. What amazes them the most, however, is a full-length mirror. Neither of the women had ever before seen herself in a looking glass, and as one says: 'you see your whole body at once. You see yourself standing in that room. They must know what they look like all the time. And now we do.'[21] With dazzling simplicity, Churchill makes clear the sensory and cognitive differences that separate those who own property and those who do not. These women had not felt the softness of linen on their beds nor the warmth of three woollen blankets, not had they had the experience of seeing themselves in a full-length looking glass, making them whole beings in their own eyes, linking consciousness to bodily form.[22] Other scenes describe how soldiers destroyed the crops that the Diggers had attempted to plant on waste land and the struggle of an emaciated woman to leave her dying baby on the doorstep of a rich man who might be able to keep it from starving.

Cumulatively, these short vignettes provide a thoroughgoing critique of the various forms of social injustice and inequality that spring from a social system that concentrates the ownership of property in the hands of a few. Yet more fully than in *Owners,* Churchill also gives space to the ideas of those who espouse alternative social arrangements, to the radical democracy sought by the Levellers and to the communism of the Diggers. Historically, these visions failed to be realized, and the second half of *Light Shining* is sobering (see also Luckhurst, Chapter 4, pp. 61–2). It dramatizes the defeat of the Diggers at George Hill in Surrey, the funeral of the Leveller, Lockyer and the disillusionment of many of the common men who had joined the New Model Army or joined radical religious movements in the hope of attaining new heaven and new earth. Claxton, a common man, was one such convert. Having heard the preaching of a radical cleric, he left his wife and his property to move 'more certainly towards God'.[23] Sleeping with whatever woman he met, he was both alone, unfettered by property, and joined with new communities who were rushing toward 'the infinite nothing that is God'.[24] Claxton gets the last lines of the play. Having emigrated to Barbados and hearing still of the strife and contention back in England, his 'great desire is to see and say nothing'.[25]

But despite such images of defeat, *Light Shining*, as play and as theatrical event, does not give up on the possibility that in the renunciation of property lies the road to something better, a something sometimes called God, but just as often represented as freedom from the tyranny of desire that ownership brings with it. In the penultimate scene, simply called 'The Meeting', a number of common characters gather in a tavern and enact something that is a cross between a communion service and a prayer meeting. They remember their dreams and those who have been killed, and some persist in their hope that despite the betrayals by Parliament, by Cromwell and by their preachers, Christ is coming soon to establish his kingdom on earth.[26] What surprises most are the acts of kindness the scene depicts: above all, the sharing of precious food and the inclusion in their circle of the lowest among them. Even in defeat, these outcasts enact a generosity of spirit that serves as the play's riposte to the coldness of those who worship mammon.

Some of these visionaries continue to act on the ideals of the thwarted revolution in their own idiosyncratic ways. Briggs, a common man who joined the New Model Army only to become disillusioned with its failure to live up to its own principles, gradually stops eating ordinary food and begins to live in the fields. After ceasing to consume meat, then cheese and eggs, then porridge and vegetables, he finally forces himself to eat only grass, reasoning that because '[a] few people eat far too much', 'if a few people ate far too little that might balance'.[27] Briggs is, on the one hand, as mad as Nebuchadnezzar who, like a beast of the fields, ate grass; on the other hand he is a holy fool who has negated desire, has freed himself from the craving for meat, for oranges, for wine, for land, for mirrors, for wool blankets – for all those things that elsewhere in the play drive human beings to turn themselves into beasts of another kind: people who in the defence of their property will whip, imprison, and kill those who ask for a share.[28]

Yet the represented action, what is encoded in Churchill's playscript, tells only part of the story of this remarkable theatre event and its relationship to the question of property and ownership. While the play bears Churchill's name, she has often called attention, as I have indicated above, to the collaborative way in which it was first imagined and brought into being. *Light Shining in Buckinghamshire* was a communally generated product both as script and as performance. Drawing on the collective labour of the actors in creating the play as well as in rehearsing and performing it, and drawing on the words of historical figures and texts from another era in moulding the play's dialogue, Churchill's work engages with issues of property and ownership not only in thematic terms, but also in terms of how, by whom, and of what it is made. *Light Shining* is self-consciously presented as the work of many hands and mouths and bodies, both those from a distant past and those who workshopped and performed the play in Britain in 1976. The script itself is thus like the hardened shell of property: something that bears the name of Caryl Churchill, but which, through its communal production and its tissue of borrowings, casts an ironic light upon any claims to 'own' either the script, the performances that spring from it, or the past it both creates and recreates.

A final aspect of the play deserves comment because it signals how thoroughly in this work Churchill's stagecraft had become intertwined with the thematic questions she was addressing. The play refuses a basic convention of most theatrical practice, namely, that characters are embodied by a single actor. Instead, a number of different actors play a given character. Doubling is quite different. Actors often play more than one character in a performance; the practice is a tribute to the actor's craft and versatility and not a challenge to the ontology of personhood. But in her production notes, Churchill writes of *Light Shining*:

> The characters are not played by the same actors each time they appear. The audience should not have to worry exactly which character they are seeing. Each scene can be taken as a separate event rather than part of a story. This seems to reflect better the reality of large events like war and revolution where many people share the same kind of experience.[29]

Churchill's justification for the practice she describes may or may not be the whole story. Her emphasis on shared experience, which wipes away the individuality of any one person's experience of war and revolution, is probably at least part of what motivates her decision to cast her play in this way. But the practice also radically dissolves the inherent unity of dramatic character since more than one actor shares the proper name: Claxton, Briggs, Ireton. The proper name has lost its propriety. The script, by contrast, stabilizes identity. Each character is figured by his or her name, and nothing troubles that identification. In the performance of this play, that fundamental given is challenged; when a common name is shared by several actors, the proper name's unique link to a single human figure is challenged. Looking in the mirror for himself, the character Claxton would be confronted with the image of more than one actor, two persons or three, a little like the mystery of the trinity.

The performed play thus strives in a variety of ways to move from singularity toward a vision of bodies, property and even names in common. The play begins with everyone on stage singing the verses of Isaiah, and very near the end, all the actors again sing, this time from Ecclesiastes 5: vii–x, xii, a final protest against the regime of property and the power that derives from it, reminding the audience that 'the profit of the earth is for all'.[30] The performance invites the audience to embrace what is shared, what is held in common, what emerges when property and propriety give way to indefinition and ecstatic vision. As a critique of the regimes of property, *Light Shining in Buckinghamshire* is best encountered, not by its transformation into a script bearing Churchill's name, but by its re-enactment in the living theatre, the place of communal creation.

Trading up: *Serious Money*

Over a decade later, in 1987, Churchill's *Serious Money: A City Comedy*, was performed at the Royal Court, again with Joint Stock. A slashing if high-spirited indictment of the world of high finance in the Thatcher era, *Serious Money* is worlds away in tone and in conception from *Light Shining in Buckinghamshire*'s exploration of seventeenth-century millenarian hopes for a more equitable society. With incredible rapidity, the times had changed. For the British Left, Margaret Thatcher's ascension to power was a disaster, ushering in a period of aggressive pro-business public policy and a return to militarism with the invasion of the Falklands Islands in 1982, part of a territorial dispute with Argentina that propelled Thatcher to a second electoral victory in 1983. In the mid-1980s, the Iron Lady deregulated the London Stock Exchange in a move that came to be known as 'The Big Bang'. As a result of Thatcher's actions, foreign entities could now own up to 100 per cent of firms that were part of the London Exchange, rather than the 29.9 per cent that had been the former limit. This change encouraged a culture of corporate raiding and aggressive buy-outs at an international level. Simultaneously, the pace of trading increased by means of intensified telephone communication whereby several deals could be pursued by individual traders at one time, encouraging a younger, more aggressive group of new traders to push out more established members of the Exchange.[31]

Caryl Churchill waded into this new terrain with satiric gusto. If *Light Shining* explored the early moments of English capitalism, *Serious Money* took on the new financial arrangements of late capitalism whereby deregulated financial markets encourage speculation, risky investments and high-speed international deals.[32] In the world Churchill creates, companies are bought, sold, ruined and expanded in the twinkling of an eye, making some investors incredibly rich and putting many others at risk. What people 'own' in this play is by and large not real property in the sense of land or factories, but paper assets in the form of stocks, bonds and other financial instruments. Their value fluctuates rapidly as companies are acquired, broken and restructured. In exploring these developments, which in the midst of the great stock market crash of 2009 look as pernicious as they did in 1987, Churchill turned to the long tradition of city comedy. From 1600 on, English dramatists such as

Ben Jonson and Thomas Middleton had written plays that satirized the effects on urban life of a quickening national and international marketplace. Usurers, rapacious tradesmen and greedy merchants are central figures in works such as *A New Way to Pay Old Debts, It's a Mad World, My Masters,* or *Bartholomew Fair.* After the Restoration, the London stage continued this tradition, and Churchill begins *Serious Money* with a scene from Thomas Shadwell's 1692 work, *The Volunteers; or, The Stock-Jobbers,* which shows a group of speculators trying to buy up stocks in various ridiculous projects, such as a patent for killing all the fleas in England. Queried as to whether such schemes are legal and useful, a character replies that those questions are not relevant so long as by investing they may 'turn the penny'.[33]

Churchill modernizes the city comedy form to accommodate the realities of modern finance capital. Her characters, for a start, are not just British. Acknowledging the global reach and interconnectedness of the world of global finance, Churchill peoples her world with figures like Jacinta Condor, a Peruvian businesswoman, Nigel Abjibala, an importer from Ghana, and Marylou Baines, an American arbitrageur. Forever in motion, flying from continent to continent and moving from meeting to meeting, some of the characters, like Jacinta Condor and the banker, Zac Zackerman, cannot even find time to schedule sex. In *Serious Money,* speed is perhaps *the* central social and theatrical fact.[34] As Churchill indicates in her notes to the text, the pace of the play is to be fast with one character often starting to speak before another has finished; and the first scene, in particular – which shows a sequence of deals being made while the traders also plan their after-work drinks and cocaine hits – is cacophonous and disjointed. Regularly handling two phones at once, the traders shout bids and delivery dates at one another. In other scenes, the characters speak in rhyme, some of it comic, most of it driving the play along with a sing-song rhythm that denaturalizes daily speech. As the American trader, Marylou Baines, opines:

> Look, with his own collapse Boesky did the biggest insider deal of all:
> The SEC let him unload over a billion dollars worth of shares ahead of announcing his fall.
> So paying a hundred million dollar fine was pretty minimal.
> Which is great, because he overstepped some regulations, sure, but the guy's no criminal.[35]

The feminine rhyme of 'criminal' and 'minimal' comically understates Ivan Boesky's crimes (in the 1980s he bet on corporate takeovers using information illegally acquired from insiders within the affected companies and was eventually jailed); it also creates heavy irony as a gap opens between what Marylou's comments admit – the scandalous fact of Boesky's scams – and the offhand casualness with which she dismisses the moral and legal seriousness of those facts. The theatregoer is invited at once to be aghast at what is being revealed and delighted by its clever expression.

Churchill herself expressed ambivalence about the world depicted in *Serious Money*. Using the Joint Stock method, she and some of the group spent time on the Stock Exchange watching and learning how the current financial world worked. In an interview Churchill gave Margaret Rose in 1987, she said that while she strongly disapproved of that world, she found herself drawn to the drive, energy and stylishness of the young traders who cut deals on the Exchange and whose language was inventive and sassy.[36] Her response was to create a play that does not pull its punches in terms of what it reveals about the treachery and viciousness of this world and its destruction of human connections: 'friends' double-cross 'friends'; a sister stops exploring her brother's death in order to track down where he hid his 'serious money' and how she can get a hold of it; protégés turn on their mentors – all in the pursuit of profits, unimaginable profits. But the play cloaks its outrage in irony and satire, finding in an excess of artifice and theatricality a style appropriate to the voracious appetites of the age. In an over-the-top final musical number, 'Five More Glorious Years', a reference to another term of Tory rule, a group of characters raucously sings of the oysters, champagne and 'mountains of cocaine' that they can expect under a continued Tory regime.[37] This is serious fun – a rousing musical number that nonetheless exposes the excesses and grotesqueries of the profit-driven financial world that had emerged in the late 1980s.

While most audiences recognize its satiric intent, *Serious Money* nonetheless provoked questions about whether Churchill had somehow sold out or been co-opted by the world she was exploring.[38] Young stock traders swelled the usual left-leaning crowd at the Royal Court where the play was first performed, seemingly taking pleasure in their own skewering and leading critics to claim that the play glamorized the world it depicted. Certainly self-conscious about the issue of co-optation, within the play Churchill explores the cruder ways in which theatre can become entangled with big money.[39] For example, one of the most rapacious traders in the play, Billy Corman, is eventually appointed to the board of the National Theatre, using the cultural capital associated with elite art to burnish his own image and make contacts with other rich people. (It is important to note that during the Thatcher years theatrical subsidies were cut, forcing companies to seek corporate sponsorship, the very thing Corman seems to represent.) At an earlier point in the action, Corman is called to the National to meet at intermission with a cabinet minister, Gleason, who wants him to desist from making a particularly egregious corporate takeover in exchange for the promise that with the

Tories' re-election he can have five more glorious years of unfettered acquisition. Speaking for a minute of *King Lear*, the play on offer, Gleason admits: 'It's excellent of course, they're not botching it, / But after a hard day's work my eyes keep closing. / I keep jerking awake when they shout',[40] and he goes on to jumble Goneril and Regan, characters in the play he's watching, with Ophelia, another of Shakespeare's heroines, but from a different tragedy. Uncomprehendingly dozing their way through the National's production, Corman and Gleason are theatrical Philistines whose connection with the theatre is purely instrumental, and in her own way Churchill is making a subtle comment on those theatres that use 'the classics', like Shakespeare, to cater to such people.

Working at the edgier Royal Court and creating a play that with its comic rhymes, its slang, and racy references to sex, drugs, and money defies good taste and eschews the status of classical art, Churchill is striving for a way to retain theatre's critical edge. Here her choice, however, is not to lay out an alternative social vision as she did in *Light Shining in Buckinghamshire*, but to exaggerate and intensify the frenetic pace and psychic emptiness of the Big Bang world – in effect, to take the premises of that world and make them the object of laughter, the site of the ridiculous. It is a risky move, but one that acknowledges that there is no clear way out of the social circumstances and economic arrangements of late capitalism. What remains possible is to point up the absurdity of the world of speculation, corporate takeovers and insider trading: its addiction to speed and surfaces, its destruction of human ties and humane values, and its obliviousness to those whose lives it destroys. Churchill elected to do this by way of a high-spirited send-up of that world, finding in mockery the road to critique and creating theatrical pleasure from the shards of the social unreal that high finance had created.

Untrammelled greed: *The Skriker*

In 1994, deep into the years of Conservative rule, Churchill produced, at the very Royal National Theatre where Corman had become a member of the board, a mystifying and moving play, *The Skriker,* that took Churchill's examination of late capitalism's social effects in an entirely new direction. What could bring home, she seemed to be asking, the catastrophic global consequences of the ever-expanding reach of untrammelled greed? For answer, she created a play with three central figures: Josie, a young woman who has murdered her new-born baby; Lily, a young woman first pregnant and then mother to a young baby always under threat; and the Skriker, described in the text as 'a shapeshifter and death portent, ancient and damaged'.[41] Around these characters swirl a bevy of fantastic figures from folkfore and myth: Johnny Squarefoot, Rawheadandbloodybones, Fair Fairy, Dark Fairy and others.

In one way the play circles back to *Owners* in that it marks the threat to the natural order first through images of injured and injurious motherhood: murdered babies, murderous mothers, endangered babies, mothers without husbands.[42] But this is only the start of the play's overwhelmingly grim dissection of a world on the brink of ecological and social disaster. Everything in the play is damaged, not just the human family.[43] The Skriker itself is a figure of incredible malice and need, stalking the young women, crying for attention, transporting them across time and space without their volition, assaulting them with language at once seductive, strange, terrible and haunting. In this play, speech repeatedly goes off the tracks, becomes mutant. At one level recalling James Joyce's puns and neologisms, the speech of the three main characters constantly veers between nonsense and new sense, its fractures allowing new ideas to form and dissolve. Taken to the underworld where she has consumed a feast of cake and twigs, a feast that subsequently disintegrated and disappeared, Josie discusses with the Skriker the fact that 'now no one tastes any good', to which the Skriker replies, 'Dry as dustpans, foul as shitpandemonium. Poison in the food chain saw massacre.'[44] The syntax looks backward and forward at once, pivoting on key words like 'pan' and 'chain'. There is poison in the food chain, a bleak reference to the fact of toxic waste runoff and salmonella and antibiotic-fed beef; but there are also chainsaw massacres, and the two may be related, and maybe not. Do murderous mothers and men who saw up young women with chainsaws owe their murderous rage in part to poison in the food chain?

Something has deeply sickened the world and made nature itself afraid. In a moment of stunning lucidity, the Skriker speaks of the changes that have overtaken the world:

> Earthquakes. Volcanoes. Drought. Apocalyptic meteorological phenomena. The increase of sickness. It was always possible to think whatever your personal problem there was always nature. Spring will return even if it's without me. Nobody loves me but at least it's a sunny day. This has been a comfort to people as long as they've existed. But it's not available any more. Sorry. Nobody loves me and the sun's going to kill me. Spring will return and nothing will grow.[45]

The consolations of nature are now taken from humankind – echoes of ecologist Rachel Carson's vision of a 'silent spring'. (For a full discussion on ecology and *The Skriker,* see Rabillard, Chapter 6.)

Among the many things that the Skriker represents, and those things are legion, nothing is more telling than its links to the devastations of late capitalism.[46] The Skriker can penetrate any space, even the most private (hospital, home, nursery); it can compress time and space (Josie appears to live for years in the Underworld and returns to find that time on earth has stood still); it can create desire (as for the food that in the Underworld turns to ashes and twigs) that makes one abandon infants and homes and friends. And yet, *The Skriker* is not an abstract allegory of capitalism's workings. Instead, it intimates the destruction that capitalism brings in its wake by making use of myth and fairytale to hint at the evil that lies hidden in caves at the centre of the world and can be released to destroy the living, and by the menace encoded in the frightening figure of the Skriker itself, a character whose gender is indeterminate, but whose malice is unmistakable.

What is to be done? The play does not say. It simply uses all the resources of theatre to awaken us to what is.

NOTES

1. For a more general discussion of the play's critique of the 'reduction of children to utilitarian objects for the benefit of their owner-parents' see Lisa Merrill, 'Monsters and Heroines: Caryl Churchill's Women', in Phyllis R. Randall (ed.), *Caryl Churchill: A Casebook* (New York: Garland, 1988), pp. 71–89, here p. 75.
2. Caryl Churchill, *Owners*, in *Plays: One* (London: Methuen, 1985), p. 63.
3. *Ibid.*
4. In what is perhaps Churchill's best-known play, *Top Girls*, the protagonist, Marlene, is extremely successful running a London employment agency, but the price she pays is giving up her child who is raised by her working-class sister in a run-down section of a seaside town. Many of the historical and quasi-historical women whom Marlene assembles at a dinner party also became famous and successful only when, like Patient Griselda, they endured having their children taken from them; or, like Pope Joan, when they were able to keep the fact of pregnancy concealed. In what some have seen as a troubling essentialism, maternity often figures in Churchill's work as a 'natural condition' distorted by patriarchal society, certainly, but also by the drive for property, ownership and worldly success.
5. For brief but telling accounts of Churchill's socialist feminism see Amelia Howe Kritzer, *The Plays of Caryl Churchill: Theatre of Empowerment* (Basingstoke: Macmillan, 1991), pp. 3–5, and Rosanna Bonicelli's 'Socialist Voices in Caryl Churchill: Objections to "Bourgeois Feminism"', in *Annali Di Ca' Foscari* XL, 1–2 (2001), 31–42.
6. Churchill, *Owners*, in *Plays: One,* p. 25. In her notes to the play, Churchill famously distinguishes between the contrast she wanted to establish between the urgent energy of Marion, embodied in the hymn 'Onward Christian Soldiers', and the passivity of Alex, embodied in a Zen poem. See headnote to *Owners*, in *Plays: One,* p. 4.
7. Churchill, *Owners*, in *Plays: One,* p. 47.
8. *Ibid.*, p. 48.
9. For an interesting discussion of Churchill as a writer of a modern history play, one that attempts to recreate the past in dialogue with the present, see Brean S. Hammon, '"Is Everything History?" Churchill, Barker, and the Modern History Play', *Comparative Drama* 41.1 (2007), 1–23.

10. This quotation is taken from Churchill's account of her work on the play as recorded in Rob Ritchie (ed.), *The Joint Stock Book: The Making of a Theatre Collective* (London: Methuen, 1987), p. 119. The quotation is unattributed but probably comes from a Ranter pamphlet, of which Churchill had read a great many.
11. In writing the play, Churchill relied upon an array of books, starting with Norman Cohn's *Pursuit of the Millennium: Revolutionary Millenarians and Mystical Anarchists of the Middle Ages* (London: Temple Smith, 1970), which had an appendix of Ranter writings. See her account of her 'insatiable readings' in Ritchie's *The Joint Stock Book*, p. 119. She also turned to Marxist historiography, most notably the work of Christopher Hill whose *The World Turned Upside Down: Radical Ideas During the English Revolution* (Harmondsworth: Penguin, 1972), read the Civil War as an instance of class struggle that resulted in the firm instantiation of capitalism and the triumph of bourgeois interests against the more radical movements of the period, in particular, of groups such as the Levellers, who wanted to widen the franchise and see realized the democratic gains promised by Cromwell, and above all the Diggers, a more left-wing group that argued for communist ideals, including the collective ownership of the land and the abolition of private property. Gerard Winstanley, one of the most articulate and textually inclined of the Diggers, was a particular hero of Hill's and appears in Churchill's play.
12. For accounts of Joint Stock and its effect upon Churchill's work see Aston, Chapter 9; Ritchie, *The Joint Stock Book*, and Frances Gray's 'Mirrors of Utopia: Caryl Churchill and Joint Stock', in James Acheson (ed.), *British and Irish Drama Since 1960* (Basingstoke: Macmillan, 1993), pp. 47–59. For a somewhat critical view of the company's early lack of commitment to multi-racial casting and practice, see Joyce Devlin's 'Joint Stock: From Colorless Company to Company of Color', *Theater Topics* 2 (1992), 63–76.
13. Ritchie, *The Joint Stock Book*, p. 119.
14. Frances Gray, 'Mirrors of Utopia', p. 49.
15. Churchill, *Light Shining*, in *Plays: One* (London: Methuen, 1985), p. 191.
16. *Ibid.*, p. 206.
17. Quotations from the Putney debates are taken from Geoffrey Robertson's *The Levellers: The Putney Debates* (New York: Verso, 2007), here quoted at p. 70.
18. Robertson, *The Levellers*, p. 74.
19. Churchill, *Light Shining*, in *Plays: One*, p. 194.
20. In 'Staging Modern Vagrancy: Female Figures of Border-crossing in Ama Ata Aidoo and Caryl Churchill', *Theatre Journal* 54:2 (2002), 245–62, Haiping Yan perceptively analyses this scene and argues that through it Churchill reveals 'the inception of modern capital as not only a violent land enclosure but a violent making of a placeless community' (p. 253).
21. Churchill, *Light Shining*, in *Plays: One*, p. 207.
22. For an interesting examination of this scene as a reworking of Lacan's mirror stage see Frances Gray, 'Mirrors of Utopia', p. 47.
23. Churchill, *Light Shining*, in *Plays: One*, p. 221.
24. *Ibid.*
25. *Ibid.*, p. 241.
26. *Ibid.*, p. 233.

27. *Ibid.*, p. 240.
28. As Stephanie Pocock in '"God's in this Apple": Eating and Spirituality in Churchill's *Light Shining in Buckinghamshire*', *Modern Drama* 50.1 (Spring 2007), 60–76, states, Briggs' self-starvation is 'a final attempt to achieve what the war failed at, the redistribution of property so that everyone has something to eat. He fasts not in hopes of Christ's victorious return but for the creation of an equitable society in the present', p. 67.
29. Churchill, *Light Shining*, in *Plays: One*, p. 184.
30. *Ibid.*, p. 239.
31. For a good discussion of 'The Big Bang', see Daniel Jernigan, '*Serious Money* Becomes "Business by Other Means": Caryl Churchill's Metatheatrical Subject', *Comparative Drama* 38.2–3 (2004), 291–313.
32. For a discussion of late or postmodern capital, see Linda Kintz, 'Performing Capital in Caryl Churchill's *Serious Money*', *Theatre Journal* 51.3 (1999), 251–65.
33. Churchill, *Serious Money*, in *Plays: Two* (London: Methuen, 1990), p. 197. For a discussion of Churchill's use of the Shadwell play, see Judith Bailey Slagle's 'Shadwell's *Volunteers* through the Centuries: Power Structures Adapted in Scott's *Peveril of the Peak* and Churchill's *Serious Money*', in *Thomas Shadwell Reconsider'd: Essays in Criticism*, a special issue of *Restoration: Studies in English Literary Culture, 1660–1700* 20 (Fall 1996), pp. 236–46.
34. Klaus Peter Muller, 'A Serious City Comedy: Fe-Male History and Value Judgments in Caryl Churchill's *Serious Money*', *Modern Drama*, 33:3 (1990), 347–62, at 356. Muller gives a good account of how Churchill's play draws on but differs from earlier city comedies.
35. Churchill, *Serious Money*, in *Plays: Two*, p. 233.
36. Margaret Rose, 'The City within the City in Caryl Churchill's *Serious Money*', *La Città delle donne: immaginario urbano e letteratura del Novecento* (1992), 71–84, at 72 and 82.
37. Churchill, *Serious Money*, in *Plays: Two*, p. 308.
38. See, for example, Linda Kintz's 'Performing Capital' with its argument that in this play critique tips willy-nilly into celebration.
39. For a very smart discussion of the play's meditation on theatre's involvement in late capitalism, see Daniel Jernigan's 'Serious Money becomes "business by other means"'.
40. Churchill, *Serious Money*, in *Plays: Two*, p. 297.
41. Churchill, *The Skriker* in *Plays: Three* (London: Nick Hern Books, 1998), p. 243.
42. Katherine Perrault, 'Beyond the Patriarchy: Feminism and the Chaos of Creativity', *Journal of Dramatic Theory and Criticism* 17 (Fall 2002), 45–67, see especially p. 49.
43. For a telling analysis of the centrality of the concept of 'damage' to this play see Elaine Aston, *Caryl Churchill*, 2nd edn (Plymouth: Northcote House, 2001), pp. 96–102.
44. Churchill, *The Skriker* in *Plays: Three*, p. 271.
45. *Ibid.*, pp. 282–3.
46. See Candice Amich's excellent article on this topic, 'Bringing the Global Home: The Commitment of Caryl Churchill's *The Skriker*', *Modern Drama* 50.3 (Fall 2007), 394–413.

4

MARY LUCKHURST

On the challenge of revolution

Caryl Churchill has shown a sustained interest in the inter-connections between self-definition, identity politics and revolution. In her career she has repeatedly examined revolutionary conditions, and engaged ambitiously with the artistic dilemma of how to represent political turmoil on stage. This chapter investigates three of her plays about revolution: *The Hospital at the Time of the Revolution, Light Shining in Buckinghamshire* and *Mad Forest.*

The Hospital at the Time of the Revolution

Hospital was written in 1972 though, inexplicably, it has never been staged. It draws on the writings of the celebrated psychiatrist and champion of the Algerian struggle for independence, Frantz Fanon, who was an inspirational figure not just for black revolutionaries but also for Churchill's generation of white, western political radicals in the 1960s.

The decolonization of Africa followed Indian independence in 1947, and when, in 1960, seventeen former African colonies became independent members of the United Nations, it marked a turning point in the post-war world, re-mapping power relations between Europe and Africa. The Algerians' fight for autonomy was particularly complex since French occupation dated from 1830 and French trade and investment in Algeria had matched economic commitments in all of France's other imperial territories combined. French emigration to Algeria had far exceeded the scale of emigration to other French colonies and colonial legal policy even upheld that Algeria was an integral part of France – an ideological position that created a panoply of contradictions and paradoxes.[1] From 1954 to eventual independence in 1962, the battle by the Algerian National Liberation Front (FLN) to overthrow French imperialism captured world attention for its duration, intensity and drama.[2] Churchill, born in 1938, grew up in this new, post-imperial world and was greatly influenced by revolutionary philosophies such as Marxism. Fanon himself did not live to see Algeria's liberation,[3] but Churchill was twenty-four at the time, and it represented for her, as it did for many others, an historic moment of utopian possibility. It is no accident, therefore, that *Hospital* is the most precisely located and overtly political of her early plays.

Set in the Blida-Joinville Hospital in Algeria, where Fanon was Director of Psychiatry from 1953–6, *Hospital* offers an evocative representation of Fanon at work during the early phases of the revolution. Visually, Churchill's description of the set, 'no scenery except bare white walls', 'white upright chairs', 'white beds for patients', 'bright light', suggests that Fanon's black skin and the dark skins of his Algerian patients appear vulnerable in a symbolically imprisoning white glare.[4] Fanon is Director of the facility but, apparently, also its prisoner and warder, and the ironies inherent in his position become more complex as the play progresses. The difference between victim and perpetrator is not as straightforward as might first appear; even Fanon's mysterious silences, which at first seem to signal resistance, gradually begin to reveal something more suspect.

The characters whom Churchill's Fanon encounters have their origins in case histories studied by Fanon himself in his celebrated work on the Algerian revolution, *The Wretched of the Earth*, which was published in 1961 and rapidly came to serve as a model for other liberation struggles. In a remarkable chapter entitled 'Colonial War and Mental Disorders' Fanon anatomizes the psychiatric disorders manifested both by the 'pacifiers' and the 'pacified' and notes that there are significant similarities.[5] In fact, Fanon argues, the colonial project is itself a psychiatric phenomenon which proliferates mental illness, and necessitates abundant supplies of psychiatric specialists and hospitals. The colonial 'cure' of 'civilization' is nothing other than 'a systematic negation of the other person', the so-called missionary philanthropy concealing ruthless commercial exploitation and mass de-humanization.[6]

Churchill's construction of Frantz Fanon as a man of strategic reserve creates a stage presence that serves as a device to expose the pathologies of both the colonizers and the colonized: Europeans and Algerians alike talk to Fanon, their confessions revealing profoundly damaged psyches and a sense of self determined only by the ideology and practice of imperial aggression. Churchill's Fanon, like the actual man, cannot risk open resistance while at work without endangering his life. The hospital is a glass house of resonating tensions, a temporary refuge for the opponents and engineers of the regime, and it functions in a precarious state of limbo. The segregation enforced outside the hospital confines is not possible within its walls and Europeans and Algerians mix uneasily, always fearful of one another. The aetiology of the mental illnesses Fanon is diagnosing is rooted in the project of colonialism itself. By setting the play in the hospital Churchill highlights the paradoxical and destructive circularity of a colonial system that promises civilization but is in itself founded on a nexus of abnormal thoughts and behaviours promoting the spread of psychiatric pathologies. Accordingly, Churchill's hospital becomes a metaphor for the self-devouring machine of imperialism, a microcosm of the much larger madhouse Algeria has become under French rule.

The Algerian patients Fanon treats in the play are symbolically without name or title and appear only as A, B and C. A is a resistance fighter, driven to bomb because he can see no other way to combat the enforced removal of his individual rights. Life in the FLN has separated him from his wife, family, job and home. He is wracked by the unbearable burden of having killed but equally his sense of justice compels him to continue killing. Trapped in this grotesque torment, he has tried but failed to end his own life. B has suffered a complete emotional and physical breakdown from torture and is in clinical shock. He is terrified of further attack and cannot interact with others. He utters only a few lines and when he bumps into his ex-torturer, also receiving treatment at the hospital, he has to be prevented from committing suicide: 'Let me die. I can't go back there.'[7] C is constantly mistaken for a European because of his pale skin, experiences extreme guilt that he has not joined the resistance, and suffers paranoid delusions that other Algerians judge him to be both a coward and a traitor. C's implosion is perhaps most drastic because he cannot connect with external reality at all, and his feelings of persecution are driven by profound self-loathing: 'What am I meant to do with my skin?' he asks despairingly.[8] All three cases indicate the dispossession and disintegration of self, which Fanon's writings describe in detail. Mental health is driven to breaking point because of the colonial task to erase the Algerian, Fanon argues: 'colonialism forces the people it dominates to ask themselves the question constantly: "In reality, who am I?"'[9] Life for the Algerian is the omnipresence of death and the loss of self. The hopelessness of that logical trap is suggested in the play by the story of the fifteen-year-old Algerian boy, who, in an unprovoked attack, has stabbed to death three Europeans, one of them his friend.[10] Though the story is not pursued further in the play, Fanon interprets the original case history as a predictable behavioural display for one who has grown up among 'a whole generation of Algerians who have been steeped in wanton generalised homicide'.[11] Once 'the point of no return' for an oppressed people is reached, argues Fanon in his essay 'Concerning Violence', survival and self-definition can only be achieved through fighting back: 'The development of violence among the colonised people will be proportionate to the violence exercised by the threatened colonial regime.'[12]

The brutality of the Europeans whom Churchill's Fanon encounters is not in question: the Doctor, Police Inspector and the married couple Monsieur and Madame each demonstrate, in different ways, that torture and extermination are a norm and a patriotic duty. Monsieur was born in Algeria into a settler family but identifies himself as French: 'This is my country. [...] I am already in France. France is Algeria.'[13] Monsieur is a civil servant and his settler status and occupation as one of the elite administrators of the colony almost certainly mean that he is also a substantial landowner. He and his wife manifest a conditioned, ingrained racism, Monsieur viewing the colonial project as 'an endless struggle to curb and suppress and pacify' what he refers to as 'urban and rural elements', the children of whom are 'naturally born violent and dishonest'.[14] Monsieur's language is a rhetorically strait-jacketed, colonial double-speak which justifies the taking of ethnic Algerian lives supposedly in the name of state security:

> The violence is committed by criminals. It is not part of any revolution. The majority of the natives look to us to protect them and restore order. And it is only the French who can pacify the land. Because naturally the Algerian has criminal tendencies.[15]

Defined entirely by racial prejudice and false doctrine, Monsieur and Madame cannot contemplate the success of the revolution, a concept outside their mental frame of reference, and yet the momentum of the liberation struggle places intolerable stress on their insistent patterns of denial. The breaking point threatens to be their daughter, Françoise, whom they bring to Fanon because she claims they are trying to kill her. Slowly, a subtext emerges and the spectator, cleverly positioned with an almost silent Fanon, comes to understand that the father is conducting interrogations, torture and executions in the family home: 'You won't find an area that has been so thoroughly cleared of subversive elements.'[16] Françoise is kept awake by the torture sessions every night (the mother takes sleeping tablets). She abhors her parents' belief systems, and their denial of the fact that they are running a human slaughterhouse has triggered schizophrenia. As far as Monsieur and Madame are concerned, Françoise's trauma-induced insanity renders her a liability because it destroys her investment potential as 'a physically perfect specimen' whose unquestioning conformity will make her a natural inheritor of colonial Algeria.[17] It also overturns the premise on which they have based their entire lives: that their investment in their daughter's future has made all their actions explicable and justifiable to themselves. Françoise's worsening condition acts as an intolerable and disgusting rebuke to her parents, who themselves show increasing signs of mental and emotional disintegration. Monsieur is now caught in a compulsive spiral of violence: 'They must be beaten because they resist us and go on and on resisting us however hard we force.' Close to complete breakdown the father weeps as he acknowledges that he cannot stop because if he does he will become a non-person: 'What will become of me if I have to go? What will I be?'[18] Eventually Françoise's parents abandon her in the hospital, insisting that she cannot return home until she is engineered into the product they require. Françoise and Fanon are the only characters granted names in the play, and have a silent sympathy with one another: both are colonized in different fashions, but both are trying to resist oppression. For Churchill Françoise's fate looks bleak: her moving speech at the end of the play reveals her belief that she is dead, that when she removes her dress 'there's nobody there'.[19]

Fanon's two sessions with the Police Inspector reveal a man who, like Monsieur, is defined by duty and profession. The revolution requires the Inspector's full-time expertise as a torturer, and he frequently works overtime. He is plagued by sleeplessness and nightmares, constant irritability and cannot prevent himself from making psychotic and brutal attacks on his wife and young daughters. His transformation into a sadistic killing machine is evident from the lack of empathy he has for the Algerians he tortures or murders, as well as the pleasure he extracts from terrorizing his wife and children. His own diagnosis is tiredness caused by work stress, but the stress is connected in his mind with the need to demonstrate professional excellence, and to stay ahead in the promotion stakes by exploiting what he calls his 'flair':[20] all he requires are drugs to make him function efficiently and calmly:

> My life would be perfect if there wasn't something the matter with me. The work's too hard and it's getting me down. What really kills me is the torture. No one thinks what hard work it is for the one that's doing it. The prisoners should have more consideration than to force us to go on doing that to them and just tell us quietly what we want to know. Because it's no joke torturing someone for ten hours. You get really involved in what you're doing.[21]

As unpalatably ironic and as dramatically extreme at the speech sounds, it is directly paraphrased from Fanon's original case history.[22] The play also delivers the same recommendation as Fanon's – to transfer out of the police service, but the Inspector blames his symptoms on 'the troubles' in Algeria as a whole, not the specific barbarity of torture. His job is his identity: 'What am I then if I'm not a policeman? I've always been a policeman.'[23] Fanon has described this double-bind in an examination of police savagery in *Toward the African Revolution*:

> Colonialism cannot be understood without the possibility of torturing, of violating or massacring. Torture is an expression and means of the occupant–occupied relationship [...] The police agent who tortures an Algerian infringes no law. His act fits into the framework of the colonialist institution. By torturing, he manifests an exemplary loyalty to the system.[24]

The Inspector, then, will continue to work until his own catastrophic implosion. Confronted with a man who is addicted to sedatives at night and tranquillizers during the day (which are already failing to work), Churchill's Fanon finds himself in the position of renewing a prescription designed to enable the Inspector to suppress all affect and to kill more effectively. Fanon, in other words, has become the means by which the Inspector continues to function and is uncomfortably implicated in the oppression he seeks to resist.

Fanon's complicitous double-bind is revealed most by the European Doctor, who cannot see the point in treating 'terrorists', and is deluded in his belief that by offering his medical expertise to administer pentathol (the truth drug) to Algerians under military interrogation, he will lessen their suffering and curtail the war. He identifies wholly with the colonial regime, but fails to conceive of himself as a soldier or torturer. He is steeped in the racial prejudice of Western medical science, arguing to Fanon that:

> The African is like a lobotomised European. It accounts for the impulsive aggression, the laziness, the shallowness of emotional affect, the inability to grasp the whole concept – the African character.[25]

His self-deceiving speech justifying to himself the injection of pentathol as a licensed medical experiment, which will require him to 'observe the effects'[26] in order to ascertain whether damage to the personality can be limited, is reminiscent of the medical abuses under the Nazi and Soviet regimes. To the Doctor, Algerian 'terrorists' are useful fodder for laboratory testing, and Fanon's silences have exposed him as an enemy of the state – the Doctor making it clear that his days are numbered: 'I'm not threatening you [...] I just hope very much I never meet you as one of the superintendent's patients.'[27]

In Chapter 4 of his work, *A Dying Colonialism*, Fanon examines the status of the European doctor during the Algerian revolution. He concludes that European doctors were economically invested in the maintenance of colonial oppression because they were mostly landowners. Invariably, argues Fanon, they were militia chiefs or organizers of 'counter-terrorist' raids.[28] Many European doctors were simply war criminals – a fact, Fanon writes, that has not been grasped by world opinion. On the strictly technical level, the European doctor actively collaborates with the colonial forces in their most frightful and their most degrading practices.[29] Fanon's position as a psychiatrist was complicated by the fact that he was a black doctor born in Martinique, but educated in Paris. His education and accent gave him a status and authority not accorded to other black doctors, but the institutional racism of colonial medical practices coupled with systematic torture and terror tactics by the authorities made it impossible for him to adopt an effective mode of resistance while remaining in post. Churchill's play ends with Fanon under threat. The real Fanon resigned and joined the FLN. His letter of resignation provides a context for the silences which are so poignant in the play:

> If psychiatry is the medical technique that aims to enable man no longer to be a stranger to his environment, I owe it to myself to affirm that the Arab, permanently an alien in his own country, lives in a state of absolute depersonalisation. What is the status of Algeria? A systematised de-humanisation. [...] Hope is then no longer an open door to the future but the illogical maintenance of a subjective attitude in organised contradiction with reality [...] The events in Algeria are the logical consequence of an abortive attempt to decerebralise a people. [...] There comes a time when silence becomes dishonesty. [...] The decision I have reached is that I cannot continue to bear a responsibility at no matter what cost, on the false pretext that there is nothing else to be done.[30]

Light Shining in Buckinghamshire

While *Hospital* focuses on the pathological difficulty of self-definition during the Algerian revolutionary struggle, *Light Shining* explores the explosive potentialities for self-invention during the years of the English Civil War from 1642–6 and the period of the English Republic from 1649–60. *Light Shining* is ambitiously experimental, the product of a famous collaboration with actors from Joint Stock, and an attempt to find a more dynamic means of representing revolutionary phenomena.[31] The carefully patterned narrative threads of *Hospital* are replaced by flashes of character, glimpses into mental and physical states, and fragments of different worlds. The play is both kaleidoscopic and epic with documentary inserts and direct quotation from seventeenth-century pamphlets, juxtaposed with vignettes of everyday encounters and political and religious debates extraordinary for their frankness. Some characters are recreations of historical figures, most are inventions, indeed the notion of 'character' is in itself problematized by Churchill's stage notes that explain how 'characters are not played by the same actors each time they appear' and that '[e]ach scene can be taken as a separate event rather than part of a story' so as 'to reflect better the reality of large events like war and revolution where many people share the same kind of experience'.[32]

For the historian Christopher Hill, the 1640s and early 1650s represent 'the greatest upheaval that has yet occurred in Britain' and saw 'a great overturning, questioning, revaluing of everything in England'.[33] Churchill concentrates on 'the revolution that did not happen'[34] (what Hill terms 'the revolt within the Revolution'[35]) and explains the trajectory of the play in her foreword:

> For a short time when the king had been defeated anything seemed possible, and the play shows the amazed excitement of people taking hold of their own lives, and their gradual betrayal as those who led them realised that freedom could not be had without property being destroyed.[36]

If the revolt within the Revolution had succeeded, it would have radically changed England's political course, perhaps ultimately legalizing communal property, disestablishing the church and disavowing the protestant ethic, as well as instituting a far more extensive legal and political democracy. By contrast, the Revolution that took root established the sacred rights of property (with the abolition of feudal tenures), gave political power to the propertied (through sovereignity of Parliament and common law), and 'removed all impediments to the triumph of the ideology of the men of property – the protestant ethic'.[37] These changes ensured a new focus on capital and prepared the way for England to become the first industrialized great power.

Churchill's attention is on the religious radicals, and on powerfully renewed millenarian beliefs exacerbated initially by Charles I's defeat and then his execution in 1649. The millennium, believed to be imminent, meant the fall of the Antichrist, the second coming, and a period of heaven on earth when Jesus would reign for a thousand years.[38] *Light Shining* provides evocative glimpses of the anti-clerical worlds of such sectaries as the Levellers, Diggers and Ranters, the radical elements in Oliver Cromwell's New Model Army, the laity, the vagrant and the poor, as well as Cromwell and his Commissary General, Ireton.

It is not difficult to see why the intellectual and moral revolution begun in the years of Civil War, and incited further by millenarianism, came to be regarded as seditious by the politicized, land-owning hierarchy. The main subjects of debate were religion, liberty and property – all three were inextricably linked and the efforts of agitators such as the Levellers centred on examining the preconceptions behind their inter-relationship. In his well-known book, Morton describes the Levellers as 'the first fully democratic party in the Revolution', whose insistence on 'freedom of the pulpit' ensured the dissemination of democratic and revolutionary ideas.[39] Leveller influence was powerful in the socially mobile Model Army and helped to turn it into a 'short-lived school of political democracy', where social injustices were hotly debated and significant numbers of soldiers became political educators and preachers, speaking to peasants of civil liberties, religious toleration, election issues and of the wrongs of private land enclosure and disafforestation, which had penalized the poor and starving.[40]

The play crackles with the energy of numerous characters exchanging incendiary ideas and embarking on journeys of unprecedented self-discovery.

Hoskins, for example, argues with a preacher that Calvinist notions of predestination are unfounded and unfair, and suggests that sickness and death have a great deal more to do with mismanagement by those in power than with sin and divine purpose: 'How can God choose us from all eternity to be saved or damned when there's nothing we've done?'[41] Claxton, based on the real-life Laurence Clarkson, known as Captain of the Rant, explains that God is 'an infinite nothing', and that 'sin' has to be committed to demonstrate that it is non-existent: 'I have come to see that there is no sin but what man thinks is sin.'[42] Two women, inside the house of a rich landowner who has fled, talk of burning the legal papers that detail how the property was consigned to him: 'That's like him burnt. There's no one over us.'[43] The scene establishes a fundamental link between identity and property. The women's realization that they and other commoners are standing on the brink of an extraordinary revolutionary moment is symbolized by their discovery of a large mirror. Neither has ever seen herself before because mirrors are luxury items, and Churchill uses the image to convey them in a moment of transformative personal and political self-knowledge: 'You see your whole body at once. You see yourself standing in that room. They must know what they look like all the time. And now we do.'[44]

The war of ideas is played out in the remarkable scene that completes Act I, which represents an edited snapshot of the so-called Putney debates, when members of the Model Army assembled at a church in Putney, London, on 28 October 1647. At this time the Army included delegates at both senior and junior officer level elected by the rank and file, and Leveller ideas were at their most pervasive. The issue of central importance was the question of franchise, namely, the question of exactly who was entitled to elect the sovereign parliament. Churchill represents just six of the original participants: Colonel Rainborough, Edward Sexby, John Wildman – all Levellers – and Cromwell, General Ireton and Colonel Rich. Rainborough argues that the poor and unpropertied live in a state of complete subjection, as do soldiers who have fought for parliament against the monarchy but are disbarred from any process of direct election:

> all Englishmen must be subject to English law, and the foundation of the law lies in the people [...] The old law of England [...] enslaves the people of England – that they should be bound by laws in which they have no voice! And for my part, I look upon the people of England so, that wherein they have not voices in the choosing of their governors they are not bound to obey them.[45]

Sexby, a private, is even more critical, voicing the betrayal felt by thousands of soldiers who have not fought primarily to protect property but for their status as citizens:

> It seems now except a man hath a fixed estate in the kingdom, he hath no right in this kingdom. [...] If we had not a right to the kingdom, we were mercenary soldiers. [...] If this thing be denied the poor, that with so much pressing after they have sought, it will be the greatest scandal. It was said that if those in low condition were given their birthright it would mean the destruction of this kingdom. I think the poor and meaner of this kingdom have been the means of preservation of this kingdom.[46]

But it is Ireton who wins the day, covertly supported by Cromwell, who postulates that property is neither bestowed by the law of God, nor by the law of nature but 'is of human constitution': 'I have a property and this I shall enjoy.'[47] Ownership of land, for Ireton, invests its proprietor with a right to govern, and, in turn, commoners have a right to be governed by those 'that have the interest in the kingdom'.[48] The meeting is a defeat for the Levellers, and Rainborough sums up his despair with a poignant observation: 'I see it is impossible to have liberty without all property being taken away.'[49] In this moment of history possession of private property is enshrined as greater than a man or woman's legal enfranchisement.

Act II opens with a narration of one of the most celebrated, radical stands against private property – the Diggers protest at St George's Hill in Surrey in 1649, when Gerrard Winstanley spearheaded the digging and sowing of private land. In a speech that was predicated on republican beliefs and a pro-active bid to address the needs of the poor, Winstanley argued that England could not be free until commoners had the licence to cultivate the land and feed themselves. Winstanley's model of a self-sufficient community living according to its own religious and political philosophies was an early example of communism: 'there can be no universal liberty till this universal community be established'.[50] Significantly, the title of the play, *Light Shining in Buckinghamshire*, refers to a Leveller pamphlet calling for equality of property in 1648. Cromwell wasted no time in routing the Diggers and destroying both their houses and their cultivated land; Leveller resistance was finally crushed at Burford in the same year. After 1649 parliamentarians became more hard-line and radical elements in the Army and amongst the people were either marginalized or brutally stamped out. Act II reports the steady stream of defeats and the decline in radicalism and its material effects. A wide range of characters testify to the regression. Ideologically opposed to the war in Ireland, Briggs deserts the Army, his views now regarded as dangerously dissident. Brotherton, a vagrant, is still destitute and symbolically cannot shake herself free of the belief that she is damned for killing the baby she could not afford to nurture. Another woman cannot abandon her baby even though she knows it will die of starvation if she keeps it. The Ranters briefly find a form of utopianism in the sexual liberty that they espouse: 'we'll have no property in the flesh'[51] but are later pursued and persecuted. In an epilogue set after the restoration of the king in 1660, characters reveal their broken spirits in a moving lamentation. Briggs has become a fugitive and survives by eating grass. Brotherton is still forced into criminality to make a living. Claxton rues the curtailment of free speech, Hoskins wonders how they missed their opportunity for change, and Cobbe, the Ranter, reflects on the introduction of legislation to reinforce protestantism.[52] As Churchill says in her foreword, this is far from heaven on earth: 'what was established instead was an authoritarian parliament, the massacre of the Irish, the development of capitalism'.[53] In her play Churchill gives a set of vivid insights into the failed struggle for liberty. Hill has given a trenchant summation of how different the world might have been if, say, the Ranters had won:

> We can discern shadows of what this counter-culture might have been like. Rejecting private property for communism, religion for rationalistic and materialistic pantheism, the mechanical philosophy for dialectical science, asceticism for unashamed enjoyment of the good things of the flesh, it might have achieved unity through a federation of communities, each based on the fullest respect for the individual. Its ideal would have been economic self-sufficiency, not world trade or world domination.[54]

Expressed thus, it is clear that Churchill has depicted worlds and characters that may initially seem remote from us, but in fact continue to have striking contemporary relevance.

Mad Forest

In *Mad Forest* Churchill takes the challenge of representing revolution to new levels of sophistication, draws a great deal more attention to the mechanisms of narrative in performance, and places the act of spectatorship under particular stress. The play is an inspired endeavour to offer glimpses of life in Romania before, during and after the revolution, which culminated in the notorious execution of the dictator Nicolae Ceauşescu and his wife, Elena, on Christmas Day in 1989. Fuelled by the rapid collapse of communist government in Poland, Hungary, Czechoslovakia, Bulgaria and East Germany, and by the breaching of the Berlin wall in November 1989, which had been a symbol of the separation between the communist East and the capitalist West, Romanians began mass demonstrations in Timisoara in mid-December. Protest spread, and reprisals by the Securitate, the secret police, were fierce but the Romanian army sided with the people and less than a fortnight later the dictator, along with 1,000 others, was dead. Ceauşescu's communist dictatorship lasted from 1965–1989, brought severe privations to Romanian people, including systematic persecution of Hungarian and Romany populations, and was renowned for its terror tactics.[55] Churchill's drama is an extraordinary and unique attempt to reflect on the end of his regime from an outsider's point of view. Directed by Mark Wing-Davey, *Mad Forest* was first performed by acting students in June 1990 at the Central School of Speech and Drama (CSSD) in London, then at the National Theatre of Romania in Bucharest. It finally transferred to the Royal Court in October 1990, and to New York City in December 1991.

Churchill's decision to experiment with clashing performance styles, her juxtaposition of the surreal with the real, of the imaginary with eyewitness accounts, of the dead with the living, and her subtle use of the micro-political to illuminate the macro-political, make *Mad Forest* a remarkable play. Her creative relationship to the generation of *Mad Forest* was more personal than her relationship to *Hospital* and *Light Shining*, and connected with her own political disillusion. She visited Romania only a few weeks after Ceauşescu's death and conducted research directly with people who had experienced the revolution. The idea of making a play about the Romanian revolution had first occurred to Wing-Davey as he absorbed events from the news in 1989. At the time he was the Director of CSSD:

> I realised the people dying were the same age as my students at Central. I knew Caryl well from our time together at Joint Stock. [...] As a socialist who had followed the collapse of communism in other countries, she felt it was important to go and see what was happening for herself.[56]

What emerged from their trip to Romania was a collaboration between students at CSSD and staff and students at the Caragiale Institute of Theatre and Film Arts in Bucharest. The Romanian students related their own experiences, and both groups conducted interviews with other Romanians. The play evolved from improvisations, field-work and other workshop exercises invented by Churchill and Wing-Davey.

Churchill's first-hand experiences in a newly liberated Romania had a profound impact on both the content and form of *Mad Forest*. According to Wing-Davey, everyone in the British party was overwhelmed by feelings of disorientation and incomprehension. One aspect of the workshops in Romania, therefore, focused on the expression of the culture shock felt by the British visitors. Common motifs emerged and heavily informed the play. These included the constant rebuttal of expectations and the difficulty of everyday living, such as the non- or erratic functionality of power sources and the challenge of finding simple foodstuffs. The Britons also found that they misread and misunderstood Romanian people and apparently everyday situations. They observed the Romanian habituation to queuing for basic items for extremely long hours and found it hard to grasp Romanian 'paranoia' about the change in regime. The intense suspicion surrounding the circumstances of Ceauşescu's death, and whether a revolution had taken place or not, struck all the British participants, Churchill herself later commenting that Romanian society demonstrated 'a whole spectrum of paranoia at one end, stretching through to a very reasonable suspicion at the other'.[57] Workshops also explored covert methods of communication, which had been in operation for Romanians living under dictatorship. Indeed, the difficulties or impossibilities of communication, both in times of dictatorship and its aftermath, and in particular the problems experienced by the British participants of trying to negotiate a language barrier as well as immersion in a totally unfamiliar culture, all served to shape Churchill's dramaturgical ideas for the play.[58]

In the published play-text of *Mad Forest* Churchill includes an epigragh to explain its title:

> On the plain where Bucharest now stands there used to be 'a large forest crossed by small muddy streams ... It could only be crossed on foot and was impenetrable for the foreigner who did not know the paths ... The horsemen of the steppe were compelled to go round it, and this difficulty, which irked them so, is shown by the name ... Teleorman – Mad Forest.'[59]

The play's title alludes to the impossibility of foreign visitors navigating their way through 'impenetrable' paths to Bucharest, and Churchill's play mirrors both those thwarted journeys to the centre of the city, and her own sense that she managed to catch only glimpses of what she was trying to write about. In *Mad Forest* Churchill's fragmentary scenes, broken narratives and unapologetic juxtapositions of performance style constantly challenge the spectator's perception of the material. The subtitle is specifically 'A Play from Romania', not '*about* Romania' and Wing-Davey is clear that:

> The key thing about *Mad Forest* is that it's not a play about Romania, it's a play about what it's like to watch a play about Romania. Not-knowing, not understanding were themselves very important ideas in its making. The play tries to generate a sense of cultural dislocation in the audience.[60]

It is precisely this cultural dislocation which is inscribed into the play through the multiple role-play of the eleven actors (who play over thirty-seven parts), through its linguistic self-referentiality, and its collapsing together of radically different theatrical and performative styles. Churchill's own attempts to learn Romanian provided the inspiration for the scene headings, which are cited first in Romanian and then in English, and styled in the manner of a tourist phrasebook.[61] The headings were read out by members of the company and instantly encoded the idea of a Westerner's attempts to get to grips with a foreign language and culture, again emphasizing that the play is an outsider's view and that language itself is under particular scrutiny.

The sonic patterns of the play are also complex. In a production note to *Mad Forest* Churchill describes the dramaturgy of the play as going 'from the difficulty of saying anything to everyone talking', indicating that the premiere production contained long silences at the beginning.[62] Mirroring the freedom of speech that has come with the revolution, Churchill's play shows a sonic landscape that moves from uneasy silences and snatched moments of freedom of expression to a Romanian Tower of Babel that is far from utopian. The physical plotting of the play mirrors linguistic patterns, moving from scenes of stasis to wild bursts of activity in Act III, including the madcap mock execution of the Ceauşescus in Scene 6 and the frenzied final scene which zanily juxtaposes a classic silent slapstick routine with the volcanic eruption of dancing, the outbreak of physical violence and inter-cutting voices.

Mad Forest adheres to a three-act structure, Act I Lucia's Wedding, Act II December, Act III Florina's Wedding, but is far from conventional. In Acts I and III actors play multiple roles in snapshot scenes that steal glances at the situation of two families, the Vladus who are artisans and the more educated Antonescus. Act I is set before the revolution under Ceauşescu and ends with Lucia's marriage to an American, the symbol of her 'escape' to the West. The sixteen fragmentary scenes in Act I all explore the complexities of lives policed by excessive state controls, and the impossibility of communicating anything meaningful without resorting to covert or non-verbal exchanges, deploying coded language, or retreat into the self. In scene 1 all dialogue is obscured by a loud radio designed to foil bugging devices, but we understand from the family's varying reactions to Lucia's gifts of eggs and American cigarettes, that her fraternization with her US boyfriend is bringing hardship and stress. In scene 5 Radu's one whispered line 'Down with Ceauşescu', uttered in a shopping queue, hints at underlying revolutionary fervour. In scene 7 Lucia arranges an illegal abortion with a doctor who pretends to admonish her but is simultaneously pocketing her bribe. In scene 8 men tell each other cryptic jokes which implicitly critique the regime. Significantly, the longest monologues are an official panegyric of Ceauşescu delivered by a schoolteacher and an interrogation by a member of the Securitate, who forces Lucia's father to inform on her. State-sanctioned rhetoric prevails and, like the ceremonial music which serves as a prologue to the play, it acts as a lethal weapon, brainwashing the gullible or ensnaring and terrorizing dissenters. The most emotionally invested exchanges occur only in the realms of the imagination: between Flavia and her dead grandmother, and between a priest and an angel, the latter proving to be a sympathizer of the fascist Iron Guard.

The priest voices the dilemma of speaking out, and its cost – both spiritual and mortal:

> Someone says something, you say something back, you're called to a police station, that happened to my brother. So it's not safe to go out to people and when you can't go out sometimes you find you can't go in, I'm afraid to go inside myself, perhaps there's nothing there, I just keep still.[63]

Nothing is what it seems in these scenes. Silences are cavernous and might be assenting, dissenting, at odds with the surrounding action and words of the scenario; they edge towards the treacherous, or even the murderous. A surreal though apparently innocent exchange between the angel and the priest, for example, also appears to be a coded death-threat, the collapse of personal responsibility, and the stirrings of political complicity:

> ANGEL I try to keep clear of the political side. You should do the same.
> *Pause.*
> PRIEST I don't trust you any more.
> ANGEL That's a pity. Who else can you trust?
> *Pause.*
> Would you rather feel ashamed?
> *Pause.*
> Or are you going to take some kind of action, surely not?
> *Silence.*
> PRIEST Comfort me.[64]

The priest's descent into terrorized silence, the very opposite of protest, is all too clear. But, as ever with Churchill, there is more to this scene than an example of everyday individual fallibility. Behind it stands her meticulous historical research and her knowledge that the Catholic Church in Romania, unlike the organized religious resistance in neighbouring communist countries, was suspiciously quiescent during Ceauşescu's dictatorship.[65] Apparently straightforward cameo scenes are, then, complex, layered cryptograms which allude to historical and political grand narratives, as well as to the pain and suffering of ordinary people.

Act II fractures the play into two discernible parts: it is a collection of direct-address speeches delivered by characters who appear nowhere else, and who describe what they did when the revolution broke out and how it affected them. While it bridges the play in terms of narrative and historical chronology, Act II is otherwise a radical disjuncture and a stark alienation device, interrupting stylized fiction with stylized verbatim accounts from real interviewees. Wing-Davey deployed a documentary style which eschewed acting behind a fourth wall, and performers stood in front of the safety curtain as if for a group photograph. The form of Act II was therefore made to stand in ironic relation to its content: stasis replaced action and actors resisted heightened vocalization. In a production at the York Theatre Royal in March 2007 actors spoke and moved into individual and group tableaus, slow motion scenarios and freezes, while film footage of the fighting on the streets of Bucharest played on a vast screen behind them, and a soundscore of rolling tanks, shots and screams gradually drowned out their testimony.[66] Given the astonishing power of the verbatim reports it is understandable that Churchill felt an ethical responsibility not to try and re-tell these revolutionary stories in her own words.

Act III is located post-revolution and ends with Florina's marriage to Radu, not previously sanctioned by Radu's family for political reasons (namely, her sister Lucia's 'unpatriotic' love-match). The American Dream having proved empty, Lucia has returned to Romania, and in a mercenary manouevre, tries to revivify a relationship with Ianos, a Hungarian. Florina's wedding ends with an apocalyptic scene of families at war, and the outbreak of violent recrimination and feelings of betrayal. The revolution has brought with it a new set of uncertainties and material problems and the war between the families only symbolizes the dangers of civil war on a larger scale.

The first scene in Act III has foreshadowed this ending. An encounter between a dog and a vampire, it is a clear alienation device and clashes with the verbatim delivery of Act II. But to dress the vampire as a vampire is to miss the point, as Churchill indicates in her production note. The scene title 'Cîinelui îi e foame. The dog is hungry' explains the situation with Brechtian formality, but unlike Brecht the ensuing scene is set in ironic counterpoint to its descriptor. The dog pleads pathetically for food and a master, quite willing to submit himself to the life of a vampire dog, and the scene ends by showing their new alliance as the vampire '*puts his mouth to the dog's neck*'.[67] Packs of wild dogs were common on Romanian streets[68] and the deeply embedded folklore about vampires and Transylvania is well-known. But the vampire is also a manifest allusion to Ceausescu himself, since he had overseen the re-writing of Romanian history, placing himself at its centre by restoring the reputation of Vlad the Impaler and rehabilitating Dracula as his direct precursor with the aim of providing a historical precedent for political tyranny. Post-revolution, the vampire is directly implicated in the shedding of blood, but the dog, now free, is disoriented and starving, suffering a self-destructive longing for authority. The dog, habituated to subjugation, simply takes the next opportunity to become a servant – even to a master who only promises more killing:

> VAMPIRE All that happens is you begin to want blood, you try to put it off, you're bored with killing, but you can't sit quiet, you can't settle to anything, your limbs ache, your head burns, you have to keep moving faster and faster, that eases the pain, seeking. And finding.[69]

A symbolic scene of self-immolation, it is also a reminder that material deprivation and poverty provide a dangerous engine to the political machinery of state. Questions about complicity and collaboration abound. It is significant that this encounter opens an Act that teems with doubts, paranoia, conspiracy theories and terror about whether the change in regime will be lasting and meaningful. The fact that the vampire's words are repeated, indeed are the last words to resound clearly from the cacophony of voices at the end of the play, is a dark and doomladen note: in Churchill's view, the Romanian past and present place heavy burdens on the future.

The oblique interrogations at the heart of *Mad Forest* place many demands on its audiences but that confounding of expectations requires spectators to re-tune their intellectual engagement, and is a critical part of Churchill's ambitious quest to find ways of representing the sporadic, chaotic and diverse narratives of revolution. In this play Churchill pushes experiments evident in *Hospital* and *Light Shining* considerably further, extending her examination of what might come after revolution. All three plays amount to an astonishingly radical theatrical enquiry of their own, and make Churchill one of the most significant political playwrights alive today.

NOTES

1. See Martin Evans and John Phillips (eds.), *Algeria, Anger of the Dispossessed* (New Haven and London: Yale University Press, 2007), p. 27; Benjamin Stora, *Algeria, A Short History, 1830–2000* (Ithaca, NY: Cornell University Press, 2001); William B. Quandt, *Revolution and Political Leadership: Algeria, 1954–1968* (Cambridge, MA: MIT Press, 1969).
2. FLN, *Front de Libération Nationale.*
3. He died of leukaemia in 1961.
4. Caryl Churchill, *The Hospital at the Time of the Revolution* in *Churchill: Shorts* (London: Nick Hern Books, 1990), p. 97.
5. Frantz Fanon, 'Colonial War and Mental Disorders' in *The Wretched of the Earth* (Harmondsworth: Penguin, 1967), pp. 200–50. Fanon's use of inverted commas for 'pacification' and 'pacified' indicate his scepticism about an official term which, in effect, meant wholesale economic and political oppression.
6. *Ibid.*, p. 200.
7. Churchill, *Hospital*, p. 146.
8. *Ibid.*, p. 142
9. Fanon, *Wretched of the Earth*, p. 200.
10. Churchill, *Hospital*, pp. 118–19.
11. Fanon, *Wretched of the Earth*, p. 202.
12. *Ibid.*, p. 69.
13. Churchill, *Hospital*, p. 135.
14. *Ibid.*, pp. 100–2.
15. *Ibid.*, p. 110.
16. *Ibid.*, p. 115.

17. *Ibid.*, p. 100.
18. *Ibid.*, p. 138.
19. *Ibid.*, p. 146.
20. *Ibid.*, p. 143.
21. *Ibid.*, p. 130.
22. Fanon, *Wretched of the Earth*, p. 216.
23. Churchill, *Hospital*, p. 144.
24. Frantz Fanon, *Toward the African Revolution: Political Essays* (New York: Grove Press, 1964), pp. 66 and 71.
25. Churchill, *Hospital*, p. 119.
26. *Ibid.*, p. 132.
27. *Ibid.*, p. 133.
28. Frantz Fanon, 'Medicine and Colonialism' in *A Dying Colonialism* (New York: Grove Press, 1965), p.136.
29. *Ibid.*, p. 137.
30. Fanon, *Toward the African Revolution*, pp. 52–4.
31. For information on processes of production in *Light Shining* see Rob Ritchie (ed.), *The Joint Stock Book: The Making of a Theatre Collective* (London: Methuen, 1987).
32. Churchill, 'A Note on the Production', *Light Shining*, in *Plays: One* (London: Methuen, 1985) pp. 184–5. See Howard, Chapter 3, pp. 38–44, for further discussion.
33. Christopher Hill, *The World Turned Upside Down: Radical Ideas during the English Revolution* (London: Penguin, 1991), pp. 13–14. See also Christopher Hill, *God's Englishman: Oliver Cromwell and the English Revolution* (London: Weidenfeld and Nicolson, 1970) and *The Intellectual Origins of the English Revolution Revisited* (Oxford: Clarendon Press, 1997).
34. Caryl Churchill, *Light Shining*, in *Plays: One*, p. 183.
35. Hill, *The World*, p. 15.
36. Churchill, *Light Shining*, p. 183.
37. Hill, *The World*, p. 15.
38. See Norman Cohn, *The Pursuit of the Millennium* (London: Temple Smith, 1970).
39. A. L. Morton, *The World of the Ranters* (London: Laurence and Wishart, 1970), p. 12. In the seventeenth century the sermon was the most important means of spreading politico-religious ideology. Pamphlets and improvements in printing presses were also extremely significant in the battle of ideas. See also H. L. Brailsford, *The Levellers and the English Revolution* (Stanford, CA: Stanford University Press, 1961).
40. Hill, *The World*, p. 128 and pp. 50–6. See Morton on 'Leveller Democracy', *World of the Ranters*, pp. 197–219.
41. Churchill, *Light Shining*, pp. 202 and 205.
42. Churchill, *Light Shining*, p. 221. Walwyn, a Leveller leader, echoed widespread antagonism to the invasiveness of the Church in ordinary lives when he referred to Presbyterian ministers as 'a company of Mountebanks', see Morton, *World of the Ranters*, p.12.
43. Churchill, *Light Shining*, in *Plays: One*, p. 207.
44. *Ibid.*, p. 207.

45. Churchill, *Light Shining*, in *Plays: One*, pp. 213–14.
46. *Ibid.*, pp. 215–16.
47. *Ibid.*, p. 215.
48. *Ibid.*, pp. 216–17.
49. *Ibid.*, p. 216.
50. *Ibid.*, p. 219.
51. *Ibid.*, p. 234.
52. *Ibid.*, pp. 240–1.
53. *Ibid.*, p. 183.
54. Hill, *The World*, p. 341.
55. See, for example, Dennis Deletant, *Ceausescu and the Securitate: Coercion and Dissent in Romania 1965–1989* (London: Hurst and Co., 1995); Martyn Rady, *Romania in Turmoil* (London and New York: I.B. Tauris, 1992); and Tom Gallagher, *Romania after Ceausescu* (Edinburgh: Edinburgh University Press, 1995).
56. Mark Wing-Davey, public interview with Mary Luckhurst, the Dixon Drama Studio, University of York, 14 March 2005.
57. Ceridwen Thomas, 'Not out of the Wood', *Plays and Players* (August 1990), pp.18–19.
58. Information on workshop processes supplied by Wing-Davey, 14 March 2005.
59. Caryl Churchill, *Mad Forest* in *Plays: Three* (London: Nick Hern Books, 1998), p. 103.
60. Wing-Davey, 14 March 2005.
61. *Ibid.*
62. Churchill, *Mad Forest,* in *Plays: Three*, p. 104.
63. *Ibid.*, p. 115.
64. *Ibid.*, p. 116.
65. Though, interestingly, it was the Government's and the Church's attempt to suppress the priest and human rights champion, Laslo Tökes, that initially prompted the demonstrations in Timisoara.
66. This was an Out of the Blue Theatre Company production directed by Mary Luckhurst. Tony Mitchell has written a fascinating account of his production in Australia. See Tony Mitchell, 'Caryl Churchill's *Mad Forest*: Polyphonic Representations of Southeastern Europe', *Modern Drama* (1993), 36.4, 499–511.
67. Churchill, *Mad Forest,* in *Plays: Three*, p. 139.
68. Wing-Davey, 14 March 2005.
69. Churchill, *Mad Forest,* in *Plays: Three*, p. 139.

5

LIBBY WORTH

On text and dance: new questions and new forms

'Playwrights don't give answers, they ask questions. We need to find new questions, which may help us to answer the old ones or make them unimportant, and this means new subjects and new form.'[1] Caryl Churchill builds on this assertion from 1960 by stressing the need to use the theatre medium more fully, an ambition pursued subsequently with a passion clearly in evidence in the series of collaborative projects she undertook between 1986 and 1997. In the performances to be considered, *A Mouthful of Birds* (1986), *Fugue* (1988) made for television, *The Lives of the Great Poisoners* (1991), *The Skriker* (1994) and *Hotel* (1997), Churchill included dance and movement choreographed by Ian Spink and it is this particular interweaving of text and dance that is the focus of this chapter. How, for instance, can simultaneity of action or the specific temporal and spatial qualities of dance contribute to Churchill's evocation of such elusive, yet crucial experiences as remembering and forgetting? In different ways issues of memory permeate these plays as recollection, re-writing of narrative, intentional forgetfulness and desire for memory retention seep into the more obviously dramatic thematic concerns of the supernatural, violence, transformation, poisoning and death. Churchill's desire to share the stage/screen with a dance-based performance maker over the course of five performances suggests a sustained preoccupation with the way that dance, in the hands of Spink, could contribute to her general drive for new forms to explore persistent as well as new questions.

A selection of this kind is always in danger of appearing reductive by seeming to imply that Churchill's engagement with dance and movement is located in only these pieces, but as Churchill notes: 'Les Waters and I asked Ian Spink and Siobhan Davis to work with us on the project that became *Fen*, but neither of them was free.'[2] *Fen*'s compositional mode of action, gesture and character transformations, combined with Annie Smart's open stage design covered in earth that framed and gave sufficient open space to set movement sequences, suggest that Churchill was anticipating the dance-theatre collaborations that would begin three years later. Geraldine Cousin observed that the end of the performance 'had a dancelike quality: movement and gesture were as important as the words, and the physical attitude of each character made a clear and distinct visual statement'.[3] It is, therefore, more appropriate to see Churchill's sustained process of working on text and dance in performance as part of a continuum that has had an impact on Churchill's subsequent writing, even where dance is apparently absent. For example, in *A Number* (2002), the possibility for the character, Salter, to stay on stage between scenes was exploited to the full in the original production directed by Stephen Daldry. No dance was required, but rather an acceptance that the smallest alteration of gesture or posture can create subtle content in a quiet moment. In *Far Away* (2000) the repetition of the hat-making scenes and the parade of hat-wearing prisoners gesture towards Bauschian[4] imagery of dislocation and alienated actions rooted in movement rather than text. Churchill experiments again with dance through writing an intriguing monologue for Siobhan Davis' *Plants and Ghosts* (2002)[5] and in her translation of August Strindberg's *A Dream Play* (2005) that received a physically based treatment under the direction of Katie Mitchell and choreographer Kate Flatt.

Similarly reductive would be an assumption that the term 'collaborative', in reference to Churchill's work with Spink, is code for a specific methodology that progressed steadily over the course of their joint projects. Quite the reverse seems to be the case, since the process of performance making has followed a range of patterns from the simultaneous creation of dance and play text (*A Mouthful of Birds*), to text being entirely written before dance creation (*The Skriker*). The challenge for the critic writing on interdisciplinary performance could be said to parallel that of cross-arts collaborators, since theoretical perspectives developed over the last few decades in relation to theatre, literature, dance and music both share many fundamental approaches and also have distinctive differences. Churchill notes that in interdisciplinary performance the 'writer has an unfair advantage because the words can easily be reproduced in a book'[6] whereas music scores and to an even greater extent dance notation, though potentially useful, are restricted to specialist readers. Aside from the play-text, the record of these performances is inconsistent, with an interesting performance dossier produced for *The Lives of the Great Poisoners*, a video of the danced element for *A Mouthful of Birds* and basic video recordings made of *The Skriker* and *Hotel* by the venues in which they were performed.[7]

All performance is ephemeral but scanty documentation of dance has been a contributory factor in its failure to be taken seriously. Much has been done to right this balance by dance scholars who insist, as Ellen Goellner and

Jacqueline Shea Murphy do, not only on close analysis of dance's non-verbal means of communication, but also on engaging 'in reading choreographic texts and dance practices as things-in-relation rather than as things-in-themselves'.[8] Given the interdisciplinary focus of this chapter, this is the approach I have adopted: to 'write in' the dance whilst seeing it in relation to other contributory media.

Surface tension: *A Mouthful of Birds*

A Mouthful of Birds (1986) was arguably the most collaborative of the performances to be considered here since it was co-written with playwright David Lan and the workshop research was combined with a continuous twelve-week rehearsal period, a departure from the usual Joint Stock process where there would be a writing gap between the workshop and production. Collaboration was also heightened by inviting all three dancers and four actors to participate in dialogue *and* dance. The degree of integration was so marked, as evident in the hugely demanding format of the performance, that it could be argued that form as well as content explore disruptions and breaching of role delineation and behavioural boundaries.

The original catalyst for the project was a shared interest in Euripides' *Bacchae* but both Churchill and Lan were keen to work with contemporary resonances of the themes that the *Bacchae* includes, in particular violence in women and the idea of possession. The play is structured around each of the seven main characters' experience of what Churchill termed an '"undefended day" in which there is nothing to protect you from the forces inside and outside yourself',[9] while woven into these episodes are fragments of the *Bacchae*. The retention of Greek narrative traces meant that something 'bursts from the past into these people open to possession'.[10] With only seven performers swift transformations were essential across contemporary and the Greek narratives, thus embodying the link between them and ensuring a visual cue for the audience that past and present are not so easily disengaged.

Spink's experience in working with theatre and opera practitioners as well as composers was already extensive by 1986, making him an obvious choice of collaborator for Churchill and Lan. In particular his work as artistic director and choreographer for Second Stride revealed openness to cross-arts experimentation, with dances such as *Further and Further into the Night* (1984), loosely based on Alfred Hitchcock's *Notorious* (1946), and *Bösendorfer Waltzes* (1986) in which he combined traditional ballet narrative such as *The Firebird* with stimuli from surrealism, dream and myth. Earlier he had worked with a wide range of musical and textual combinations, with significant collaborative input from designers such as Craig Givens and later Antony McDonald.[11] Stephanie Jordan suggests that his early pieces signal a 'recurring theme ... of isolation and tension between people'.[12] This, together with a proclivity towards creating dances with multiple threads rather than a single narrative, suggests why he might be in sympathy with Churchill and Lan's project.

In *A Mouthful of Birds* isolation is emphasized structurally through the separation of the main characters' mini-narratives, with each one created from quite contrasting performance elements. As in his earlier dances, Spink based his choreography in *A Mouthful of Birds* on a formidable range of training that spans a range of styles and supports a versatile approach to movement making. He trained with the Australian Ballet School, danced with The Australian Ballet (1969–1974) and took classes with Merce Cunningham while he was on tour in Australia. After moving to Britain in 1978 he worked with, amongst others, Mary Fulkerson and Richard Alston.[13]

Spink's ability to traverse movement styles contributed to the specificity of each example of possession in *A Mouthful of Birds*, as shown in the physical theatre style of movement developed for Lena's scenes (Act I, Scene 9, i–iv). For these, rather than use stylized dance, the moves Spink choreographs would look familiar in the playground, but with uncomfortable moments of sexually explicit gestures and positioning. The challenge of this section of the play is to convincingly shift Lena out of domestic routine to infanticide. The way it is achieved, I suggest, is through maintaining several registers of interaction between Lena, the Spirit and Roy. The verbal device of Lena carrying on a stilted conversation with Roy while attempting a far more desperate response to the Spirit has her trapped in a domestic setting by male attempts at domination. The pressure is increased as her distraught mental state takes physical form fighting the Spirit. In these moments it is interesting that Lena shows physical strength, imagination and assertiveness, signalling the power, albeit corrupt, that leads both to the horrific murder of her baby and to the awareness she expresses in her coda to the play: 'I haven't forgotten anything. I remember I enjoyed doing it. It's nice to make someone alive and it's nice to make someone dead. Either way. That power is what I like best in the world. The struggle is every day not to use it.'[14] In these physical encounters the combination of desire, playfulness and violence provide a sharp contrast with domestic activity, a reference to the Bacchants' escape to a place of ecstasy and destruction.

Stephen Goff, the dancer who played the Spirit in the original production, also took one of the main character roles, Dan. In Dan's scenes, as in Lena's, the play relies on simultaneity of action to unsettle a restrictive view of identity and although structurally both sections are comprised of short, interrupted scenes, in Dan's section the movement component runs in parallel to the spoken dialogue and at a physical distance from it. Where Lena and the Spirit had confronted each other beneath the kitchen table, in Dan's scenes the sense of disturbance beneath life's surfaces is increased through taking full advantage of Annie Smart's versatile and imaginative stage design of the exposed innards of a two-story house and placing the prison officers in an upstairs room and Dan and victims in the lower recesses of the house. This contrast in spatial dynamics is consistent with the abrupt change of identity Dan has undergone, from vicar collecting jumble in Scene 6 to imprisoned, multiple murderer at the start of his section 'Dancing', Scene 15. Whereas the six other main characters excuse themselves from their daily obligations but retain contact with the everyday world, Dan appears from the outset to operate in a world of his own. Thus he can barely engage with his parishioners in the introductory scenes, his life is reported by warders and he dances with strangers.

In a video interview Spink discussed the creation of *Bösendorfer Waltzes*, the piece he made just prior to working on *A Mouthful of Birds*, and spoke forcefully of how his desire that the audience should be able to create their own meaning when watching the piece, to make 'even structural and moral decisions', had had implications for both content and process.[15] This attitude is in evidence in Dan's scenes, which seem designed to seduce the audience into experiencing dramatically conflicting perspectives of the same event.

Logocentricity is emphasized in the Prison Officers' dialogue that consists of discussion about the offences, the gender identity and the diary of Dan, their prisoner. Even though the tone is bantering, ultimately expressing exasperation and bewilderment, the attempt to explain gender dysphoria is nevertheless seductive. Does the conversational tone or the wearing of a uniform contribute weight to the meaning of the officers' words? Is the eye drawn to the officers and the diary entries they read, in which Dan declares that his killings will be 'good deaths' as 'these are the deaths the earth needs to grow strong',[16] and away from the largely silent dance that proceeds on the stage floor below? This is Spink's point: structurally and morally an audience has the freedom to choose and to determine a path through these multiple narratives but these choices are contingent on societal and cultural norms that can, without care, become blindly observed imperatives.

Equally seductive are Dan's dances that seek to destroy, but in the process provide the victims with unbearable pleasure. The choreography is for a trained dancer given its alluring combination of balletic stance, lightness and extensions combined with fluid, spiralling, weighted sequences that effortlessly travel between the floor and the vertical. Goff, as Dan, enmeshes each of his/her victims through circling the chair in which they sit. In one memorable section Goff, on the lap of his first victim with one leg stretched over her shoulder, gradually extends back to the floor and, with a backward head over heels, lands coyly turned away from her. Just as she leans back from stroking his hair he turns and springs forward full length with his head face down in her lap; she dies. The wooden, minimal movements from the victims serve to increase the fluid power 'Dan' appears to have across levels and space. Dance has so frequently been associated with seduction and distraction that Spink's controlled focus on easy flow of movement and Goff's accomplished lightness of execution seem both familiar and deeply disturbing within the murderous context in which they are set.

Dan's costuming, a woman's slip over plain trousers, symbolizes gender confusion and links him to Dionysus who, with bare chest and long skirt is presented throughout as the uncategorizable, androgynous god. The split shown in the *Bacchae* between Pentheus' rigid control of the state and Dionysus' violent disruption of the status quo receives a precise and rigorously layered representation in these scenes, but not through stark polarization. Dan's diary entries, fantastical and illogical, interweave with the Prison Officers' colloquialisms, while the dances of ecstasy are precisely controlled and contained movement sequences, a choreographic illusion of lightness and fluidity. There is no ready path offered to the audience, more a provocation that allying with one side or the other has a nasty habit of inducing forgetfulness. It seems appropriate, therefore, that the seven characters' statements at the end of the play are not neat closures but meditations on the power or occasionally pain of memory together with the desire for, and sometimes impossibility of, forgetfulness.

Memory, remembering, individual and collective – *Fugue*

Remembering and forgetting is central in Churchill and Spink's next collaboration, *Fugue*, a piece made for television (Dance-lines Productions, Channel 4). The subject matter seems simple enough (Spink even suggests the opening section is like a 'soap opera')[17] but the combination of writing and choreography enters a very different phase of collaboration when compared to *A Mouthful of Birds*, with choreographic strategies, inspired in part by the music for the piece Fugue No. 10 from J. S. Bach's *The Art of Fugue*. The piece centres on the death of a father and how this impinges on his wife and children, but unlike a soap, there is no straightforward narrative drive, rather a series of fragments which allow stories to emerge dependent on each viewer's focus. Sarah Rubidge describes how Spink 'asked Churchill to structure her script using the musical principles which underpin Fugue No 10'[18] a familiar method for a choreographer but unusual for a playwright. She produced a script that 'used two sets of very short sentences ... which passed from one character to another'[19] whilst Spink followed a similar process with movement sequences and everyday gestures. This has the effect that both Churchill and Spink favour of disrupting linear narrative, but the use of such an abstract structural device rather than a proliferation of stories sourced from different times and places (evident in *A Mouthful of Birds* and *The Lives of the Great Poisoners*) has intriguing temporal repercussions.

Fugue opens with a series of repetitions with slight variations on the news of the father's death being relayed to each of the adult sons and daughters. The short sentences such as: 'he'd just got out of the bath', and 'he was already falling down the stairs – when I heard him' are reiterated with shifts in emphasis, rhythm and order.[20] *Fugue* appears to use the structure of the piece to reference the need of the newly bereaved to repeat in order to grasp the enormity of the event. Through the series of reflections on the same moment of time, narrative forward motion is interrupted with time held open vertically and the attention of the camera focuses instead on posture, gesture and reaction of each family member as they receive the news. In miniature this is like the flashbulb memory that occurs in response to a major public catastrophe and fixes a moment in time. As Barbara Misztal suggests in her analysis of theories of social remembering, emotional response has a powerful effect on what is recalled: 'such strong sensations help to overcome memory distanciation and make the recalled memories vivid and somatic'.[21] In *Fugue*, the common, collective experience is both shown and eclipsed through the intensity of the gestural specificity of each character's reiteration of the news.

Flurries of Churchill's half sentences create a specific rhythmic pattern that can, like Bach's music that plays through the piece, become material to be manipulated, deconstructed and re-built. This echoes the way that memories are susceptible to dislocation and reformation in sudden, unexpected ways, with the trigger often lying in a kinaesthetic experience. So, for instance, the young adults are shown towards the end of the piece in a vast empty room each making a private gesture that gradually transmutes into a sequence of dance in which the momentum of a sweeping arm or a leg turns the body into a series of spins. Each dancer's trajectory ends in impact with the wall where a moment of private and intense recall seems to extend in time and across space.

Rubidge suggests that *Fugue* is a flawed piece. Its rather basic use of the televisual medium allowed Spink fast switches between outdoor and inside locations, including dreamlike spaces of a sand-filled room or another with four grand pianos being played simultaneously. These spaces are intriguing but what remains impressive are the subtle ways in which *Fugue* combines text and dance/movement to reflect on the instability of memory and how intensity of emotion opens up tensions between individuals and their family narratives that define social cohesion. Spink's directorship and choreography ensure that memories are not just reformed in words but re-embodied, literally re-membered. Some of the most poignant moments are those with the baby grandchild with whom family members dance, and, in a poetic moment, whom the young father holds over the piano so that its toes touch the keyboard. As the baby's fingers clutch the man's wrist, the close-up shot signals a new cycle of cultural and social identity being inscribed on the body.

Re-collecting memories of movement: *Lives of the Great Poisoners*

For *Lives of the Great Poisoners*, Spink and Churchill were joined by composer Orlando Gough and designer Antony McDonald, both of whom had worked previously with Spink in Second Stride productions. Closer in structure to *A Mouthful of Birds* than *Fugue*, the piece relies on narrative sequences that share thematic strands without overlapping. Poisoning rather than possession link the episodes which extend across time and place: Dr Crippen from London in the early twentieth century, Medea from ancient Corinth and Mme de Brinvilliers from Paris in the seventeenth century. One character, Midgely, traverses the scenes in a somewhat surreal manner, engaging with each of the Poisoners. Churchill loosely based him on an early twentieth-century American industrial chemist, who 'put the lead in petrol and CFCs in fridges, two inventions that seemed a good idea at the time but were inadvertently poisonous'.[22]

Not having seen *Lives of the Great Poisoners* must inevitably hamper writing about it, yet this also offers an opportunity to consider how to engage with the physicality of a multi-disciplinary performance when only the traces are left. Susan Leigh Foster, in her introduction to *Choreographing History*, argues forcefully that writing a historical text inclusive of past bodies and movement 'rather than an act of verbal explanation, must become a process of interpretation, translation and rewriting of bodily texts'.[23] Above all she examines the bodily relationship between writer and subject and through emphasis on the physicality of writing and the agency of bodies moving, suggests that 'verbal discourse cannot speak *for* bodily discourse, but must enter into "dialogue" *with* that bodily discourse'.[24] As mentioned earlier, Churchill is quick to acknowledge the advantages for the writer in such collaborative work, having ready access to a recorded form in the play text, but dialoguing with the 'bodily discourse' of *Poisoners* is aided substantially by the contributors' desire to produce a recorded form that would better reflect their joint creative undertaking. The resulting performance dossier includes a commentary on the making process from each collaborator, the full text with detailed stage directions, the musical score for the *a capella* singing and a substantial number of photographs that indicate design images, the set design and moments of performers' movement, dance and interaction.

Reading each of the artists' accounts reignites the kinds of debates that seemed to permeate their collaboration. As you 'listen' to each of the voices in the four introductions the differing preoccupations and disciplinary perspectives begin to illuminate both process and performance. What might have seemed a rather conventional process of set text, set music and dance relegated to responding to each of these, begins to unravel as the emphasis moves in the artists' accounts from making the work to putting it into production. It seems clear that in making their own component each artist held spaces open, in imagination, for the other 'voices'. For Spink this involved creating dances that 'fitted into the written scenes' since completion of the choreography was reliant on working with the dancers.[25]

The dossier's detailed record of process reveals how early creative decisions determined a highly distinctive method and outcome, simultaneously setting up certain limitations. The decision to have 'singers who sang, dancers who danced and actors who spoke' for instance brought the inter-disciplinarity directly onto the stage with the challenge that performers would need to become adept at communicating seamlessly across disciplines.[26] This became a catalyst, as Spink suggests, to produce 'a subtler kind of dance, one that could appear out of the action as if from nowhere' to prevent 'a flagging in the narrative line [or] indeed in the layers of the texture'.[27] Gough recognized a similar need to accommodate through using counterpoint more frequently than harmony to reflect the characters' disputes and tensions. He observes that a disadvantage lay in a certain thinness of texture but, similarly to Spink's innovation, this gave performers a degree of versatility in moving 'between spoken and sung text'.[28] If this form of work places special demands on the performers this is surely also true of the audience who are required to call on a parallel openness of response.

Poisoners, performed at Riverside Studios (March 1991), incited a cacophony of contradictory voices.[29] Thus for Clare Bayley, Churchill 'sure-footedly combines anachronistic frivolity with high poetry'[30] while John Percival writes that she 'has a few neat one-liners but most of them are repeated to distraction'.[31] Gough's composition is variously labelled 'problematic', 'torturing', 'endlessly inventive', 'quirky', 'rich in pastiche and parody', while Spink's choreography is viewed by some as virtually absent with only 'moments of pure dance' – 'when he actually puts in some dance steps they look irrelevant' – while Bayley sees that it 'enhances the total effect, at times jokey, at times deadly serious'.[32] Even in moments when the critics agree that specific sections of the performance are forceful and memorable, there is a frustrating lack of analysis to account for these high points. Two reviewers, however, do respond to the different media and, as Foster suggests, bring themselves into dialogue with the physicality of the piece. Bayley for instance suggests that the choreography 'works best when integrated into the narrative; small, isolated sub-sets of activity can be distracting, but Spink uses his dancers provocatively and in true postmodernist style, to represent fragments of experience disjointed to but simultaneous with the main action'.[33] Alastair Macauley develops the concept of unison work and what this achieved: 'As often with Second Stride, there are suggestions of alter egos, and – with song, speech, mime and dance – different layers of the psyche. Cross-references and parallels between the three stories are subtly woven in and the multiple role-playing hints wonderfully at connections between killer and victim and between observer and observed.'[34]

Richard Cave takes up and extends this idea of connections through his analysis of *Poisoners* in which he argues that the audience is confronted by 'structuring devices' that 'seemed designed to activate moral discrimination'.[35] He illustrates this through a detailed exploration of how Creusa's dance of death after donning the poisoned dress ensures that the 'spectators are required to watch and imaginatively engage with the victim's experience of murder as the process in its horror is defined through dance and mime'.[36] When the audience 'dialogues' with the physicality of the piece the meaningfulness of the choreography is asserted.

Different worlds – permeable walls: *The Skriker*

Thematically all the performances considered so far are linked through focus on the puncturing of everyday life by acts of violence and death. Each piece incorporates threads from the past, whether a mythic story that erupts into the present as in *A Mouthful of Birds*, a series of memories and reconstructions as in *Fugue* or the parallel narratives of different ages deployed in *Poisoners*. While the use of such historical interventions is evident in other of Churchill's plays, in these which are reliant on mixed media, the spaces she leaves open in the text invite a fluid and complexly layered approach to the stage representation of time. In *The Skriker*, Churchill again leaves space in her writing in anticipation of music and dance interventions and observes that she would never have written it 'that way if I hadn't already worked on other shows with dancers and singers',[37] but there is no attempt this time to document the other media in such a way as to tie them to the play post-production.

Churchill invited Spink to create the movement for (but not direct, to his disappointment)[38] *The Skriker* (1994), which, unlike the other performances discussed, was written by her as solo creative project over the course of many years. It concerns the nightmarish underworld of dark fairies and hobgoblins intervening in and running parallel to a contemporary world based partly in London and focused on two young women: Josie who appears to have killed her baby and Lily who is pregnant and gives birth in the course of the play. The performance format is distinguished from her other mixed media work through having the women of the contemporary world interact primarily through the spoken word, with dance and operatic music assigned to the underworld and folkloric characters. Churchill states unequivocally that 'it seems all right that the movement will be developed differently for each production' and that different music could be used, although she 'strongly recommend[s] Judith Weir's'.[39] This somewhat formulaic approach to working across media serves Churchill well in this play since she is able to highlight a main narrative, while suggesting that 'a number of stories are told but only one in words'.[40] These enigmatic other narratives are scantily fleshed out in the stage directions and libretto, acting more as triggers for spectators' imaginative completion than significant parallel stories.

More significantly perhaps, this sharp division of disciplines establishes a strong theatrically expressed separation between worlds which, throughout the performance, is breached and threatened. Reviewers of the first production expressed bewilderment at the choice of subject that involved dredging up characters from folklore such as Brownie, Kelpie, Black Annis and Yallery Brown, but those most excited and convinced responded to the play's ambivalent quality. Without direct reference to global events it seemed to inhabit the unease of an age. While the tearing down of walls, literally in Berlin and metaphorically through the dismantling of apartheid in South Africa might be greeted euphorically, Churchill's *Skriker* seemed to play upon the destabilizing fear that accompanies the forming and breaking of boundaries. The specific social vulnerabilities of psychologically unstable Josie and lone mother Lily are heightened by the presence of an even darker level of existence that hovers threateningly around them.

Straddling the two worlds is the Skriker, who describes herself to Josie as 'one of many, not a major spirit, but a spirit'[41] and whose ability to move between worlds is emphasized in performance by the facility with which she uses movement and dialogue to transform through a range of shapes, such as a derelict woman, American woman, a pink fairy, a young businessman, a child, a teenager and a sick old woman. From the opening of the performance the language of the Skriker, described as 'a shapeshifter and death portent, ancient and damaged'[42] careers off in a multitude of directions as one phrase, word or sound triggers a new line of thought. Throughout her opening monologue there is no respite from the frantic multi-referentiality of her language that spits in so many directions that the sense conveyed is of a mind so fractured that it is unable to form boundaries or follow the rules of spoken language. Kathryn Hunter's performance of the Skriker in the original production was recognized as extraordinary by all the critics, no matter how confusing they found the play. Yet the power of both the character and the performer as she shifted through the range of shapes created to lure, tease, torture and tempt, the two vulnerable young women into the underworld would lack conviction without the layered and subversive depths shown running parallel to contemporary society.

In *The Skriker* dance and music are employed to hold open the spaces within a more linear narrative; to interrupt and intrude. Several reviewers suggested that the final result might not have been as consistently forceful as intended. Spink seemed to concur in his rather critical view of the rehearsal process in which they (director Les Waters and himself as movement director) 'would work for days and days without actually seeing what each other were doing', despite Churchill making a piece that was in his view 'like two pieces occurring simultaneously in the same space'.[43] Nevertheless there were many moments in the Cottesloe performance where movement and music conveyed the invasive threat of a nether world. Nicholas de Jongh's review notes 'Judith Weir's eerie, thin music and Ian Spink's spare, stately choreography enhance the dreamstruck atmosphere',[44] while Judith Mackrell comments 'Much of the movement is closer to gesture and image than to dance, but Spink is particularly adroit at finding ways of capturing the play's collision between the real and spirit worlds.'[45] At various points Spink has two spirits hurl themselves time and again onto a wall that from the impact seems solid enough but then suddenly opens to allow a giant form on bone-shaped stilts to stride through. Annie Smart's design of a moveable small white box stage within a larger white box contributes to the confusions of space and time as the spirits hang in a corner, fling through a wall or sit above the action. Just as important as the larger set pieces of spirit banquet and beach picnic amongst blue men are the smaller dance sequences which prise open the normality of a London park, hospital or kitchen and infect them with the dangerous presence of children's fairytale nightmares.

Intimate ritual in public space: *Hotel*

From the weird, spirit-strewn, doubled world of *The Skriker* to the apparently mundane space of a hotel room in which its occupants do nothing more than prepare for bed could hardly be more of a contrast. And yet *Hotel* (1997), particularly in the first half 'Eight Rooms', moves between dimensions in a way that is different from *The Skriker* yet with a magical quality. In this Second Stride production with Spink as director/choreographer, Gough composer, Churchill writer and Lucy Bevan designer, music was placed centrally to create what Gough termed a 'music-theatre piece, opera almost, which required a very sophisticated contribution from a choreographer'.[46] Split into two separate sections, the first was based on the simple premise of six couples, two single guests and a ghost occupying a hotel room for a night, but instead of characters being separated sequentially or with divides in the stage space, they all pursue their nightly routines in one large, bland hotel room oblivious of each other. Thirteen of the performers for this piece were singers, two dancers and to one edge of the stage three musicians played piano and double bass. 'Two Nights', the second section, focused on dance with the interweaving of three narratives, two expressed by each of the two dancers and the third sung by the chorus of singers based on extracts of a diary that had supposedly been left in the hotel room.

To try to envisage the fifteen performers of 'Eight Rooms' pursuing their own preparations for bed as if in their own room while singing, suggests chaos or farce but the performance was subtly modulated, moving fluidly through a range of emotional registers. This, I believe, is testimony to the degree of experience the collaborators had established in working with different arts media, both separately and together. The roles of Churchill and Spink seem muted by comparison with earlier pieces, but the delicacy and precision in both the words and choreography are impressively crafted to allow the performance to contain individual intimacy and collective experience. Against the institutional backdrop of the hotel room the micro-dramas being played out are imagined with such humanity and performed so expertly that it is possible to absorb the oddity of the theatrical device and see each couple and individual with clarity.

As Gough suggests, Spink's 'sophisticated contribution'[47] was essential in this process to ensure that the emotional and expressive range of the music and text were echoed in the movement. The split-second timing that allows the occupants to traverse the hotel room and bathroom while doing everyday activities of brushing teeth, hanging up clothes, reading, arguing and watching TV is clear terrain for a choreographer and this interweaving of paths is managed perfectly. Equally significant is Spink's sensitivity to proxemics, his understanding of how physical detail can evoke character identity and vitality. Thus, as the US woman, about the eighth person, squeezes and snuggles into a double bed, the audience laugh, but it's a complex response, not the belly laugh of farce, but a laugh of pleasure in the absurdity of the gesture: and, on a deeper level, recognition of the common experience of feeling alone amidst a host of people that anticipates her sung repetition of 'are you there? because I'm lonely'.[48]

The demands on the singers in 'Eight Rooms' are formidable since they must work with absolutely focused awareness of their partner and dramatic vignette whilst following the musical score that requires by turn duets, solos, dissonance and harmony of many voices. When achieved, Gough has a rich palette with which to create a highly textured expression as personal moments of song are repeated and amplified with the addition of other voices. Interwoven but not merely illustrative of the music and text, Spink worked with similar versatility and wit, as for instance when the timorous but loving lesbian couple begin to strip off their clothes and move from the bed to the sofa that has just been vacated by two separate book readers. The place the women leave on the bed gives the hot, amorous affair couple space to roll. The three media are skilfully manipulated throughout to allow the night to take on a darker tone, as sleeplessness, sleep-walking, a ghostly visitation and a strange ritual involving lining up of shoes punctuate the calm.

A different emphasis is evident in 'Two Nights' with two dancers the focus of the action backed by the thirteen singers in supporting roles and throughout as a chorus. Darker, more obviously dramatic, the performers draw on earlier everyday gestures but now they are laden with threat. 'Man' spends a suspiciously long time on washing and drying his hands, whilst the 'Woman' shifts rapidly from showing him her wrists as if slashed, to re-entering in a nurse's uniform with a gun. Although there are moments of interaction these characters seem locked in their own worlds defined by distinctive movement styles. She employs arm swings, extensions, turns and face-covering, which are repeated to a point where they become strangely ritualistic. He battles with gravity in a series of contortions and movements along a vertical axis contrasting her precision and control with dispersed, irregular movements which threaten complete collapse. Throughout these dark actions the chorus sing the fragments of a diary that recounts how the writer is gradually disappearing.

The violence and death of the second half is all the more shocking for its abrupt contrast with the homely rituals in the public space of 'Eight Rooms'. The threat intrudes, not on an established contemporary scene as witnessed in *A Mouthful of Birds*, *Poisoners* and *The Skriker*, but on the audience's memory of what has taken place in the first half of the piece in the same hotel room. Thwarting anticipated content is characteristic of the series of artists' collaborations considered here, that have consistently and inventively strained at the boundaries of what is possible for each art form. Never merely experiments in form, each performance confronts issues of threatened identity, isolation and alienation prevalent in contemporary society. Churchill's drive for interdisciplinary collaborations has entailed a degree of complexity that, on occasion, has led to unevenness in performance as well as yielded powerfully dramatic encounters. Experimenting with form provoked new questions for the collaborators which in turn made special demands on both performers and audiences. Although there is much that is bleak in these pieces, they are relieved and lightened by humorous and witty elements. These combine with a tangible sense of tenacity in the realization of cross-disciplinary performance that in the final analysis is uplifting in its humanity.

NOTES

1. Caryl Churchill, 'Not Ordinary, Not Safe: A Direction for Drama?', *The Twentieth Century* (November 1960), 443–51, 446.
2. Churchill, *Plays: Three* (London: Nick Hern Books, 1997), p. 184.
3. Geraldine Cousin, *Churchill the Playwright* (London: Methuen, 1989), p. 55.
4. In her Tanztheatre pieces, Pina Bausch often includes parades of dancers who weave across both stage and auditorium whilst meticulously repeating the same gestural and step sequences. Such iteration of action, divorced from obvious function or narrative, paradoxically highlights each dancer's individuality and human commonality. See for example *Kontakthof* (1978), *1980* (1980) and *Masurca Fogo* (1998).
5. Churchill's monologue for the dance *Plants and Ghosts* starts with a reference to a woman biting her tongue but gradually, over a series of repetitions, extends the narrative through cumulative descriptions of events prior to and post the original action.
6. Churchill, *Plays: Three*, p. viii.
7. Videos of *The Skriker* can be viewed at the National Theatre Archive and of *Hotel* at the Laban Dance Centre (where there is also a good collection of videos of Ian Spink's and Second Stride's performances).
8. Ellen W. Goellner and Jacqueline Shea Murphy (eds.), *Bodies of the Text: Dance as Theory, Literature as Dance* (New Brunswick, NJ: Rutgers, 1995), p. 8.
9. Caryl Churchill and David Lan, *A Mouthful of Birds* (London: Methuen, 1986), p. vii. The play is also anthologized in Churchill's *Plays: Three*, but the advantage of the single text edition for the purposes of this chapter is its inclusion of photographs from the original production, several of which capture movement sequences.
10. Churchill and Lan, *A Mouthful of Birds*, p. 5.
11. For a detailed account of his work up to 1991 see Stephanie Jordan, *Striding Out: Aspects of Contemporary and New Dance in Britain* (London: Dance Books, 1992), pp. 182–206.
12. *Ibid.*, p. 189.

13. US dancer Mary Fulkerson was central in introducing release dance work and contact improvisation to the UK through her teaching at Dartington Hall. Richard Alston combined an eclectic range of dance techniques and styles in his work and has choreographed for companies such as London Contemporary Dance Theatre, Strider, Ballet Rambert, Scottish Ballet and with Ian Spink for Second Stride.
14. Churchill and Lan, *A Mouthful of Birds*, p. 70.
15. Ian Spink, Digital Dance Interview by Stephanie Jordan (Reading: Digital, distributed NRCD, 1989).
16. Churchill and Lan, *A Mouthful of Birds*, p. 39.
17. Spink, Digital Dance Interview.
18. Sarah Rubidge, 'Recent Dance Made for Television', Stephanie Jordan and Dave Allen (eds.), *Parallel Lines: Media Representations of Dance* (London: John Libbey for the Arts Council of Great Britain, 1993), pp. 185–215, p. 193.
19. *Ibid.*, p. 193.
20. *Fugue*, Ian Spink and Caryl Churchill, for Dance-Lines 2, Dance on 4, 1988.
21. Barbara A. Misztal, *Theories of Social Remembering* (Maidenhead: Open University Press, 2003), p. 80.
22. Caryl Churchill, Orlando Gough and Ian Spink, *Lives of the Great Poisoners: A Production Dossier* (London: Methuen, 1993), p. x. As a 'dossier' this edition contains more production detail – including photographs and music – than the anthologies script in Churchill *Plays: Three*.
23. Susan Leigh Foster (ed.), *Choreographing History* (Bloomington: Indiana University Press, 1995), p. 9.
24. *Ibid.*, p. 9.
25. Churchill *et al.*, *Poisoners*, p. xiv.
26. *Ibid.*, p. ix.
27. *Ibid.*, p. xv.
28. *Ibid.*, p. xii.
29. *Theatre Record* (12–25 March 1991) pp. 306–7. Six reviews of *Poisoners* refer to the Arts Council's impending withdrawal of funding from Second Stride. This adds immediacy as both the production and nine years' work by the company are evaluated.
30. Clare Bayley, *Theatre Record* (20 March 1991), 307.
31. John Percival, *Theatre Record* (14 March 1991), 307.
32. For full reviews see *Theatre Record*, 306–7.
33. Bayley, *Theatre Record*, 307.
34. Alistair Macaulay, *Theatre Record* (20 March 1991), 307.
35. Richard Cave, 'Caryl Churchill and Ian Spink: "allowing the past ... to speak directly to the present"', in Fiona Macintosh (ed.) *The Modern Dancer and the Ancient World* (Oxford: Oxford University Press, forthcoming).
36. *Ibid.*
37. Churchill, *Plays: Three*, p. viii.
38. For extended discussion see Ian Spink, 'Collaborations', Interview with Richard Cave, in *Border Tensions: Dance and Discourse: Proceedings of the Fifth Study of Dance Conference* (Department of Dance Studies: University of Surrey, 1995), pp. 293–303, p. 299.
39. Churchill, *Plays: Three*, p. viii.

40. *Ibid.*
41. Churchill, *The Skriker*, in *Plays: Three*, p. 257.
42. *Ibid.*, p. 243.
43. Spink, 'Collaborations', p. 300.
44. Nicholas de Jongh, *Theatre Record* (28 January 1994), 97.
45. Judith Mackrell, *Theatre Record* (29 January 1994), 95.
46. Orlando Gough email interview with Libby Worth, 27 May 2008.
47. *Ibid.*
48. Caryl Churchill, *Hotel* in *Plays: Four* (London: Nick Hern Books, 2008), p. 22.

6

SHEILA RABILLARD

On Caryl Churchill's ecological drama: right to poison the wasps?

Caryl Churchill's drama shows a sustained and deepening engagement with ecological issues from her 1971 radio drama *Not Not Not Not Not Enough Oxygen*, through *Fen* (1983) (developed for the stage with the members of the Joint Stock theatre company), to the collaborative combination of dance, song and drama *Lives of the Great Poisoners* (1991), the more recent plays *The Skriker* (1994) and *Far Away* (2000), and her 2006 choral work *We Turned on the Light*. Her focus moves from localized environmental concerns (as in *Fen*) to the ecological effects of globalization and the alienated consumerism of late capitalism (for example, in *Far Away* and *The Skriker*), but there is not so much a simple progression in her work as a recursive, intense dialogue in which elements of her earlier plays are repurposed and complex issues are revisited. In particular, Churchill returns to the idea of the commons – which can be understood both as a localized place, a plot of land unenclosed and of equal access, and also as a planetary concept of shared resources,[1] where the nature of the sharing (perhaps beyond the human?) is open to philosophical inquiry. Churchill works with time as well as place in her ecological dramaturgy, deploying temporal shifts which hint at the multiple rhythms of biology and of capitalist exchange, exploring conceptual legacies of the past which inform current understanding of our relationship to the natural world, and historicizing in the Brechtian sense as she shows paths not taken. The temporal element of her ecological drama invites further development in theatrical eco-criticism, a field in which much of the richest work has emphasized the staging of place.[2] Similarly, she works innovatively with the non-visual senses in ways which may allow her to disturb some of the anthropocentric structures of perception built upon sight.

Over the course of her body of ecological work the tension between what might be called 'environmental justice' and 'deep ecology' constitutes a complex and developing argument. That is, she brings into dialogue two opposed extremes of ecological thought: the politics of the environmental justice movement (and its cognate, though crucially distinct, movements outside the US such as the Green movement in Europe), which emphasize legal and ethical responsibility for the effect of human actions on the environments of other human beings;[3] and a philosophical impulse ('deep ecology', for example) to get beyond anthropocentric thinking,[4] a mode of thought which critiques even the term 'environment' as tending to suggest that the purpose of the whole ecological web is its use in sustaining human life and which reminds us of the disastrous past effects of ideologies assuming the right to human dominance (see Howard, Chapter 3, and Luckhurst, Chapter 4, respectively on this point). The power and obligation to act so urgently invoked by ecological dystopias operating within the framework of environmental justice is distinctly human-centred, emphasizing right use of the environment and just distribution of its resources. Yet this is a kind of blindness or hubris, seen from the perspective of deep ecology. But to move beyond a human-centred focus on use of the environment (if this is even possible) risks debilitating the ethical impulse to act, and – perhaps more dangerous still – risks succumbing to preservationist thinking: fantasies of recovered utopias and attempts to create places where nature is untouched by humanity. Ramachandra Guha is perhaps the most eloquent critic of such preservationism, and points out its inevitable elitism, as areas are set aside for the scientific or aesthetic use of a few.[5] The potential conflict within ecological thought, then, constitutes part of the interest of Churchill's plays; an avowed socialist, she is drawn to issues of just use of the environment at the same time as she confronts a countervailing need to challenge all ideologies, socialism as well as capitalism, that have assumed human dominance and taken human use as the measure of justice.

Environmental crisis and consumer capitalism: *Not Not Not Not Not Enough Oxygen*

Churchill's ecological engagement is perhaps most obvious in *Not Not Not Not Not Enough Oxygen*, *Fen* and *Lives of the Great Poisoners*. These are plays that participate in what the ecological literary theorist Glotfelty labels consciousness raising:[6] they draw attention to ecological disaster – immediate or impending – and they dramatize responsibility, staging the causal connections of systems and attitudes to environmental exploitation. The earliest of these, *Not Not Not Not Not Enough Oxygen*, is a dystopian fantasy of a future world (the year is 2010) in which England itself has become 'the Londons', the ultimate extreme of urban sprawl; almost everyone lives in tower blocks; and pollution is so extreme that people must buy bottled oxygen which they spray about the room as literal air freshener.

In *Not ... Enough Oxygen*, Churchill emphasizes the commodification of what had once been a common good, thus deftly pointing to capitalist, consumerist attitudes as a cause of environmental degradation: the profit motive leads to short-sighted exploitation of a world seen purely as a resource, and the capitalist response to pollution is simply to exploit resulting scarcities. Even attempts at a 'green' solution to the lack of oxygen are subsumed within the logic of consumer capitalism: when it is suggested that plants might be installed in every room to improve air quality, it appears that all plants are now confined to parks and both the parks (the nearest is four days away) and the plants in them are in very short supply and hence vegetation is very costly. 'Plants plants would take money. Earth plants earth would all have to come in from the park and the park park authority wouldn't permit. Because hardly any park hardly any park left.' If one has enough money, we learn, it is possible to buy a cottage in one of the parks but as a result 'the park is mostly rows of cottages mud a little little grass'.[7]

The action of this one-act radio drama takes place inside the small, cluttered room of Mick, aged sixty, who is waiting for a rare visit from his son, Claude, nineteen, who appears to be a wealthy celebrity (Mick mentions watching his son on television, and speculates that thousands of little girls must kiss his screen image). Vivian, Mick's married girlfriend half his age, keeps him company as he waits. The pair hope that Claude will give his father enough money to buy one of the park cottages so that they will have a place large enough to live together. Vivian, it seems, still lives with her husband ('Mick you know I only only I only live with him for the room')[8] because Mick insists that his own room is too small for two (although Vivian points out that all of the rooms are the same size). This anticipation, which structures the slight plot, points to the ways in which an ethos of consumption has infiltrated even emotional life. Mick cannot enjoy a life with Vivian without the right sort of (purchased) environment; and his feelings for his son are thoroughly confused with admiration for wealth and fame, and expectation of a gift. Indeed, he imagines his son feels and judges in the same way: 'Yes, spray [the oxygen] all about. Let's have plenty of it. Don't spare. Claude will see his poor old dad knows how to live. He can give me all the money he likes and be sure I'll make good use of it.'[9] When Claude arrives, we learn that he has just given away all of his money and decided to follow the example of his mother (Mick's estranged second wife) and opt out of the capitalist, totalitarian system. What will happen to him is uncertain: Vivian thinks he has become one of the 'fanatics' who are shown on television trying to change the status quo through violent shock tactics, trying to stop war and mass starvation through killing and dying themselves. It is not at all clear, however, that the television version is accurate; although Vivian and Mick can see blocks on fire when they look out the window, Claude does not attack them as Vivian expects. 'Not going to kill anyone else. Just came to see my father' says Claude. However, he is certainly in the process of risking his own life, one of the last children born in the Londons, by abandoning his housing and car and breathing the polluted outdoor air: the walk to Mick's room brings him close to collapse. When he leaves to live with his mother in whatever open country spaces still exist, Claude admits, 'Risk is you starve of course like most people.'[10]

In the span of this short drama focused on exploitation of the environment as a resource, Churchill plays out the capitalist logic of supply and demand. She presents ecological crisis perceived as a crisis of scarce commodities requiring state control (even birth is strictly regulated and priced), and producing increased competition for resources (resulting in war, starvation and heavily-armed elites who can buy themselves out of scarcity, like Mick's briefly mentioned first wife). The plot offers a couple of ways of resisting this disastrous logic: the violent revolution of the fanatics (if such exist) or an almost suicidal refusal of the system and resort to mere subsistence-level use of environmental resources. Neither is made to look very attractive, though a certain glamour is associated with Claude's youth and courage. After Claude's departure, the conclusion of the plot is left to Mick who decides to invite Vivian to live with him in his small room after all. This plot resolution offers a tiny degree of hope: at least in this small gesture Mick has broken free from a consumerist measure of personal happiness.

Environmental justice and the commons: *Fen*

Not ... Enough Oxygen, with its darkly comic picture of oxygen and plants obtainable by purchase only, hints at Churchill's historical interest in past transformations of 'commons' – common spaces, shared freely by humans and other animals – into land owned and intensively farmed chiefly to the benefit of the few.[11] This is the territory she explores in *Fen*, a play which was rooted in the human ecology of the fenlands agricultural workers and their exploitation. As they developed the play, Churchill and the other members of the Joint Stock theatre company lived in the fens, researched their history, interviewed the workers, drew on local newspaper accounts and traditional stories. The shared creativity of the theatre company was a practice pointedly opposed to the hierarchical exploitation of the local workers, just as the play itself unearthed the historical process whereby the local people had been gradually subjected. Once, they hunted and fished freely in the marshlands, supporting themselves independently. The play opens with a prologue in which a visiting Japanese businessman speaks of the 'wild people, fen tigers'[12] who walked the marshes on stilts and lived on fishes and eels. Then in one of the earliest manifestations of capitalist investment in land, seventeenth-century projectors bought, drained and ploughed the fens, turning the people into employees; the stage is haunted by ghost-figures crying out against hundreds of years of privation; and during the course of the play, which is set in the present, global capital buys out the local landowner and the workers no longer know even to whom they can protest their exploitation. 'Nell: So who's the boss? Who do you have a go at? Acton's was Ross, Ross is Imperial Foods, Imperial Foods is Imperial Tobacco, so where does that stop?'[13]

This play is intensely local, and very much focused on the plight of the agricultural workers, especially the women, for Churchill is concerned to show the mutually reinforcing parallels among gender, class and environmental exploitation:[14] 'You're good workers', says Tewson the former farm owner to the gang of women picking stones from a field. 'Better workers than men. I've seen women working in my fields with icicles on their faces. I admire that.'[15] The loosely constructed plot follows the lives of several women, centring on the frustrated love affair between Val and Frank. Val has left her husband for her lover Frank, but cannot bring her children with her and cannot live without them. This emotional impasse provides a metaphorical equivalent for the condition of all the fen workers whose livelihood traps and stunts them rather than sustaining them: the point is made particularly effectively through the figure of May, Val's mother, who always wanted to be a professional singer but could not and therefore refuses to sing at all. *Fen* makes an appeal for environmental justice in the sense that it compels the audience to feel that there must be a better way of getting a living from the fens, and invites them to recognize how closely bound together are the lives of the labourers who live here and the earth that they work, both ruthlessly exploited by intensive farming methods. In the immensely effective original staging, the surface of the playing space (designed by Annie Smart) was entirely covered in soil; the tables, chairs, and so forth indicating interior scenes sprouted from the dirt which progressively dusted the costumes of the actors. In a telling stage direction, Shirley, one of the staunchest workers, irons the soil as if it were laundry, a *Gestus* economically binding home and workplace drudgery but also connecting human inhabitants of the fen to the source of their sustenance even though that relationship has been vitiated by capitalism; the inappropriateness of ironing soil suggests workers alienated from their labour and the labour itself transformed into a harsh subjugating of the land.

Yet for all its concern with the immediate demands of human justice, its concern that the land is used to sustain a good life for a few investors rather than the many workers, *Fen* also has something to say about the mentality, the ecological understanding (or rather, lack of same) underpinning exploitation of land and people. There are hints that ownership itself may be an expression of a mind-set dangerous to the environment: an assumption of the human right to dominate and transform. This is suggested by the strategies Churchill uses to prevent us from locating the cause of harm solely in globalization per se (though she clearly dramatizes its inimical effects). Among these strategies: she introduces the Japanese businessman at the outset as a tempting target of anger – he sees no human suffering, and no disturbing domination of the environment, just good investment, efficient farming and 'beautiful English countryside' to photograph when the fog clears.[16] Yet if we isolate global capital for condemnation *as foreign*, we find ourselves uncomfortably allied to the character Geoffrey, who directs the anger resulting from his harsh life against 'Pakis' (i.e. Pakistani immigrants, or citizens of Pakistani descent), the French, the common market and 'Argies' (this was the era of the war against Argentina).[17] And of course, there are those ghosts and tales recalling centuries of local exploitation of the poor men and women of the fens. By implication, then, claiming ownership of the earth may lie at the heart of the problem.

This exposition might be taken to suggest that Churchill slips into preservationism, her layered images of miseries generated by successive forms of capitalism potentially evoking a utopian dream of nature untouched by humanity. Note, however, that her target is capitalist ownership and the concepts of dominance it entails, rather than human (and non-human) sharing in the world's resources. I argue that here, as elsewhere, Churchill presents an ethical vision comprehending both the human-centred responsibilities of environmental justice and the ethical demands of deep ecology. That is, she evokes a dream not of human absence but of a deeper integration – an integration hinted in the intimate kinship she shows between human and animal suffering.

A glimpse of hope in the final scene of this bleak play is afforded by the indomitable Nell, who throughout voices direct protest against the miseries of her life as an agricultural labourer rather than internalizing or displacing her anger as do many of the other characters. She strides across the stage on stilts, as if the common marshlands were still there, and she is able to hear the sun speak: 'Nell: I was walking out on the fen. The sun spoke to me. It said, "Turn back, turn back." I said, "I won't turn back for you or anyone."'[18] Though the ability to hear a non-human voice implies a promisingly responsive rather than dominating attitude toward the environment, what the sun has said sounds ominous. Perhaps there's an analogy to be found between its obscure warning of some trespass, and the lines immediately following in which the layered actions of the play are summed up, actions in which pain felt by the characters past and present is expressed and transmitted in acts of violence towards self and vulnerable fellow creatures. Shirley recalls ancient tales about mutilating animals as a form of protest against oppression – animals who, in a different world, might have been treated kindly; and Frank says: 'I've killed the only person I love', for he has done Val the desperate kindness of helping her commit suicide.[19] Perhaps trespasses against the environing earth and sky are of a like kind, ultimately born of suffering and possible to imagine otherwise; perhaps it is possible to turn back. In the final moment of the play 'May sings, i.e. she stands as if singing and we hear what she would have liked to sing.'[20]

Global commons and the myth of human dominance: *Lives of the Great Poisoners*

In *Fen*, then, Churchill's focus is local. The play is grounded in the specific physical, economic and social environment of the fenlands, dramatizing the history of human interaction with place and setting up a suggestive opposition between a lost commons and intensive highly capitalized agriculture, an opposition which hints at a flawed assumption of the human right to exploit the earth inherent in the very idea of land ownership. With *Lives of the Great Poisoners* Churchill's horizon expands to the global commons of atmosphere and ocean because the environmental threats she considers here affect the natural interchanges and transmissions in air, water and land which respect no political boundaries and for the moment escape any effective legal imposition of responsibility. 'We played around for some time with the idea of a toxic waste ship of fools unable to put into any port', Churchill recalls, and the rejected plan indicates the transnational, global theme which remained when 'That faded but poison stories stayed'.[21] In this performance piece, combining dance choreographed by Ian Spink, song scored by Orlando Gough, and spoken word by Churchill, the playwright and her collaborators investigate the lives of Dr Crippen, Medea and Madame de Brinvilliers, a trio of poisoners from Edwardian London, Greek myth and seventeenth-century France. Around and through their stories moves the greatest (though accidental) poisoner of them all: Thomas Midgley, 1940s inventor of leaded gasoline and CFCs.

A full discussion of this fascinating work would require equal attention to the contributions of all three collaborators (see Worth, Chapter 5 for details). I will focus instead on Churchill's text, emphasizing three aspects in particular which develop and extend her ongoing ecological engagement. I propose, first, that there is a dialectical relationship between *Poisoners* and *Fen* at least insofar as the depiction of a commons is concerned. For if in *Fen* there was some danger of an unexamined, nostalgic idealization of the

England of common lands[22] – an ecological pastoral, because the commons is represented as already lost, rather than subjected to dramatic analysis – in *Poisoners* the global commons provides no Arcadian vision, but a warning against its ongoing collective abuse. Indeed, the structure of the piece turns sharing or commonality into a kind of contagion. A prologue featuring Medea is followed by a sequence of scenes concerning the Edwardian-era wife murderer Dr Crippen, then four scenes devoted to Medea's deeds in the mythic past, succeeded by Mme de Brinvilliers' poisonings and intrigues in seventeenth-century France; throughout the piece the 1940s industrial chemist Midgley interacts anachronistically with all of the characters. As mythic and historical figures of different eras share the stage (Midgley discusses fuel additives with his landlord, Dr Crippen), and characters share embodiment by the same performer (for example Cora, the wife murdered by Crippen, comes back for her revenge as Medea, and subsequently plays the poisoner Mme de Brinvilliers), the common urge to poison is seemingly communicated from one element of the performance to another. (Stage directions indicate that a singing chorus of Poisons assists Medea with a metal box of ingredients, and later hands it on to Brinvilliers, the same performer.) This performative contagion is emphasized in the play's closing scene when it is reported that the body of the executed Brinvilliers has been burnt. Mme de Sevigne comments (in song): 'She is in the air. Her body burnt, her ashes scattered to the winds. Now we all breathe her in so we'll all catch a mania for poisoning which will astonish us. She's in the air.' At this point in the performance, there is something actually in the air of the theatre: just before the burning is described, a character enters with a tray of coffee and amaretti, which he serves to everybody on stage. Churchill directs: '*People unwrap their amaretti and roll up the papers and Sainte-Croix sets fire to them so that the burning paper floats up into the air and the ash floats down.*'[23] Sevigne's lyrics, then, can apply to the audience as well as the characters – they too are potentially exposed to ashes – and they are thus invited to consider whether they are catching or have already caught the mania. In his final speech Midgley, affected by grief for the dead woman (and perhaps by her ashes?), expresses a very contemporary version of the poisoning mania, a kind of poisoning with an unknown outcome.

The second ecological aspect of Churchill's collaborative composition concerns the breathed-in ashes. These ashes, along with the prominent role played by song and the rhythms of dance, are instances of important non-visual elements of Churchill's dramaturgy in general. I propose that her appeals to senses other than sight are part of an affective art which may potentially unsettle the workings of what Agamben calls the anthropological machine[24] – the ways in which we produce ourselves as not-animal and hence position ourselves as users of the environment, paradoxically outside the system that contains us, and is within us, so to speak. There are many other junctures in Churchill's work where she addresses the non-visual senses and the performative environment penetrates us, the audience, as it does not when we merely gaze from a distance at spectacle or hear words simply as bearers of meaning. She fills our noses with the smell of fresh earth in *Fen*, she overlaps dialogue in many of her plays so that we are compelled to hear the yawp and cry of utterance, and in *The Skriker* she penetrates our ears with a sustained, siren-loud shriek.

Third, I suggest that the accidental character of Midgley's achievement – in this, as well as his modernity, he contrasts with the other poisoners – not only adds to the black comedy of the piece but constitutes one of Churchill's most incisive critiques of the effects of the modern union of science and technology. As Churchill herself points out, Midgley's inventions of leaded automotive fuel and CFCs for fridges 'seemed a good idea at the time'.[25] Midgley's refrigerants helped to preserve food for many and thus prevent hunger and disease; Churchill chooses as her central figure a scientist whose poison would have been very difficult to detect and reject when it was first offered. If *Fen* hinted at the philosophical blindness of assuming humankind's right to own and use the earth, this play suggests that the use itself, the control, may be illusory. Churchill returns to the theme of technology as something the effects of which we do not understand (rather than a tool we control) in *The Skriker*.

Beyond environmental justice: *The Skriker*

The Skriker revisits the theme of pollution explored in *Not ... Enough Oxygen* and *Lives of the Great Poisoners*, and incorporates the concern with global capitalism touched upon by *Fen*. It presents the story of two young, poor, single mothers, Josie and Lily, who are friends. When the play begins, Josie has killed her baby and is confined to a mental hospital; Lily is pregnant. The Skriker, a supernatural creature, speaks a tangled, punning, poetic prologue and proceeds to haunt the two girls, first Josie and then – when Josie wishes her away – Lily. There are strong hints that the Skriker is connected to the prior baby-killing. Throughout the play, she appears in various guises and appeals to Lily for affection or help; she also tries to persuade Lily to make wishes. Her malevolence is unmistakable; when she assumes the guise of a small girl, for example, she is jealous of the unborn baby and strikes Lily's belly. It becomes clear that the appeals for affection are dangerous temptations, that wishes (as in many tales) will put one in the power of the fairy; and, when each girl in turn goes with the Skriker to a fairy underworld, there is danger of entrapment if she tastes fairy food or drink. An underworld glamour feast which looks attractive turns out to be sticks, beetles, and dead bodies. Josie eats, and though she is able to return from fairyland she slides increasingly into insanity. Eventually she engages in a mad attempt to appease the Skriker and perhaps distract her from Lily by providing her with news of bloody deeds, some of which she commits herself. Lily, finally, agrees to go with the Skriker to the underworld in order to make her leave Josie and her own baby alone. But while Josie's visit took no time in the real world, Lily returns to find generations have passed and she is confronted by her granddaughter, now an old woman and accompanied by her own grandchild.

Although this play initially drew attention because of the ways in which it tested the limits of representation, it has more recently been discussed as one of Churchill's most important ecological statements.[26] Its eco-logic centres upon the role of the fairy characters. In addition to the Skriker, a shape-shifter and death portent from Yorkshire or Lancashire lore whose alternative traditional name most appropriately is 'Trash', there are a great many non-speaking, supernatural figures who appear on the stage: the list of characters includes Johnny Squarefoot, The Kelpie, Bogle, Spriggan, Rawheadandbloodybones, Thrumpins and more.[27] All of these derive from British folklore and all are traditionally malevolent; they originate in a period before the decline of magic, when human beings struggled for survival in the natural world and often peopled the environment with imagined creatures, personifying what were felt to be opposing forces in the world around them. The Skriker, who claims to be hundreds of years old, is an updated version of human opposition to the natural environment projected onto it as anthropomorphized malevolence. People used to propitiate the spirits of the land – 'They used to leave cream in a sorcerer's apprentice' says the Skriker – but no longer, and now they insult the land itself: 'Now they hate us and hurt hurtle faster and master. They poison me in my rivers of blood poisoning makes my arm swelter.'[28] The Skriker refers freely, and with evident relish, to human mishaps such as car crashes and especially to ecological disaster: 'toxic waste paper basket case'; 'poison in the food chain saw massacre'; 'up in the war zone ozone zany grey?'[29] In the guise of an intrusive American tourist in a bar, she asks Lily repeatedly to explain how the TV works. Lily can't, and her incomprehension recalls the great accidental poisoner Midgley, and the dangers of technology which can almost magically magnify the impact of human actions on the world beyond our understanding of their ultimate effect. In addition, the trick with time in the fairy underworld – first no time passes, then generations – suggests that real time, too, is misperceived and that our attempts to master the environment are hurtling us towards disaster. Elin Diamond's recent essay reads the temporal manipulations of Churchill's play as evoking the compressed space–time of globalized market forces, and their implications for subjectivity as well as the environment.[30] The deceptive, horrid foodstuffs in the fairy underworld suggest 'poison in the food chain' and the danger of the false feast ('Don't eat or you'll never get back' a girl trapped in fairyland warns)[31] evokes the myth of Proserpine, whose confinement in the underworld is associated with earth's periods of sterility.

I have mentioned that the fairy creatures operate according to the Freudian logic of projection.[32] This means that they are not so much Churchill's representations of nature as dramatizations of the human relationship to nature; this is why the Skriker is associated with both the ecosystem as damaged object of human actions ('Skriker: They poison me in my rivers of blood poisoning makes my blood swelter') and the desires of the human subject which lead to poisoning the earth ('Skriker: Don't you want to feel global warm and happy ever after?').[33] In keeping with the logic of projection, human aggression against the natural world is (mis)perceived as malevolence directed against humankind by a natural world conceived in the human perceiver's own image. And the process of projection belongs not to the psyche of any individual human character in the play, but to the structure of the play as a whole – hence, by implication, drawing attention to generalized patterns of displaced guilt characterizing human relations to the non-human world.

The logic of projection explains why Churchill has altered traditional fairy morality in her supernatural creatures. There is a strong tradition in fairy lore which associates fairies with the punishment of socially unacceptable behaviour such as greed or slovenliness. In this play, however, Lily is in danger when she responds to appeals for aid or love, when the Skriker entices her in the guise of a needy child, a lonely older woman in a bar, a disturbed man seeking a lover. How then does it make sense for Lily to suffer for her kindness or sympathy? Perhaps Churchill presents again her undeceived view of the way in which the injured take out their anger and frustration on vulnerable fellow-creatures (as in *Fen*), including those who care for them. Thus the anthropomorphized image of the natural environment, the Skriker, behaves according to human motivation. And in some respects, the Skriker's human guises indicate once more that Churchill sees the oppression of human and non-human intertwined. In her commitment to environmental justice she suggests via her plot structure that the poor, single mum is more likely to be exposed to contaminated food and polluting toxins – the 'anger' of the damaged, anthropomorphized environment. Of course this is not fair; and the unfairness is encoded in the poetic injustice of the dire consequences Lily risks in responding to the Skriker's appeals.

At a deeper level still, if we see the play as in some sense organized by the psychic structure of projection governing human perception of the non-human world, then perhaps Churchill also hints at the philosophical difficulty of escaping a human-centred vision. As feminist eco-theorist Catriona Sandilands puts the matter, although constructing nature as a subject in all senses of the word is the task of environmentalism, 'there cannot be an authentic voice of nature without profound revision of either the notion of speech or the notion of the speaking subject'.[34] The Skriker is clearly a warped version of the natural world, her speech a tangle of familiar human phrases given ominous and peculiar twists, her malevolence an image of human aggression. As we reject her as a voice of nature, we gain an intimation of the task of constructing the Real subject.

Churchill was recently commissioned by the BBC Proms to compose the lyrics for a choral work on climate change, with music by Orlando Gough. The piece, titled *We Turned on the Light*, premiered in London on 29 July 2006. It adapts a device from the close of *The Skriker* and serves as something of a coda to the earlier play. In *The Skriker*, Lily confronts her aged granddaughter who appears accompanied by her own grandchild; here the granddaughter of the granddaughter of the present-day protagonist speaks to the protagonist. The repeated device of confrontation across the generations emphasizes Churchill's concern with our ethical responsibility to the future. The later version also clarifies why the child in the final scene of *The Skriker* directs a bellow of wordless rage at Lily, and suggests another facet of the Skriker's pursuit of affection; for in *We Turned on the Light* the granddaughter of the granddaughter, suffering the effects of climate change, asks the present-day protagonist 'Didn't you love me?' The protagonist answers 'I'm sorry ... It's hard to love people far away in time.'[35] Ecological ethics require a kind of love that extends far in time, in space, and beyond our own species.

Far Away and close to home: global ethics

The theme of distance and ecological ethics is precisely the core concern of Churchill's play from 2000, *Far Away*. This play begins with a young girl, Joan, questioning her aunt Harper about having seen her uncle in the garden hitting people with an iron bar. It moves on to Joan as a young woman, employed in the city along with her friend Todd in making elaborate hats which are worn by prisoners paraded to execution. It concludes several years later with Joan and Todd, now married, taking temporary refuge at the aunt's house in the country, before returning to their roles in a pervasive conflict; the whole world is apparently at war, including the animals. The aunt comments on the situation: 'Mallards are not a good waterbird. They commit rape, and they're on the side of the elephants and the Koreans. But crocodiles are always in the wrong.'[36] Horrific as this statement may be, it's also very funny. And as we smile at the story-book absurdity of crocodiles who are always in the wrong, we catch a glimpse of another way of perceiving the world – a way that does not calibrate everything by the measure of man. Indeed, Una Chaudhuri has proposed that the disjunctive animal presence in this play 'resonates with posthumanist programs like Agamben's which seek to interrupt the obsessive and ideologically fraught distinguishing of humans and other animals in Western thought'.[37]

This evocative and somewhat cryptic play returns to the dystopic vision of a threatened global ecosystem Churchill first examined in *Not ... Enough Oxygen*. In several ways her ecological dramaturgy has grown in breadth and intimacy. As just noted, Churchill now indicates the anthropocentrism underpinning environmental crisis which, it appears, has precipitated a more than Hobbesian war of all against all. Interestingly, she doesn't present accounts of environmental disaster directly. Using a strategy like her evocation of the psychic structures of projection in *The Skriker*, she suggests such disaster by including animals, grass, rivers, weather, among the opponents mentioned by the characters: in the final speech of the play, as Joan describes her difficult journey to join Todd, she comments that 'It wasn't so much the birds I was frightened of, it was the weather, the weather here's on the side of the Japanese' and a few lines later remarks that she 'didn't know whose side the river was on'.[38] Without any explicit discussion of global warming or allusions to competition for diminishing resources in the dialogue, Churchill can now rely on her audience's familiarity with current news reports of scientific studies.

There is a new grimness here, as Churchill probes the ethics and psychology of a global struggle for resources – nature perceived as the object of human dominance, as a hellish commons ruled by might. And if her drama of a future universal combat seems too fantastic to bear upon the actual relations between Britain and the rest of the human and non-human world, it is useful to note columnist Gwynne Dyer's ironic commentary from 2006, in which he speculates that, given the dire predictions of the Inter-Governmental Panel on Climate Change, the British government may be developing its new generation of nuclear weapons in order to prevent refugees of catastrophic global climate change from swamping lifeboat Britain.[39] In Joan's closing speech previously innocent elements of the natural world have become weaponized – suggesting the deployment of atoms, and serving as a synecdoche for the violence people do to one another by controlling the means of sustaining life: 'The Bolivians are working with gravity [...] But we're getting further ahead with noise and there's thousands dead of light in Madagascar. Who's going to mobilize silence and darkness?'[40] This poetic device also conveys an all-pervading aggression transforming the global environment.

Churchill uses a number of strategies to show how easily such extraordinary aggression becomes familiar and acceptable and in so doing hints at a need to revise judgment of common forms of violence against people and the environment, as well as the commonplace ethical divide between human and animal. At first, when Harper tries to keep the child Joan from knowing what her uncle has been doing in the garden, we assume she sees herself as an accomplice guiltily concealing a crime. But as the play unfolds, and Joan the young woman does not seem greatly distressed by the execution of the prisoners whose hats she designs, the suspicion grows that Harper was simply withholding information that adults deal with comfortably. In Joan's closing speech there's no distinction to be made between human and animal slaughter: 'Of course birds saw me, everyone saw me walking along but nobody knew why, I could have been on a mission, everybody's moving about and nobody knows why, and in fact I killed two cats and a child under five so it wasn't that different from a mission ...'[41] By means of this juxtaposition of cats and child Churchill suggests that Joan, her hearers Todd and Harper, indeed a whole society familiar with 'missions' accept as normal virtually every kind of violence.

Churchill also uses this device to challenge the audience's ethical awareness. For if we judge Joan to be morally desensitized partly because she doesn't seem to distinguish between killing humans and animals, Churchill hints that the presumed distinction between the status of human and animal (which of course permits her to create the effect of a shocking fantasy world by dint of characters who refer to animals as if they are national or military opponents) may itself be a means by which the audience makes its own familiar acts of violence against the natural world acceptable. At several junctures, the characters discuss the fantastic scenario of animal military opponents in disturbingly familiar terms which remind us of ways in which we often distinguish 'good' and 'bad' animals because of their usefulness to us, or their aesthetic appeal: the attractive eyes of deer, the capacity of ants and wasps to sting.

Churchill also includes many homely details to bring the audience to recognize that aggressively laying claim to a large share of the Earth's resources and thus depriving others is part of our daily, familiar actions, not a fiction of far away. The garden – emblem of normal suburban English life – is the setting for the first, gradually revealed, violence. There are touches, too, in the closing scene recalling the clichés of wartime domestic sacrifice used in so many British movies: as Joan walks into Todd's arms, Harper asks her niece 'What are you going to say when you go back, you ran off to spend a day with your husband? Everyone has people they love they'd like to see or anyway people they'd rather see than lie in a hollow waiting to be bitten by ants.'[42] Here, through allusion to the celebration of Mrs Miniver-style self-control, Churchill adds subtlety to her exposure of the role played by the arts in normalizing aggression, a theme asserted more obviously in the hat-making scenes.

If in *The Skriker* human aggression was projected onto the natural world which was transformed into a damaged, poisoned, devious enemy combatant, here a similar psychic structure allies deprived nations and depraved natural phenomena in an opposing axis. In a sense, then, this play brings together Churchill's concern with environmental justice – now seen as a global as well as a local issue – and her philosophical exploration of the possibility of a post-human ecological understanding. The issues Churchill deals with in her succession of ecological dramas are both far-reaching and close at hand, and through these plays she transforms our understanding of the ethics of even very ordinary statements such as the once seemingly innocuous assertion with which the final scene of *Far Away* begins: 'You were right to poison the wasps.'[43]

NOTES

1. Debate concerning the economics and ecology of the commons in this latter sense was spurred by Garrett Hardin's 'The Tragedy of the Commons', *Science*, 162 (1968), 1243–8. George Monbiot published a riposte: 'The Tragedy of Enclosure', *Scientific American* (1994) available at his website: www.monbiot.com/archives. Significant discussions of the topic appear in, for example, Ramachandra Guha, *How Much Should a Person Consume? Environmentalism in India and the United States* (Berkeley: University of California Press, 2006) and David Harvey, *Justice, Nature and the Geography of Difference* (Oxford: Blackwell, 1996).
2. See for example Una Chaudhuri, *Staging Place: The Geography of Modern Drama* (Ann Arbor: University of Michigan Press, 1995), and Chaudhuri, 'Animal Geographies: Zooësis and the Space of Modern Drama', *Modern Drama*, 46.4 (2003), 646–62.
3. See Joni Adamson, Mei Mei Evans and Rachel Stein (eds.), *The Environmental Justice Reader: Politics, Poetics, and Pedagogy* (Tucson: University of Arizona Press, 2002).
4. Philosopher Arne Naess is the founder of the deep ecology movement; see A. Naess, *Ecology, Community and Lifestyle* (Cambridge: Cambridge University Press, 1989).
5. Ramachandra Guha, 'Radical American Environmentalism and Wilderness Preservation: A Third World Critique', in Ramachandra Guha and J. Martinez-Alier (eds.), *Varieties of Environmentalism: Essays North and South* (Delhi: Oxford University Press, 1998), pp. 92–108.
6. Cheryll Glotfelty, Introduction, Cheryll Glotfelty and Harold Fromm (eds.), *The Ecocriticism Reader: Landmarks in Literary Ecology* (Athens, GA: University of Georgia Press, 1996), pp. xxii–iii.

7. Caryl Churchill, *Not Not Not Not Not Enough Oxygen* in *Churchill Shorts: Short Plays by Caryl Churchill* (London: Nick Hern Books, 1990), pp. 39, 55.
8. *Ibid.*, p. 40.
9. *Ibid.*
10. *Ibid.*, p. 50.
11. Prior to *Fen*, Churchill's *Light Shining in Buckinghamshire* (1976) explored attempts by the Diggers and Levellers during England's civil war to challenge ownership and re-establish rights of common access to enclosed land. The play also presented a religious reformer who rejected the doctrine of divine sanction for human dominion over the earth. See Howard, Chapter 3, and Luckhurst, Chapter 4, for full discussions of *Light Shining*.
12. Caryl Churchill, *Fen*, in *Plays: Two* (London: Methuen, 1990), p. 147.
13. *Ibid.*, p. 181.
14. See Sheila Rabillard, 'Churchill's *Fen* and the Production of a Feminist Ecotheatre', *Theater* 25.1 (1994), 62–71.
15. Churchill, *Fen*, *Plays: Two*, p. 171.
16. *Ibid.*, p. 147.
17. *Ibid.*, p. 170.
18. *Ibid.*, p. 189.
19. *Ibid.*
20. *Ibid.*, production note, p. 145.
21. Churchill, Introduction in Caryl Churchill, Orlando Gough and Ian Spink, *Lives of the Great Poisoners: A Production Dossier* (London: Methuen, 1993), p. ix.
22. Raymond Williams warns against the nostalgic myth of the enclosures, in which 'the transition from a rural to an industrial society is seen as a kind of fall, the true cause and origin of our social suffering and disorder'. This myth, he argues, is 'a main source for that last protecting illusion in the crisis of our own time: that it is not capitalism which is injuring us, but the more isolable, more evident system of urban industrialism'. *The City and the Country* (New York: Oxford University Press, 1973), p. 96.
23. Churchill, *Poisoners*, p. 65.
24. Giorgio Agamben, *The Open: Man and Animal*, trans. Kevin Attell (Stanford, CA: Stanford University Press, 2004).
25. Churchill, Introduction, *Poisoners*, p. x.
26. See, for example, Candice Amich, 'Bringing the Global Home: The Commitment of Caryl Churchill's *The Skriker*', *Modern Drama* 50.3 (Fall 2007), 394–413; Elin Diamond, 'Caryl Churchill: Feeling Global' in Mary Luckhurst (ed.), *A Companion to Modern British and Irish Drama 1880–2005* (Oxford: Blackwell, 2006), pp. 476–87; and Elaine Aston, '"A Licence to Kill": Caryl Churchill's Socialist–Feminist "Ideas of Nature"', in Gabriella Giannachi and Nigel Stewart (eds.), *Performing Nature: Explorations in Ecology and the Arts* (Bern: Peter Lang, 2005), pp. 165–78.
27. Names and characteristics of the supernatural creatures can be found in a standard folklore reference work such as Katharine Briggs' *A Dictionary of Fairies* (London: Allen Lane, 1976).
28. Caryl Churchill, *The Skriker* in *Plays: Three* (London: Nick Hern Books, 1998), p. 246.
29. *Ibid.*, pp. 271–2.

30. Diamond, 'Feeling Global', p. 477.
31. Churchill, *The Skriker*, *Plays: Three*, p. 270.
32. Freud first articulates the concept of projection in his analysis of Schreber, the case study on which Churchill bases her play *Schreber's Nervous Illness*. See *The Standard Edition Complete Psychological Works of Sigmund Freud*, trans. James Strachey (London: The Hogarth Press, 1953), vol. XII, p. 66.
33. Churchill, *The Skriker*, in *Plays: Three*, p. 270.
34. Catriona Sandilands, *The Good-Natured Feminist: Ecofeminism and the Quest for Democracy* (Minneapolis: University of Minnesota Press, 1999), p. 80.
35. These lines are quoted in a synopsis of *We Turned on the Light* in The Ashden Directory (www.ashdendirectory.org.uk).
36. Caryl Churchill, *Far Away* in *Plays: Four* (London: Nick Hern Books, 2008), p. 155.
37. Una Chaudhuri, abstract of 'The Anthropological Machine in Overdrive: Zooësis and Extremity', a paper presented at Tel Aviv University, January 2008, www.environment.tau.ac.il/_Uploads/416UnaAbstract.pdf.
38. Churchill, *Far Away*, in *Plays: Four*, p. 158.
39. Gwynne Dyer, 'British Nukes: Taking the Long View' (17 March 2006), www.gwynnedyer.com/articles.
40. Churchill, *Far Away*, in *Plays: Four*, p. 159.
41. *Ibid.*, p. 158.
42. *Ibid.*
43. *Ibid.*, p. 152.

7

R. DARREN GOBERT

On performance and selfhood in Caryl Churchill

Theatre is born in its own disappearance, and the offspring
of this movement has a name: man.
Jacques Derrida[1]

In 'The Work of Art in an Age of Mechanical Reproduction', Walter Benjamin argued that technologies of mass reproduction had undermined the work of art's 'originality', rendering ideas of its 'authenticity' and its 'authority' increasingly irrelevant, however nostalgically they might be mourned.[2] These ideas concatenate in Caryl Churchill's play *A Number*, whose Bernard worries about human identity under threat from cloning technology. Having met his genetic double – one, he learns, of a number – Bernard frets that 'someone else is the one, the first one, the real one', neatly tying together essence, origins and authenticity. Salter answers, 'no because ... I'm your father'.[3] He guarantees Bernard's uniqueness with a *sui generis* paternal authority, merely by reiterating the son's patrilineage. But unsurprisingly Salter's balms turn out to sting rather than soothe. Of course, all of the clones are genetically descended from him; in fact, Bernard is not 'the first one'; and, in time, Salter's paternal succour will fail even the first one, also Bernard, who turns up in the play's second scene and who eventually ends his own existential conflict in suicide.

Throughout her career, Churchill has married thorny theoretical content (whether colonialism and sexual politics in *Cloud Nine*, social regulation in *Softcops*, or the logic of terror in *Far Away*) to stunning dramatic form, using the language of the stage – words, but also living bodies – vividly to conjure, in her words, 'worries and questions and complexities'.[4] Here I consider five plays, each from a different decade, whose central dramatic impulse is the difficulty of self-knowledge – 'How do I know who I am?' – that has long preoccupied Churchill. I trace her interrogation of 'identity' through *Identical Twins* (1968), *Traps* (1977), *Icecream* (1989) and *Blue Heart* (1997). These plays' complexities we might see as postulates for the conclusion she reaches in *A Number* (2002): that the problem of identity is shadowed by the problem of performance and thus best contemplated in the evanescent realm in which performance resides.

Identity, subjectivity, uniqueness

A Number situates itself in a long tradition of domestic dramas that interrogate the family structure, whose role in identity construction is as fundamental as it is problematic; like Hedda Gabler, chafed by her ill-fitting role as Tesman's wife, Bernard 2 falls prey to a crisis of self. Identity hinges on a subject-position, and, as Hedda knows too well, we begin as sons and daughters. The twentieth century's most compelling articulations of subjectivity show that the subject originates in, and is reinforced by, its difference from others. Thus, the family proves crucial, since the 'I' that anchors the subject is produced early, either by linguistic opposition to 'you' or against the mother whose unlikeness the child recognizes as a necessary precondition for language.[5] In other words, the subject is fundamentally defined in relational and negative terms, against what it is not.

The conceptual difficulties these terms present are laid bare in Churchill's radio play *Identical Twins*, first broadcast on 21 November 1968 on BBC Radio 3. The title characters, Clive and Teddy, find their processes of subject-formation impeded precisely because of a lack of difference: they are identical. Churchill amplifies the claustrophobia of the twins' early childhood by vacating it of other characters – particularly significantly, their mother, whom the play invokes only by two references. The first is Teddy and Clive's dual declaration that she couldn't tell them apart; the second, their memory of her three-way mirror:

> TEDDY AND CLIVE When I was very small I would stand with him in Mummy's triple mirror. If we stood very close we could almost shut it round us. There were hundreds of reflections, all the same. (*Clive's voice gets fainter*) Then I was terrified to move (*Clive silent now*)
>
> TEDDY not knowing which reflections would move with me.[6]

Rather than seeing himself as whole, each twin sees himself (as Bernard 2 comes to) as a number of identical reflections. Thus, his process of individuation is thwarted rather than facilitated – a thwarting perpetually reinforced by the reflection that does indeed 'move with' each: Teddy for Clive, Clive for Teddy. Churchill captures this existential crisis not only by perpetually overlaying Teddy's 'I' with Clive's 'I' – much of their text is shared, delivered in unison – but also by asking that the twins be played by the same actor.

Containing no other speaking characters, the play gives the twins no space of difference against which to define themselves, which manifests in a desire to harm the reflection that begins in childhood ('every day, with bricks in our playpen and knives once when we were sixteen') and continues into adulthood ('I leapt at him and we fell on the pavement and rolled over and over into the road, I wanted to hurt him.').[7] Their identical voices remind us that 'I' and 'him' are functionally useless both in their lives and in the radio play's reception; like Teddy and Clive, the audience struggles to keep separate track. Appropriately, then, and as their tandem monologues make clear, violence offered to the other twin is expressed and experienced equally as violence offered to the incomplete self. The situation reaches a climax in the play's suicide scene, in which the two sit at a table contemplating a bottle of sleeping pills. With only one bottle between them, the two finally find a twisted sort of individuation, marked materially on the page as the text splits, for the first time, into parallel columns:

TEDDY	CLIVE
Clive takes more pills. This is one of those stupid things you regret later. I go on watching. Then I get up without a word and go straight out for a walk, the night is quite mild as the day has been and I feel better for some fresh air.	I take more pills. This is one of those stupid things you regret later. I take some more pills. And some more. Then I lean over the table and hide my face in my arms and hope I'll go to sleep quickly and whether it works or not is out of my hands now.[8]

Clive thereafter disappears from the play, as his fading voice in their shared monologue about the mirror had portended. Teddy seems, at last, to have singly claimed the 'I' that will anchor his subject position and his identity.

However, the play's events leading up to this climactic moment make clear that suicide will not fully resolve the twins' identity crisis; it offers only false hope, like earlier plot incidents that seemed to provide a basis for identity-consolidation. For example, when we learn that 'when I was twelve I was seduced by an oaf of sixteen', Teddy and Clive narrate in unison, finally noting that 'a friend told me the same boy had done the same to Clive/ Teddy [each says the other's name] that same summer'.[9] The twinned *same*s aggregate the joint failure of their sexual initiation. Similarly, the twins recount that '[a]t seventeen I began to be myself ... The day I came nearest to feeling fond of him was when I realised we were both separately planning to run away from each other.'[10] Their shared delivery and shared 'I' enfeeble the act of 'be[ing] myself', as does their collective and unsettling insistence on the adjective *both*, which corrodes the adverb *separately*. They go to the station together, effecting a physical but not psychic separation.

While they flee to find difference, to city and country respectively, in adulthood their notions of identity continue to be unsettled precisely because of its relational nature. Defined too similarly as husbands, lovers and fathers of two children each – a reminder of the role ideology plays in defining relationships – the twins inexorably drift towards reunion and, eventually, the mitigated success of Clive's suicide. Teddy takes Clive's mistress and children and moves into his country home, asserting not individuality but lack of difference. And the play ends with Teddy considering his own suicide. 'Sometimes I think I'll make one effort, not to kill myself', he declares.[11] The phrase, spoken by a solo voice, emphasizes its unitary nature, its uniqueness: it will be 'one effort'. But the interposed negation 'not' disquiets, a shadow of the negative terms on which identity is founded and a reminder of the peculiar psychodynamics of his brother's death. Clive needed Teddy not to save him. Who will not save Teddy?

Identical Twins prefigures the schizophrenic world of Churchill's *Schreber's Nervous Illness*, visiting the existential question 'How do I know who I am?' by figuring it as 'How do I know I am not someone else?' (Or, as Salter puts it in *A Number*, 'if that's me over there who am I?')[12] The troubled uniqueness Teddy possesses at the play's end he procures by metaphorically smashing the mirror, by systematically honing doubles, as *A Number*'s homicidal Bernard 1 will attempt. Two wives become one when Clive's depressive spouse, Janet, kills herself; two mistresses become one when Teddy's tenant, Dawn, is abandoned; two twins give way to one. But Teddy is still an identical twin, and the play's final lines draw the contours of his attenuated accomplishment. On the one hand, these lines remind us that his single house and mistress are Clive's, and that he is still haunted by the play's remaining set of doubles, the children. (His own live in the city while he raises his brother's.) On the other hand, the lines suggest that his children have made possible the very difference which the triple mirror had denied. 'Clive's children are sweet and I'm fond of them but my own are the ones I love', he says, his *ones* marking their unitary distinctness from their shadows in the country.[13] Thus *Identical Twins* ends by reiterating the centrality of family relations in establishing a unique identity. It ties this establishment directly to patrilineage, an idea whose vexations *A Number* will theatricalize with particular brilliance.

Family relations and citationality

The relationship between selfhood and patrilineage provides the dramatic impetus for *Icecream*, first staged by Max Stafford-Clark at the Royal Court in 1989. Whereas the picture Churchill paints in *Identical Twins* represents identity as mired in the deep psychoanalytic terrain of subject-formation, the picture in *Icecream* reflects 'identity' off the shallow surfaces of a postmodern landscape, bereft of psychology. This difference resonates generically. *Identical Twins* is an unsettling psychic drama about one split character; *Icecream* is a satire about family relations, as announced in the character list, which folds 'Lance and Vera' and 'Phil and Jaq' into two units: 'husband and wife' and 'brother and sister'.

Icecream burlesques the search for identity by employing the hoariest cliché of self-discovery: the road trip. Lance, whose existential anxiety is figured as his lack of 'history' as an American, travels to England in a quest to find familial roots, which he imagines as stretching back before 1066. But early in the play, as he surveys a castle with Vera, she precisely diagnoses his epistemological error: 'Just because someone doesn't know who their grandparents are doesn't make them not exist.'[14] The proliferating negation in her phrase ironically traverses the fraught terrain of any quest for identity even as it refuses its corollary, positive, claim: knowing one's grandparents doesn't necessarily make one exist, either. Nonetheless, Vera is along for the ride, a genealogical blank patrilineally attached to Lance. 'If it's mine it's yours', as he puts it.[15] Indeed, when third cousins, Phil and Jaq, are located in East London, Vera naturalizes her familial bond with Phil, explicitly brushing aside his caveat 'in law' and thus making possible the mock-flirtation with incest that will serve as one of *Icecream*'s many red herrings. '[W]hat's Lance's is mine', she jokes.[16]

The scene in which Lance and Phil uncover their shared 'origins' is the play's funniest, as the two men compete to articulate their ostensibly natural bond:

> LANCE So great aunt Dora was my great /
> PHIL was your greatgrandfather's –
> LANCE grandmother's brother's daughter – mother's, great / grandmother's –
> PHIL – mother's, right,
> LANCE she was my greatgrand*mother*'s brother's daughter and your greatgrand / *father's*
> PHIL father's
> LANCE brother's daughter.[17]

Churchill's satirical register reveals itself both in the text ('I think it was Madge. Unless it was Elsie. Let's go for Madge')[18] and in its delivery, with the two men's accents – a mark of their cultural and class differences – wrapping together like the ancestral roots they struggle to separate. Churchill's trademark overlapping dialogue here serves the precise opposite of its function in *Identical Twins*. The American and the Briton could scarcely be more dissimilar, and the bond they forge is as unnatural as their two-dimensional images of one another's countries: Lance adores England's fields, accents and pubs, while Phil derides America's hamburgers and television. (He does admire, however, America's fanciful icecream flavours and concedes: 'The idea of Oregon, the word, just the word Oregon really thrills me.')[19]

Their tenuous bond is cemented not by the money that Lance begins almost immediately to lend his 'cousin', but by the intrusion of a more brute material reality: after Phil kills a man, Lance and Vera must help him and Jaq dump the body in Epping Forest. 'You don't go to the police about your own family', Lance reasons.[20] The image's ironies ripple. Having come to England to explore his family tree and to uncover kin, Lance ends up in a dark forest, covering a dead (and, significantly, un*identified*) body with fallen leaves – before being quickly shuffled back to America for the second act. Finally, Lance is a tourist and without roots, whatever his genealogical claims. Identity as he sought it fails. This failure is reflected in the unmoored plot of Act II and especially Lance's increasingly erratic characterization. 'Lance', like 'Vera', 'Jaq' and 'Phil' – none of whom has any other family, either – coheres only as one more shifting image in the kaleidoscope that constitutes *Icecream*, a territory whose simulacral similarities to his 'Britain' and Phil's 'America' unsettle. Identity seems a series of citations, a string of clichés like those Vera unapologetically celebrates.

Critics have described the play as spare, but this assessment is entirely wrong. In a postmodern trick, Churchill keeps *Icecream* uncharacteristically busy: a theme-park panorama of hollow attractions. Spanning twelve speaking parts, seventeen settings and twenty scenes in under seventy-five minutes, the play deploys its dramatic and cinematic tropes with a kitchen-sink glee. Homecomings, recognition scenes and voyages of discovery come and go alongside Vera and Phil's drunken entanglement and other red herrings. Indeed, as Una Chaudhuri has noted, Churchill kills off not only Phil's victim but Phil himself (in an 'accident', between scenes, after he and Jaq follow their new relations to America) entirely without motive, dramaturgical rationale or dramatic consequence. Critics who identify the dead man as Jaq and Phil's landlord or who claim that Phil dies from looking the wrong way while crossing the street, connect dots that Churchill has left unconnected with a wilful offhandedness.

Veering from the story to the question of the story's meaning, the second act opens with Vera in mid-monologue, confessing to her 'shrink' – the word is Churchill's; his character name, Shrink – her role in the murdered man's disposal. '[N]obody ever did find him', she reports, adding tellingly, 'Didn't he have a family?' 'Go for the police. I'm a murderer', she demands.[21] The psychiatrist's response turns on the inter-relationship of family and selfhood:

> The man in the wood is your dead ancestors, your unborn children and the part of yourself you fear to have discovered. When you ask me to go for the police you are asking me to discover this self and help you to face the consequences. Which is what I am trying to do now.
> *Pause.*
> The man in the wood is also me.[22]

In this metatheatrical moment, Churchill shifts her focus to *Icecream*'s audiences by figuring the Shrink as their onstage surrogate. Having heard the story that we have seen represented in Act I, he provides an earnest reading. Thus Churchill can ironize two tendencies of spectatorship. The first is the longing to make coherent meaning, to find depth, even as it is what it is. (Chaudhuri delightfully calls it a 'burial for burial's sake'.)[23] After all, Vera's confession is neither symbol-laden dream nor fantasy but a straightforward admission that leads nowhere, just as *Icecream*'s settings and characters remain steadfastly two-dimensional. The second tendency Churchill ironizes is the impulse to identification, so central to our dramatic tradition, that runs parallel to our longing to make meaning.

In Aristotelian dramatic theory, theatrical identification serves precisely to consolidate the subject-position of the spectator. Acknowledging his similarity with the hero, the spectator fears; recognizing his difference, he concomitantly pities. Since we learn as we look, in Aristotle's immortal formulation,[24] presumably the theatregoing impulse inheres partly in the desire for a refined self-knowledge, gained in contemplation of the theatrical Other. In *Icecream*, the psychiatrist claims to interpret the dead body but actually deduces that the story is all about him. That he is male is of course no accident; the vast majority of the theatrical tradition, as various feminist thinkers have shown, is decidedly masculinist – perpetually reinforcing its male-centred perspective and thus its male spectators' subjectivity. A feminist playwright might then offer an alternate perspective, as Churchill does in *Top Girls*. Here, however, ridiculing the audience surrogate, she flouts the possibility of anchoring any perspective at all on *Icecream*, whose spotlights on 'identity' reveal it to be in flux, perpetually displaced, lost in citation. Jaq puts it this way: 'I feel I'm in a road movie and everyone I meet is these interesting characters'.[25]

We could read this revelation as allegorizing women's subjectivity in general, remembering Simone de Beauvoir's formulation that 'He is the Subject, he is the Absolute – she is the Other.'[26] And indeed, Chaudhuri finds hints of a new kind of identity, implicitly feminine, in the play's final encounter, when at the airport returning to England Jaq meets a 'South American Woman Passenger' who urges her to '[c]hange your destination'.[27] The play's second act has been largely preoccupied with Jaq's American road trip. After her brother's death, and shorn of the familial identity Churchill's character list had assigned her, Jaq has remained literally in transit – in Lance and Vera's car, which she steals – and dramaturgically in freefall, shown in unsatisfactory engagement with a series of mismatched scene partners: a hitch-hiker, his mother, a professor who offers sexual violence. (That he teaches history, Churchill's slyest joke, reminds us of the opening scene. Jaq pushes him off a cliff.) But what new basis for identity her airport encounter might offer remains entirely unclear, and the South American Woman Passenger proves just another implausibility in two dimensions: *Icecream* offers new flavours, new travels, all the time. Ricocheting from setting to setting, its dramaturgy untethered to any discernible logic, the play provides no more grist for the spectator's self-knowledge than it provided to Lance, just a reflection of its characters' perpetual disconnection.

Space and time

In *Icecream*'s opening scene, Lance and Vera mangle the song 'The Heather on the Hill' from *Brigadoon*. It is a particularly cunning citation, not only because Lerner and Loewe's musical concerns two American tourists but also because it so casually thematizes extreme temporal dislocation. (Churchill's Americans aren't even in *Brigadoon*'s Scotland, another wry joke that amplifies the spatial dislocation of the scene's setting: in a car on the 'Road to the Isles'.) In the play's closing scene, Jaq hesitates in the transitional space of the airport's departure lounge, destined for somewhere uncertain. These two moments, bookends to the play, remind us that another dimension to identity follows on its relational fluxes. Benjamin explicitly links the death of originality to the loss of time and space. And the answer to the question 'Who am I?' depends on where and when 'I' is, the very contexts which the postmodern *Icecream* denies. This postulate is the central subject of Churchill's still-startling *Traps*, first staged by John Ashford at the Royal Court in 1977.

Traps announces its concern with identity early, when Reg arrives at the living room that is the play's only set. He is looking for his brother-in-law:

ALBERT Jack isn't married so how could he have a brother-in-law?
REG I'm the one that's married.
ALBERT If Jack's got a sister.[28]

The exchange encapsulates the central trick of the play's opening scene, which appears straightforward on the surface but in fact obeys its own deep unreality. We read Albert to be stating the obvious: Jack, if unmarried, cannot have a brother-in-law unless he has a married sister. (The character list does announce that 'JACK is CHRISTIE's younger brother, and REG is her husband.') However, we soon come to understand Albert's more troubling propositional logic: Reg, the 'brother-in-law', ceases to exist if Jack hasn't got a sister, and Jack both may and may not have a sister at any given moment, just as, in the famous thought experiment, the cat may both live and not live within Schrödinger's box. For the ontological world of *Traps* is one in which 'the characters can be thought of as living many of their possibilities at once', as Churchill puts it in her author's note and as the play's central emblem, a

Möbius strip, makes clear. She likens the play to an image by Escher, 'impossible in life'.[29]

Traps' ruptured ontological space – the setting is both city flat and country house – is governed by a ruptured time. To choose just one example, Syl speculates about whether she'll have a child in the next five years mere minutes in stage time after she has put her baby down to sleep. Churchill has experimented with time in this way elsewhere, folding both past and future into a continuous present in *Moving Clocks Go Slow* and compressing time radically in *The Skriker*. But *Traps* ties its impossible space–time much more explicitly to the question of identity, returning again and again to the impossibility of imagining a self outside of its spatial and temporal locations.

Existing in the skewed ontology that they do, the characters become functionally unintelligible: one minute Syl is a mother, the next she is not; Jack announces he's gone when he is manifestly present; the door opens or does not open irrespective of whether it is or is not locked. The play's opening image, Syl and Jack with a baby, promises a recognizable context – again, a family structure – within which we will be able to orient ourselves and their identities. But the promise is immediately revoked by Albert's entrance. Indeed, in the course of the play, we see evidence of romantic relationships between Syl and Jack, Syl and Albert; Albert and Jack, Albert and Del; Del and Christie, Del and Jack. (The play's one, fully past-tense relationship is between Christie and Jack. 'Do you find incest a worry?' asks Del. 'We did all that a long time ago. We weren't all that good together', answers Christie – to which Jack adds, 'We were very young.')[30] These simultaneous relationships collectively result neither in a radically new family structure nor a communal bisexual harmony like that ironically promised in *Cloud Nine*'s second-act orgy scene. After all, as Del reminds us, 'Utopia means nowhere', and no-one lives nowhere.[31] Rather, it is of a piece with the play's Escher-like unreality. Moreover, the traps of their shared life keep revealing themselves: Syl and Christie's 'many possibilities' seem startlingly limited and conventionally gendered; the pain which Reg needs to 'know he's alive' disturbingly seems to leave bruises on Christie's back,[32] and, in a world outside time, the ironing needs doing even more often than in our own.

Like their Pirandellian counterparts, the six characters are trapped; and Churchill's intertextual engagement with *Six Characters in Search of an Author*, which Elin Diamond has identified elsewhere, is substantial.[33] He opposed the world of reality, including its actors and directors, to the truer world of illusion, represented by the six characters. She opposes the world of theatre, with its pre-scripted lines and cues, to the truer world of performance. This opposition begins in the play's prefatory notes in which Churchill explains the play's card trick, whose false magic is governed by predetermining the cards' order. Stacking the deck is theatre – as when Jack can be sure that Christie 'will be' 'here' precisely because the text has scripted her entrance two lines later.[34] The card trick contrasts the jigsaw puzzle, which sits onstage throughout to be worked on at will by the performers. Its near-completion by the play's end – its movement from disorder to order – defies the putatively out-of-joint time. The card trick is to the jigsaw puzzle as *Six Characters* is to *Traps*. Pirandello ends his play with the Child drowned in the onstage fountain, whereas Churchill's six onstage bodies get naked and bathe in the same bathwater. The drowning is an act of make-believe, of theatre, of non-subjectivity: no-one really dies. The bath is the world of the real, of performance: naked bodies and dirty water. In the baptismal present of performance, subjects become themselves. To be, argues Churchill, people require a world around them – a material situation, a space and time.

In this way, the bathing scene resolves the fractured ontology of *Traps*, both its insecure setting and its puzzling atemporality. Unlike staged actions such as locking the door, which are disconnected from either causes or effects, the bathing ritual celebrates its tethers to past choices and future consequences. Bodies, marked by mud (Albert) or ersatz bruises (Christie), get wet and, once clean, get dry, aided by the other bodies who wash backs and dispense towels. The temporal limbo of the set's inhabitants gives way to the real time marked by an onstage clock. The setting shifts. The ontologically unstable country-room/city-flat cedes to the material reality of the stage-as-stage, the stage itself, populated not with theatrical properties but real objects: the bath and its water; biscuits, peas and bread; the toenail clippings Jack removes.

A pivotal exchange during the first act of *Traps* serves as synoptic, sounding an alarm about a central feature of subjectivity:

JACK What are you frightened of?
CHRISTIE Time.
JACK What else?
CHRISTIE Space.
JACK What else?
CHRISTIE Me.
JACK What else? What are you frightened of?
CHRISTIE You.[35]

The passage encapsulates *Traps*' central theoretical insights, tying time and space to the positions of 'I' and 'you' that make identities possible. If identity is relational, as *Icecream* explored in its own lampooning terms, then identity is impossible within *Traps* until 'Jack' and 'Christie' give way to the performers who play them, sloshing around and threatening to soak the audience. Our failure to understand the characters' relationships to one another at the play's beginning turns out to have reflected the characters' own impossible self-knowledge. As Del alleges, twice, they 'don't correlate'.[36]

Body and language

The final moments of *Traps*, filled with concord, privilege the body as the site of subjectivity, as 'each separately, they start to smile'.[37] (The grammatically consonant 'each separately' recalls its dissonant double, 'both separately', in *Identical Twins*.) But it is the notion of a script, and not language itself, that has been left behind. Subjectivity houses itself in the body but anchors itself in language. Churchill returned to the complicated relationship between the two with a dazzling precision twenty years after *Traps* in *Blue Heart*, first staged by Stafford-Clark at the Traverse Theatre, Edinburgh in a production that opened at the Royal Court in September 1997. The play's bifurcated structure epitomizes its interests in body, language and their conjunction. The first half, 'Heart's Desire', is driven by physical action; the second, 'Blue Kettle', is told with increasingly challenging linguistic play; and the intricate kinship between the two plays mimics their shared theme of family relations.

'Heart's Desire', about a mother and father awaiting the homecoming of their daughter, revisits two aspects of *Traps*, one ontological and one epistemological. In its perpetual stopping and starting – it goes off-track and resets itself twenty-six times – the play calls attention to itself as a play, and it likens its own setting to a stage or rehearsal room populated by absurd repetitions, some unnaturally fast and some with incomplete lines. This metatheatrical play with ontology also involves a generic component, as the text's derailments repeatedly send it lurching into territory foreign to the genre, domestic drama, indicated by its opening stage directions, which announce the setting as Brian and Alice's kitchen. Churchill's attention to ontology may be amplified by the 'ten foot tall bird' called for in one interruption, which obliterates the line between theatre and performance as in the old Futurist stratagem: like the dog in Francesco Cangiullo's 1915 *Non c'è un cane*, a bird cannot know it is acting. (In Stafford-Clark's production, he opted for a representation: an actor in an ostrich costume.)

The play's derailments, such as that caused by the large bird, work twofold. By taking the play off-track, as announced by the restarting that they necessitate, they help the audience to outline what it will understand as the contours of 'Heart's Desire'. For while the different possibilities of *Traps* unfolded simultaneously, 'Heart's Desire' is rigorously teleological; each time the play resets, it returns to an earlier, stable moment and then proceeds along its 'correct' course. Churchill of course writes the play to include all of its errors, but our conditioned apprehension of a 'correct' plot effects her metatheatrical trick: she draws our attention to our viewing practices, the standards – whether generic constraints or, indeed, lived conventions – by which we judge 'natural' or 'deviant' behaviour. Consider the play's second correction: Brian enters donning a tweed jacket only to exit and return, on the same repeated cue, donning an old cardigan. The cardigan marks him more effectively as 'father', establishing his relationship to the woman invoked over and over in the play's repeated first line, 'She's taking her time.'[38] We are made aware that we will know who 'she' is by reading the citation. This particular bit of knowledge will be effectively tested later, when Brian answers the door and returns with a nameless young Australian woman. In staging, his body language, and that of Alice and Aunt Maisie, will alert us well before the text does that the woman is not the long-awaited 'she'. Moreover, the playwright reminds us of the iterative process by which we naturalize such semiotic conventions in the first place. She replays the donning of the old cardigan eight additional times. *Icecream*'s citations are revisited in less sardonic terms.

Churchill here thematizes performance and knowledge, asking 'How do we know who they are?' and recalling the signifiers that marked Syl and Jack as 'parents' at the top of *Traps*. As in that play, by doing so Churchill trains a spotlight on performance and self-knowledge, posing the question 'How do they know who they are?' as well as its existential twin, 'How do we know who we are?' *Traps* makes plain the inter-relationship between these two questions – and indeed, in their metatheatricality, both *Traps* and *Blue Heart* serve to theorize the absolute primacy of recognition and misrecognition tropes in Western theatre history, which stretch back at least as far as *Oedipus Rex*'s pierced heel. But 'Heart's Desire' foregrounds Churchill's particular phenomenological stance. She accents the ways in which we constitute our identities and relationships through all manner of signs; she foregrounds that we recognize someone – that is, determine an identity – by watching that someone in the act of doing things that have been done before. Indeed, she clarifies that we become someone by doing, by acting from a subject position located in time and space. One moment is emblematic: the wordless embrace between Brian and Alice that precedes Susy's first entrance, which consolidates their positions, for us and for them, as effectively as the daughter's appellative first line: 'Mummy. Daddy. How wonderful to be home.'[39]

Like 'Blue Kettle', Susy's appellation directs us to the question of language and its central role in identities such as 'mother'. In the second half of *Blue Heart*, we observe Derek convincing each of four elderly women, Mrs Plant, Mrs Oliver, Mrs Vane and Miss Clarence, that he is the biological son she had given up for adoption four decades before. As the play progresses, correct words – i.e., words that convention leads us to expect – are replaced by 'blue' or 'kettle'. Such substitutions multiply, so that by the eighth or ninth scene meaning is imperilled. A line such as 'I know it's not the kettle but why is it not the kettle, blue is the kettle' can only be made intelligible to an audience by the performances of the actors.[40] Thus we are reminded of the two foci of 'Heart's Desire': the regulation of normalcy and deviance, here linguistic, and the nature of performance, both constitutive and disruptive. The formal interest in language in 'Blue Kettle' relates directly to its undisguised concern with genealogical identity and the problem of self-knowledge. In one scene, Mrs Oliver talks Derek through a family tree, illustrating with photographs. Doing so ostensibly serves to reintroduce him to his family, but it quickly reveals itself as salve for the epistemological anxiety she betrays with the phrase 'I mean I look at you and you could be anyone.'[41] This precise uncertainty, of course, has facilitated Derek's exploitations in the first case.

In the penultimate scene, Derek exploits the relational aspect of identity, using false subject-positions as Iago uses Desdemona's handkerchief, to engender epistemological certainty. Upping his stakes, he enlists each of the unwitting Mrs Oliver and Mrs Plant to play biological mother to the other's adoptive mother. The presence of the latter, he wagers, will consolidate the former; and thus in one deft manoeuvre he may solidify his own position as 'son' relative to each 'mother'. But his gambit unravels. Mrs Oliver has authenticated her identity as his 'real' mother by means of documents Derek claims to have. But Mrs Plant has been thus authenticated too. 'No I'm that', she says.[42] This crisis elicits an ironically maternal response from Mrs Oliver – 'I'm getting a horrible kettle from this situation, Derek. I think you need to blue us what's kettle on' – and, chastened, Derek plays the child's role and dodges responsibility: 'There's been a kettle in the documentation.'[43]

Critics have connected the faltering language of 'Blue Kettle' to the disintegration of identity as Derek's ploy gradually fails. But this misreading projects the audience's own disconnection from the stage back onto its characters. Note the precision with which the scene moves to greater clarity in spite of the linguistic play. Each of Mrs Plant and Mrs Oliver in fact knows exactly what she and her scene partner say – and, indeed, the actors playing the roles must behave as if they have said the semantically 'correct' words and not *blue* or *kettle*. The epistemological concord clarifies the plot-level misunderstanding, setting up the scene's pivotal final line, which positions Mrs Oliver as wronged outsider and Mrs Plant as lovingly scolding parental authority: 'What have you done to the poor woman, Tommy?'[44] Perversely, Derek's ruse seems to have cemented his relationship with Mrs Plant, who addresses him not as Derek or as Tom – the name of the son she gave up for adoption – but as Tommy, its familiar diminutive. This linguistic act facilitates the denouement, in which the two bond as he comes clean, or at least seems to: while travelling, he met a photographer, John, who was searching for his biological mother; when John died, Derek thought to find the woman, Mrs Plant (whom he meets first in the play's action), but ended up devising his cuckoo plan. With his confession, a relationship of mutual benefit is promised. As 'blue' and 'kettle' substitute for any number of words, she substitutes for mother and he for son.

Two facts gnaw at this resolution. First, their symbiosis rests on a lie, as Derek claims that his own mother is dead: 'Tle died ket I ket a child.'[45] She is not. Senile, she is merely incapable of playing the maternal interlocutor he desires. Second, the audience is denied access to the communication that Mrs Plant and Derek share, as Churchill gradually reduces the script to phonemes. 'T b k k k k l?', Mrs Plant asks, and Derek responds, 'B. K.'[46] We were better able to understand the ravings of his biological mother in the geriatric ward than the words of Mrs Plant, which suggest the communicative babbling of a mother to her infant. She and her surrogate son speak a language that is foreign to the audience, left in the dark. But it is not a private language. As Ludwig Wittgenstein argued, no language is private, since it must signify to at least two people for it to be language at all. And, crucially, the meaning exchanged between Mrs Plant and Derek is clear not only to the two characters but to the two actors who play them. Not blood but the dialect of blue kettle bonds these actors, too, an insight that returns us to the question of performance.

Identity as performance

More directly than its predecessors, *Blue Heart* explores the philosophy of language – the capacity of 'Oregon' to 'thrill' – keenly aware that its problems relate to identity and self-knowledge. Wittgenstein adumbrated this connection himself in his concept of 'family resemblance', by happy coincidence a good name for Churchill's central preoccupation in *A Number*, in which she returned to the theme of parent/adult child relationships. Wittgenstein sought to understand how a word could have meaning if no essence unites the many things to which it refers. These many things, he explained, might not be the same, but analysing them would reveal a pattern of similarity, a 'family resemblance'. Wittgenstein's view therefore allows us to speak meaningfully about things, and about people, without lapsing into essentialism – the precise victory of *A Number*'s purview on identity. In another happy coincidence, Wittgenstein demonstrated his idea with a 'number', too:

> Why do we call something a 'number'? Well, perhaps because it has a – direct – relationship with several things that have hitherto been called number; and

> this may be said to give it an indirect relationship to other things that we call the same name. And we extend our concept of number as in spinning a thread we twist fibre on fibre. And the strength of the thread does not reside in the fact that some one fibre runs through its whole length, but in the overlapping of many fibres.[47]

To consider the many threads of a 'number' is to map the complex terrain of *A Number*. A number is a series of individual things as well as their aggregate, a quantity not exactly defined, and a grammatical category (Bernard or Bernards: singular or plural?) – as well as a distinct performance within the greater show: Churchill's next number after *Far Away*. The title's indefinite pronoun 'a' suggests what most unsettles Bernard, whose number haunts him as Clive haunted Teddy in *Identical Twins:* he worries about authenticity in a world dominated by reproductions. This anxiety derives from an essentializing mind-set, which Churchill aligns with a patrilineal logic – an alignment insinuated by Benjamin, for whom 'uniqueness' is 'inseparable from its being imbedded in the fabric of tradition'.[48] 'I got the impression there was this batch and we were all in it', Bernard frets, and Salter reassures him: 'No because you're my son.'[49] His logic tracks that of Teddy, and it will be similarly prone to collapse. A time and space may be necessary for authenticity, as Benjamin theorized, but such a location can be found without recourse to the patriarchal platitudes that govern 'originality'.

A Number rebukes Salter's claim to Bernard that 'they've damaged your uniqueness, weakened your identity'.[50] For in Churchill's picture, the art of human identity bears no family resemblance to Benjamin's work of art, whose essence Benjamin likens to its 'aura'. Rather, it is like performance, which represents without threat of reproduction.[51] It continually constitutes and reconstitutes itself through words and deeds in a process that unfolds moment by moment but which is tethered to its history and future. It coheres in the present as an aggregate of acts that necessarily disappear into the past, as *Traps'* bathing ritual makes clear and as Derek in *Blue Heart* claims to understand: 'If you didn't have any [memories] you wouldn't know who you were would you.'[52] Lance sought fake memories in the castles of England. However, anchored in the citational chain of lived experience – most palpably that of the rehearsal room – performance honours its memories by coming into being anew, night after night in space after space as the curtain rises. Since 2002, *A Number* has been performed in Australia, Canada, Italy, Japan and Russia; in Brazil as *Um Número*, the Czech Republic as *Řada*, France as *Un grand nombre*, Germany as *Die Kopien*, and Spain as *Una còpia* (but in Argentina as *Copias*). The list is inexhaustible. In the US, *A Number* was the fifth most-produced play of the 2005–6 theatre season.[53]

In other words, like Bernard, *A Number* proliferates. Its iterations share a family resemblance; they are akin but unique, like Bernard, Bernard and Michael Black tied together by a shared DNA. The clones are independent units familiarly entwined, a relationship that finds its grammatical analogue in the script, whose near-absence of other punctuation throws into relief its hundreds of commas, splicing independent clauses like genes. The first comma splice appears in the set instructions: 'The scene is the same throughout, it's where Salter lives.'[54] The specifics of this spare setting will be expressed differently by each of *A Number*'s stagings, whose myriad variations will reflect the contexts from which they emerge, the spaces and times in which they are performed and thus come into being. Churchill's disdain for didascalia – there are zero stage directions – highlight a lesson of *Blue Heart*: performance provides the supplement that brings the textual DNA to theatrical life. That play had another anti-essentialist emphasis, exposing the codes that govern performance as learned and iterative. In *A Number*, Churchill shadows each of her characters with echoes of the others. To cite only one example of many, Salter ('do you get asthma do you have a dog') unwittingly mimics Bernard 2 ('do we get asthma but what do you call your dog') as he talks to Bernard 1.[55]

In this way, *A Number* surveys the relational terms of identity with less dread than *Identical Twins* and *Icecream*. After Bernard 2's murder and Bernard 1's suicide, Salter begs Michael for 'something from deep inside your life', in an effort to effect a paternal bond; Michael describes not himself but his wife, whose 'disney elf' ears he loves.[56] The reference revisits Churchill's instructive focus on the citational nature of DNA. Our uniqueness inheres not in 'originality' – 'none of us' is the original, as the doctors have told Bernard 2[57] – but in the infinite variety of ways that we cite, combine and interpret pre-existing codes. No language is private. We become ourselves minute by minute through the actions we perform and the words we say, just, indeed, as Daniel Craig can become Bernard, Bernard and Michael Black before our eyes at the Royal Court. The actor stood to each of them as each of them stands to the others: a genetically identical person with a nonetheless unique way of being.

Thus *A Number* ends by quelling the angst that shadowed the Bernards. Their clone Michael instructs:

> We've got ninety-nine per cent the same genes as any other person. We've got ninety per cent the same as a chimpanzee. We've got thirty per cent the same as a lettuce. Does that cheer you up at all? I love about the lettuce. It makes me feel I belong.[58]

'[Y]ou like your life?' asks Salter, whose bewilderment betrays the patriarchal logic to which he clings. Michael replies, 'I do yes, sorry.'[59] Setting Michael against Salter – strangers, and yet son and father – *A Number* highlights the performative nature of identity even as it limns the longing for essences. This longing persists, pervading the play and coursing under the skin of Churchill's entire corpus, suppurating onto her stages. It ties together Lance's quest with Teddy's plight, Derek's psychological need with Bernard's existential anxiety; it haunts Albert's schizophrenia in *Traps*. Filial longing may also stand behind our own fetish for origins, which we betray in our theatre histories and the printed artefacts of plays. (The text of *A Number* is no exception, announcing it 'was first performed at the Royal Court Theatre Downstairs, London, on 23 September 2002, with ... Daniel Craig [and] Michael Gambon').[60] But this longing betrays the distinctive nature of performance.

One stress remains to be laid. Churchill once said that her radio plays, such as *Identical Twins*, sought to smash the bourgeois family structure that constricted Hedda Gabler, one reason for the playwright's iconic status in feminist theatre.[61] It is unsurprising that the sardonic Vera, like Syl and Enid, is without parents. Churchill's later plays, too, jam patrilineal lines – a potential effect of the incest fleetingly invoked in *Traps, Icecream* and even *Blue Heart*. (After all, the 'correct' plot of 'Heart's Desire' cannot get past its last hiccup, Brian's uncomfortably intimate declaration to Susy that 'You are my heart's desire.'[62] Moreover, Susy and her brother Lewis – 'Where's my big sister? I want to give her a kiss ... Dad knows where she is, don't you Dad? Daddy always knows where Susy is'[63] – will reappear as a couple, Enid and Derek, in 'Blue Kettle', thanks to the semiotics of doubling.) That all of the characters searching for genealogical relief in these plays are male is equally unsurprising. Their search for originality follows their search for origins, on a path suggested by these words' shared etymology. The Latin root stresses ancestry.

But it also stresses 'coming into being'. So does theatre, which wields an inherently anti-essentialist power. Unlike her collaborative plays, *Identical Twins, Traps, Icecream, Blue Heart* and *A Number* are all solely authored creations; and the playwright's identity is imprinted on their copyright pages: 'Caryl Churchill has asserted her right to be identified as the author of these works.'[64] The etymology of *author* stresses origination, too, and as a category it is unsurprisingly gendered; indeed, the so-called 'right of paternity' binds the legal relationship of author to text.[65] However, unlike the father – Salter, omnipresent in *A Number* – Churchill is absent from the stage. The infinite acts of performance she engenders are all her progeny, but as a theatre artist she cannot invest in the patriarchal notion that positions 'author' as the unitary source of meaning. This fact may best explain why Bernard, Lance, Derek and others look only in vain for their patrilineal origins. At least one critic has bemoaned the complete absence, in *A Number*, of the clones' mother, who is invoked only through her death before Bernard 2's birth – 'so she was already always', as he cryptically puts it.[66] It is Churchill's most fruitful provocation. The backward search for self may always turn up dead, but like the mother the performed self reveals itself, already always, only as it disappears in performance.

NOTES

1. Jacques Derrida, *Writing and Difference*, trans. Alan Bass (Chicago: University of Chicago Press, 1978), p. 233.
2. Walter Benjamin, 'The Work of Art in an Age of Mechanical Reproduction', in *Illuminations*, trans. Harry Zohn (New York: Schocken Books, 1969), pp. 217–52.
3. Caryl Churchill, *A Number* in *Plays: Four* (London: Nick Hern Books, 2008), p. 166.
4. Churchill, 'Incompatible Flavours', interview with Kevin Jackson, *Independent* (12 April 1989), p. 15.
5. For example, Emile Benveniste demonstrated that speech requires a perspective – a subject position – from which 'I' can be uttered, and each subject position and therefore 'I' is different from all others. As he puts it:

   > Each *I* has its own reference and corresponds each time to a unique being who is set up as such... The definition can now be stated precisely as: *I* is 'the individual who utters the present instance of discourse containing the linguistic instance *I*'. Consequently, by introducing the situation of 'address', we obtain a symmetrical definition for *you* as the 'individual spoken to in the present instance of discourse containing the linguistic instance *you*'.
   >
   > (Emile Benveniste, *Problems in General Linguistics*, trans. Mary Elizabeth Meek (Coral Gables, FL: University of Miami Press, 1971), p. 218)

   Jacques Lacan theorized that a child finds the possibility of a unified, coherent being by identifying itself, in a mirror, as separate from the rest of the world and especially its mother. However, this illusion of an autonomous identity is rent, first because the identification is a mis-identification (the child sees a reflection) and second by the discovery of other bodies – a discovery which makes possible language acquisition and especially the subject-position declared as 'I'. In Lacan's terms,

   > We have only to understand the mirror stage *as an identification*, in the full sense that analysis gives to the term: namely, the transformation that takes place in the subject when he assumes an image ... This jubilant assumption of his spectacular image by the child at the *infans* stage ... would seem to exhibit in an exemplary situation the symbolic matrix in which the *I* is precipitated in a primordial form, before it is objectified in the dialectic of identification with the other, and before language restores to it, in the universal, its function as subject.
   >
   > (Jacques Lacan, 'The Mirror Stage as Formative of the Function of the I', *Écrits: A Selection*, trans. Alan Sheridan (London: Tavistock Publications, 1977), pp. 1–7, p. 2)

6. Churchill, *Identical Twins*, unpublished typescript, p. 25.
7. *Ibid.*, pp. 1, 18.
8. *Ibid.*, p. 24.
9. *Ibid.*, p. 10.
10. *Ibid.*, pp. 12, 14.
11. *Ibid.*, p. 26.
12. Churchill, *A Number,* in *Plays: Four*, p. 170.
13. Churchill, *Identical Twins*, p. 27.
14. Churchill, *Icecream,* in *Plays: Three* (London: Nick Hern Books, 1998), p. 59.
15. *Ibid.*
16. *Ibid.*, p. 62. The incest discussion appears in Act I, Scene 6, 'The Kiss', pp. 67–9.
17. *Ibid.*, p. 60.
18. *Ibid.*, p. 61.
19. *Ibid.*, p. 63.
20. *Ibid.*, p. 75.
21. *Ibid.*, p. 80.
22. *Ibid.*, pp. 80–1.
23. Una Chaudhuri, *Staging Place: The Geography of Modern Drama* (Ann Arbor: University of Michigan Press, 1995), p. 131.
24. Aristotle, *On Poetry and Style*, trans. G.M.A. Grube (Indianapolis: Hackett, 1989), p. 7: 'Hence they enjoy the sight of images because they learn as they look.'
25. Churchill, *Icecream,* in *Plays: Three*, p. 96.
26. Simone de Beauvoir, *The Second Sex*, trans. H.M. Parshley (New York: Alfred A. Knopf, 1957), p. xvi.
27. Chaudhuri, *Staging*, p. 135 and Churchill, *Icecream*, in *Plays: Three*, p. 102.
28. Churchill, *Traps,* in *Plays: One* (London: Methuen, 1985), p. 77.
29. *Ibid.*, p. 71.
30. *Ibid.*, p. 106.
31. *Ibid.*, p. 87.
32. *Ibid.*, p. 103.
33. Elin Diamond, '(In)Visible Bodies in Churchill's Theatre', *Theatre Journal*, 40.2 (May 1988), 188–204, p. 192.
34. Churchill, *Traps,* in *Plays: One*, p. 90.
35. *Ibid.*, p. 94.
36. *Ibid.*, pp. 86, 100.
37. *Ibid.*, p. 125.
38. Churchill, *Blue Heart*, in *Plays: Four* (London: Nick Hern Books, 2008), p. 65.
39. *Ibid.*, p. 86.
40. *Ibid.*, p. 120.
41. *Ibid.*, p. 103.
42. *Ibid.*, p. 126.
43. *Ibid.*
44. *Ibid.*
45. *Ibid.*, p. 128.
46. *Ibid.*
47. Ludwig Wittgenstein, *Philosophical Investigations*, trans. G.E.M. Anscombe (London: Blackwell Publishing, 2001), §67 (pp. 27–28c).
48. Walter Benjamin, 'The Work of Art in an Age of Mechanical Reproduction', p. 223.

49. Churchill, *A Number*, in *Plays: Four*, p. 171.
50. *Ibid.*, p. 169.
51. See, for example, Peggy Phelan, *Unmarked: The Politics of Performance* (London: Routledge, 1993), especially pp. 146–66.
52. Churchill, *Blue Heart*, in *Plays: Four*, p. 115.
53. As is *American Theatre*'s convention, their tally excludes Shakespeare and adaptations of Dickens' *A Christmas Carol.* See Eve Zappulla,'2005–06 Season Preview: A Comprehensive Listing of Productions, Dates, and Directors at TCG Theatres Nationwide', *American Theatre*, 22.8 (October 2005), 43–50, p. 43.
54. Churchill, *A Number*, in *Plays: Four*, p. 164.
55. *Ibid.*, pp. 180, 169.
56. *Ibid.*, p. 202.
57. *Ibid.*, p. 171.
58. *Ibid.*, p. 205.
59. *Ibid.*, p. 206.
60. *Ibid.*, p. 163.
61. They are 'about a bourgeois middle-class life and the destruction of it', Churchill quoted in Catherine Itzin, *Stages in the Revolution: Political Theatre in Britain since 1968* (London: Methuen, 1980), p. 281.
62. Churchill, *Blue Heart*, in *Plays: Four*, p. 92, see also p. 95.
63. *Ibid.*, p. 71.
64. Churchill, *Plays: Four*, p. iv.
65. A superb treatment of this relationship appears in Mark Rose, 'Mothers and Authors: *Johnson v. Calvert* and the New Children of Our Imaginations', in Paula A. Treichler, Lisa Cartwright and Constance Penney (eds.), *The Visible Woman: Imaging Technologies, Gender, and Science* (New York: New York University Press, 1998), pp. 217–39, especially pp. 223–6.
66. Churchill, *A Number*, in *Plays: Four*, p. 190.

8

ELIN DIAMOND

On Churchill and terror

Of all the jingoistic terms characterizing recent US foreign policy, the 'war on terror' has endured, not only because it refers to the unprovoked bombing of Baghdad on 19 March 2003, which led to a brutal and ongoing war, but because it is such an elusive and strange idea. At first it seemed that this was typical 'Bush-speak': meaning 'terrorism', the former president loosely and inaccurately said 'terror'. Yet the *OED* states that the provenance of 'terrorism' is the 'system of terror' introduced in the French Revolution, and that 'terror' derives from the far older Latin *terrorum* or 'the state of being terrified or greatly frightened'. Can war be waged on a system of terror *and* on the affective state of being terrified? Isn't war the cause of terror? Or is terror what feeds war? And what of terror when no war is in view? Since her earliest radio plays, Caryl Churchill has explored these questions, not as ancillary to but as deeply rooted in her work. She dramatizes a provocative slippage between terrorist act and terrorized affect and invites us to discern in her theatre a unique dramaturgy of terror, a shifting aggregate of formal decisions based on the media she writes for and the times she has lived, and is living, through. 'On Churchill and terror' will trace a long arc of representative plays, from *The Ants* (1962) and *Objections to Sex and Violence* (1975), to *Softcops* (1978), *A Mouthful of Birds* (1986), *Thyestes* (1994) and *Far Away* (2000) in order to map the key coordinates of Churchill's career-long concern with both systems and affect, with terrorism and terror.

Political and literary historians approach contemporary terrorism through the French Revolution, particularly the Reign of Terror (1793–1794), and it is worth recalling why this is so. The Jacobin rebellion and its aftermath 'systematised and modernised terror', giving shape to all future discussions of the concept.[1] The fall of the Bastille led to the rise of the 'modern terrorist state' with its 'centralised power, mass conscripted army, economic and social controls, organized secret police, informers and spies', as well as a scientific method of killing (the guillotine) and a vast publicity network that spread the horror of executions.[2] The theatrical and symbolic nature of the bloody spectacles will be crucial in all discussions of terrorism, as will the view, accepted by most political historians, that the modern state and terror *rise together*. All civilized modern states have practised terror, using intimidation, abduction, torture and murder as a way of silencing dissent. As Terry Eagleton puts it: 'Terrorism and the modern democratic state were twinned at birth.'[3]

The effects of such twinning will shape Churchill's dramaturgy. If the modern state is terroristic at its inception, it breeds mirror images of itself as a condition of ordinary existence. These days state terrorism conjures up nations like Zimbabwe, Sudan, Darfur, where leaders and their armies use horrific and intimidating violence against their own citizens. Yet Churchill entered adulthood during the Cold War and knew how modern states like her own could be twinned with terrorism. Reading Fanon, Arendt and Sartre in the early 1970s, she absorbed the analysis of the anti-colonial, anti-French struggles of Algeria's FLN (1954–1962), of the IRA's violent anti-British Provisional wing (emerging in 1969), of the left-wing anti-capitalist, anti-nationalist German Red Army Faction and the Italian Red Brigade (both founded in 1970), as well as the Symbionese Liberation Army in the US which kidnapped newspaper heiress Patty Hearst (1974).[4] Modern terrorism is the targeted use of extreme violence to intimidate a population and/or to weaken state power, and it involves the relatively small writ suddenly large. If the target is symbolically huge, the acts of a small group can expose weaknesses in a vast state authority. Through worldwide media links, the act becomes an instantaneous and constantly replayed spectacle, generating global recognition, the life-blood of terrorist organizations. The anti-British violence of IRGUN (pre-state Israeli insurgents) was directed as much to New York and Washington DC as to London and Jerusalem. The FLN's terrorism 'spoke' less to local policy-makers in Algiers than to Paris and New York.[5]

Yet what interests Caryl Churchill is the relatively large writ small – the indirect atmospherics of terror, the way it leaches into the psyches of ordinary citizens and ordinary lives. Ordinary lives are always dialectical for Churchill, individually marked yet ensnared, obscurely or directly, in political and historical force fields. Her plays may not include the power brokers – *Drunk Enough to Say I Love You?* and *Serious Money* are the exceptions – but a wider terror is suggested in small acts of violence. My argument here is that the spatial logic of terror's dissemination, from here to there, there to here, has worked its way into the form of Churchill's plays. Characters, especially children, expressive and often impotent, are aware of distant wars being fought, of bombs that could annihilate them, of anxiety that also threatens (Tim in *The Ants*, Kit in *Top Girls*). The last word in Pope

Joan's speech is *terrorum* and the last word of *Top Girls*, spoken by the slow adolescent Angie (often double cast as Pope Joan), is 'frightening'.[6]

Intimate shrieks: *The Ants*

The Ants, a radio play, was produced for the BBC Third Programme and broadcast on 27 November 1962. (The BBC no longer have the recording.) The play concerns a lonely boy worried about his parents' separation who befriends the ants on the porch of his grandfather's seaside home. During the play, the father briefly joins the mother only to affirm their split. The play is dominated by the eccentric and bitter rhetoric of the grandfather who invites the boy to imagine a life of solitude like his own. While the mother sees the ants as 'disgusting' and recommends setting them on fire with petrol, Grandfather, giving sugar, sees them 'as intelligent as people ... They've got everything organized, they all work together for their society ...They've no imagination, just like people.'[7] Tim distinguishes the individual in the group, a 'reddish' ant he calls Bill. But his feelings toward the ants – first he loves them, then finds them horrifying – are shaped by Grandfather's choral-like commentary:

> GRANDFATHER You'll think you want to live in a happy ant hill ... but don't be fooled by love or vocation, you keep by yourself and you won't have to desert anyone later.
>
> TIM What do you mean? ...
>
> GRANDFATHER Desertion is when you stop loving people and see them from miles above, when you lose them and see just a lot of black ants ... I mean nobody loves anyone ... I'm an old man and it's all too late and nobody loves anyone. Out there they're all dropping bombs, bang, bang, bang. I don't know, I only know about me ...[8]

Loss of love is linked to a sudden shift in perspective, when the beloved loses singularity and dissolves into a meaningless mass. The radio play format is a perfect medium for this widening of perspective, in this case from horizontal to vertical 'views' (seeing from 'miles above'). If time is circumscribed in a radio broadcast, space is infinitely flexible. And of course radio drama has a distinguished history in producing terror, for what imagination 'sees' is far more terrifying than any embodiment.

Churchill scholars have always understood her pre-stage works as historically rather than aesthetically significant. But I would argue that the spatial expansiveness of radio had a lasting effect on her formal choices when rendering states of terror. In writing for radio she could define and redefine social space, create a situation and just as quickly dissolve it. As singular disembodied voices, characters speak intimately to the listener as much as to an imagined other; thus the minds of listeners and exterior spaces merge: the bombs are dropping 'out there' but the sound ('bang, bang, bang') is 'here' through Grandfather's speech; that is, 'there' is instantly 'here'. Tim watches his parents approach and unlike a visualized moment on stage, where the actor's indication of an offstage world is indulged by the audience but not shared, Tim's verbalized landscape *becomes* our imagined one: 'They're nearly here, they're just coming along the road ... Here they are now, here they are! Daddy, Daddy.' In the imaginary drama co-created by the listener, the father touches Tim: 'Hello Tim, up you go. You're getting a heavy boy.' But this imagined intimacy turns into quarrelling leaving Tim to reprise his vision ('I saw you on the beach. I watched you coming') as though to reverse the action to seconds before, to stabilize the image before its promise slips away forever.[9] His next act is to participate in a bit of child-sized terrorism. Implicitly following the mother's suggestion, Grandfather douses the ants with petrol, Tim lights the fuse, and as '*the petrol explodes into flame*', he 'shrieks with laughter'.[10]

In this small terroristic act, Churchill demonstrates another component in her terror dramaturgy: the decoupling of psychological accuracy from a private interiority. She *suggests* a personal psychological narrative – the boy destroys the ants (and his connection to others) out of fear and insecurity over his parents' separation. Yet what echoes in the mind is not the predictable family drama but the child's shrieking laughter, his terror/pleasure in the explosion and, by extension, in Grandfather's melancholy sadism, the pleasure he finds in viewing people (or ants) from 'miles above'. 'See the little flame go all the way down to the ants', intones Grandfather and Tim's shrieking laughter mingles with the fiery explosion as the last sound in the play. Michael Bakewell, the producer of the 1962 BBC broadcast, deliberately cast 'a real boy rather than one of the actresses who specialized in playing boys because I wanted his vulnerability to be real'.[11] He recalls that the boy's laughter 'began as if he was trying to force himself to laugh, and then it took him over, getting more and more hysterical'. It is the juxtaposition of Tim's hysteria and the explosion that interested Churchill and this, recalls Bakewell, was typical of the era: 'the Bomb ... was omni-present and at the back of everyone's minds all the time [sic]'.

In 1958, when Churchill was still a student at Oxford, the Campaign for Nuclear Disarmament was launched from a groundswell of protest against the rapid building and testing of nuclear weapons by the United States, Soviet Union and Great Britain. Just one month before the broadcast of *The Ants*, the US blockaded Cuba to prevent the Soviet Union's installation of nuclear missiles there. The Cuban Missile Crisis, the thirteen-day confrontation between the two superpowers, nearly provoked nuclear war – if not a reign of terror, this was a time when terror reigned, and many felt like ants trodden underfoot by governments that terrified their populations in the name of national defence. *The Ants* is no allegory for nuclear panic but it touches on nuclear era uncertainty, helplessness and fear. Again, we could say that Tim's thwarted desire for his parents' reconciliation quickly flips into violence and helpless rage causing him to incinerate the ants. However, through the spatial elasticity of the radio play medium, Churchill annexes a larger public terrain – not only anxiety over nuclear war but also the widespread social fantasy of not relating to the other but seeing her/him as an anonymous blob, as though from 'miles above'. In the radio format, the 'global' context presses as close as the familial one.

'Suppose you killed that man you work for': *Objections to Sex and Violence*

Churchill thematizes terrorism directly in *Objections to Sex and Violence*, first produced at the Royal Court Theatre on 2 January 1975. In her comment appended to the published text, written in 1985, she realizes how deeply worldwide terrorism affected the writing of her play:

> The Angry Brigade bombed the Post Office tower in 1972, Patty Hearst's kidnapping was in the papers, I think, the summer I wrote the play, Baader-Meinhof hadn't happened yet. I've looked through the notebooks in which I wrote it to see *where I started from and how the situations of the play gradually emerge*, and am left with a strong sense of what I was thinking about in the early seventies, of how *immediate and pressing* ideas about the anarchism, revolution and violence were [italics mine].[12]

Objections to Sex and Violence carries over from *The Ants* both the proximity of thwarted desire to violence and the social nature of that desire. Jule, the admitted terrorist, the object of desire for her sister Annie, for Annie's partner Phil, and for the old voyeur Albert, has another object entirely – the smooth icons of consumer capitalist success. These are Annie's employers and sexual exploiters, for whom Annie, according to Jule, is a 'thing' they manipulate and don't see. 'Suppose you killed that man you work for', Jule suggests. If the remark shocks her timid sister, it also shows that Jule craves recognition from those who rise to the status of symbolic target, for only a worthy target justifies terrorism. One must attack precisely those who grossly benefit from an unfair system and intimidate others who do the same.

Desire in this talky play follows the poetic course that psychoanalytic theory (also a renewed discourse in the 1960s and 1970s), decrees – it circulates endlessly because the object of desire is always misrecognized and when attained cannot satisfy. With an early interest in Freud, Churchill may have absorbed some of the psychoanalytic discussion of desire. For Jacques Lacan (here influenced by Hegel) desire is not really about an object, but rather proceeds from a lack in the subject. And while it seems to emanate from the torments of a private imagination, desire is always the desire of the other; it is *socially* mediated and thus marked by cultural proscriptions – including gender and racial proscriptions. In this sense, the taboos and titillations of our advanced capitalist system, including images and messages from consumer culture, inevitably colonize our desire.[13]

In Churchill's drama, a desire so constructed can erupt, often in self-annihilating violence. Thus Phil's imagined desire for Jule and the terrorism she espouses (and, in her sexuality, represents) causes him to implode: 'I smile, I smile, my face is beyond me. I can't spit.'[14] Desire dismembers Annie: 'I sometimes get the feeling my arms and legs and body and head aren't all joined together. I see my hands a long way away.'[15] Family is where, for psychoanalysis, lack begins, and Churchill's comical Miss Forbes gives voice to this zone of desire: 'My family burst into my flesh like shrapnel ... I sometimes feel the top of my head will blow off.'[16] When Jule resists her sister Annie's version of their common world, Annie turns on her: 'I hate you, Jule, quite often ... It would be a relief to know I was hurting you. I see why people use knives ... I'd enjoy slashing your face and knowing it was too late, that I couldn't be sorry and change my mind. The blood would be pouring out, frightening us.'[17] Jean Baudrillard glosses Annie's pleasure in an act of violence about which 'I couldn't be sorry and change my mind.' That the terrorist act cannot be recalled is one of its potent appeals. He writes: 'In a system of generalized exchange' (social reality under advanced capitalism), terrorism restores 'an irreducible singularity'.[18] And this, Churchill implies, may be a relief from the circumnavigations and displacements of desire.

But terrorism is the extreme option. Between fantasies of attack and self-annihilation Churchill's characters succumb to inertia – Miss Forbes' metaphorical drawer of 'things that are impossible ... bills I can't pay, library books I can't take back'.[19] Churchill notes a political correlative for inertia in the words of radical mid-century economist Vilfredo Pareto, cited in Hannah Arendt's *On Violence*: 'freedom ... by which I mean the power to act shrinks every day',[20] a line Churchill borrows verbatim and gives to Eric, Jule's fellow terrorist-in-making. Yet Churchill ends the play by handling desire rationally, as if it were possible to do so. She offers an example of playwriting she will abjure for the rest of her career: a naturalistic dialogue between Terry and Jule in which social questions – the difference between communism and anarchism – are self-consciously raised, explored and resolved, however unsatisfactorily.

Terror's docile bodies: *Softcops*

Softcops was written in 1978, with a revised version staged by the Royal Shakespeare Company at the Barbican Pit in 1984. Coming after Churchill's brilliant theatrical innovations and collaborations of the 1970s (*Traps, Vinegar Tom, Light Shining in Buckinghamshire*) *Softcops* could be seen as a further gloss on Pareto's notion that 'freedom [or] the power to act shrinks everyday', although the focus shifts to institutional mechanisms of regulation and how we learn to discipline ourselves. Written just as the Conservative Margaret Thatcher was poised to become Prime Minister, Churchill was, she writes in a prefatory note to the original published text, casting about for a way to write about 'soft methods of control, schools, hospitals, social workers [*sic*]'.[21] As testimony to her excitement at finding Michel Foucault's *Discipline and Punish* (1978, 1979; *Surveiller et Punir*, 1975), *Softcops* contains dozens of references to Foucault's study, especially from his final chapters which review, as does the play, the disciplinary gamut from spectacular rituals of punishment to Enlightenment reform where, as Churchill puts it, instead of 'tearing a victim apart with horses ... [you] simply watch him'.[22] Vidocq and his opposite number Larcenaire, the chain gangs, the sectional discipline of Mettray, and finally the carceral city's production of 'docile bodies' all skip off Foucault's pages into *Softcops*.

But Churchill's self-reflexive theatricality provides additional layers of insight about 'soft controls'. *Softcops* is structured like a vaudeville with Pierre as the Enlightenment's bumbling master of ceremonies ('Reason is my goddess').[23] Pierre represents what Foucault calls 'the gentle ways of punishment' or 'penalty representations' wherein each punishment becomes a fable, teaches a moral lesson.[24] Rejecting the 'sheer horror' of hackings and dismemberment Pierre espouses a 'balanced' presentation – 'Terror, but also information. Information, but also Terror'[25] – and requires an orderly audience of submissive schoolboys who will learn from it (their 'soft minds [will] take the impression').[26] Pierre opens the play decorating a public scaffold but dreams of a colour-coded 'Garden of Laws' displaying 'every kind of crime and punishment', with a suspended iron cage for the most heinous crime, parricide.[27] Baffled in later scenes by the fashion for prison chain gangs and utterly blind to a growing carceral apparatus, Pierre recovers his ebullience upon meeting Jeremy Bentham whose panopticon (1785), a means of prisoner control through surveillance, replaces the criminal in the iron cage with the guard who is watching him. Pierre doesn't grasp the irony of the change in the cage's personnel – from despised prisoner to trusted guard – but Churchill's audience might, marking the moment when, in Foucault's words, 'criminality becomes one of the mechanisms of power'.[28]

As Churchill well understood, Foucault's tropes for the panopticon, and throughout *Discipline and Punish*, are theatrical – the panopticon's cells are backlit like 'so many small theatres, in which each actor is alone, perfectly individualized and constantly visible' – implying theatre's collusion in social discipline.[29] Although Foucault's genealogy of punishment never speaks directly to the social regulation required for industrial capitalism, the goal of modern punishment is to 'normalize' social deviants into docile, productive bodies capable of supplying the 'apparatus of production – "commerce" and "industry"'.[30] Foucault's trope of 'docile bodies' – how we learn to terrorize ourselves into social obedience – was already suggested in Phil's rhetorical implosion in *Objections to Sex and Violence*, and later, far more concretely, in *Fen* (1982) when the worker Frank fearfully imagines slapping his boss and slaps himself instead. In *Softcops*, terror as affect, terror as act converge in the docile body, normalizing it for use – a social and theatrical trope Churchill will explore again and again. And yet if she believes in the ubiquity of disciplinary networks that reach beyond penal systems into the social institutions of family, school, hospital, factory, the military, that 'mark the body, train it, force it to carry out tasks, to perform ceremonies, to emit signs',[31] she never tires of exploring resistance to this process. If *Softcops*' theatre of 'Terror and also information' produces docile bodies, *A Mouthful of Birds*, written just two years later, locates terror/terrorism in bodies that are decidedly undocile. Theatre may be part of a Foucaultian disciplinary network, subtly normalizing our spectatorial pleasures, but Churchill's dramaturgy pushes theatre's limits, summons the extraordinary, and, in *A Mouthful of Birds*, stages a theatrical invasion.

Terror's pleasures: *A Mouthful of Birds*

A Joint Stock production of 1986, *A Mouthful of Birds* pivots on the Janus-faced notion of possession. On the one hand, possession refers to the act of owning or taking control, including control of the self (self-possession) or of a thing owned; on the other hand, in its anthropological sense, possession means temporary but complete loss of rational control, as in the familiar expressions 'I was beside myself' or 'I don't know what got into me'. In this dance and word play developed through thirty-two scenes, characters from Euripides' *The Bacchae* 'get into' the individual stories of seven ordinary Londoners and extraordinary things happen. Churchill, co-creating with anthropologist and playwright David Lan and choreographer Ian Spink, asked their Joint Stock actors to take an '"undefended day" in which there [was] nothing to protect you from the forces inside and outside yourself'.[32] As Foucault found the link between mechanisms of punishment and 'mechanisms of normalisation', Churchill and Lan de-exoticize spirit possession and discover it in ordinary lives. They looked for 'possession by forces within us as well as without: [possession] by memory, by fear, by anxiety, by habit ... by alcohol, by love, by past trauma.'[33] Inviting *The Bacchae* to invade their work, Churchill recovers the there-to-here structure she'd abandoned in *Softcops* and imagines another iteration of terror and terrorism, for Euripides' drama depicts a violent attack on state power and its disastrous consequences.

The Bacchae (406 BC) is an eccentric tragedy. In this last extant play of Euripides the multiple deaths in the royal house of Thebes receive neither dignity nor meaning; neither state law nor religion provides guidance in human affairs. The action of *The Bacchae* seems to be precipitated by mere revenge – Dionysus' ancient grievance against Thebes for not recognizing his mother Semele, daughter of the Theban king Cadmus, as the consort of the god Zeus, and therefore not revering Dionysus as the son of god. But the larger context is far more interesting. *The Bacchae* dramatizes an invasion of Thebes by adherents of a religious cult from the East. In contrast to the Greek rule of law, based on rational order, and to Greek ceremonies based on religious hierarchies, the Bacchantes embody ecstatic worship and trancelike states where human and animal intertwine in violent orgiastic dances and nature rituals. *The Bacchae*, then, depicts the subversion of patriarchal rule in the Greek city states – Cadmus was historically the first king of Thebes – by women who exchange domestic lives for ecstatic religious abandon in the woods and hills beyond the borders of the city. Churchill noted that Jule, her terrorist from *Objections to Sex and Violence*, was as subversive in her sexuality as in her terrorist ambitions. In the Bacchantes Churchill finds a more intense merging of sexual and social subversion. Further, Dionysus not only transgresses identity – he is both god and man – he radically subverts masculine authority by appearing to Pentheus as an effeminate boy while his female adherents have become stronger and more fearless than average men. When their women's rites are disturbed by the spying Pentheus, who is seduced by Dionysus into wearing women's clothing, they rip him to pieces as they would dismember an animal for sacrifice. According to Jan Kott, Pentheus is 'the only great unburied corpse' in all of Greek tragedy.[34]

This is why Eagleton calls Dionysus 'one of the earliest terrorist ringleaders'.[35] Like the violent groups whom political scientists have studied over the past three decades Bacchantes are imbued with the transcendent rightness of their cause and readily take on Dionysus' *ressentiment* over Thebes' rejection of him. In *A Mouthful of Birds* terrorism erupts both in the tearing of Pentheus and in the 'irreducible singularity' that possession, or violent loss of control, brings to lives mired in what Baudrillard calls the 'generalized exchange' of consumer culture. Lena shakes off the pain of a belligerent husband, listens to an abusive spirit (a schizoid projection of her own self-loathing?) and, a latter-day Agave, drowns her child. Marcia, working as a telephonist, desperately tries to reconnect with her Trinidadian medium Baron Sunday, but she is instead possessed by Sybil, a British spirit who subjects her to anthropological investigation. Paul, like the child Tim in *The Ants*, restores narrative *and* singularity to the porcine commodities he sells on the international market: he falls in love with a particular pig. In the logic of the commodities market Paul's pig and all the others are slaughtered for profit, but in the logic of Dionysian possession Paul dances with his pig, '*tenderly, dangerously, joyfully*'.[36] Dionysus, played by two of the actors, orchestrates these isolated encounters.

And under the sign of Dionysus, Churchill and Lan are liberated from the imperative of causality that renders bodies docile in a conventional plot. *I* have broken possession's law by narrativizing Lena's spirit – she drowns her baby *because*, I suggested above, she experiences a schizoid break. In the logic of terror, argues Baudrillard, there is 'no ideology, no cause'.[37] Desire, too, lacks causality and its eruptive force is again synonymous with self-annihilation. Playing Dionysus, the vicar Dan dances to a woman sitting in a chair wearing a hat. '*This dance is precisely the dance that the woman in the chair longs for. Watching it she dies of pleasure.*'[38] Only in the unreal precincts of possession can desire hit its precise target. The woman is fulfilled. But the result for her, as for the mortal Semele, is lethal violence, immediate death. Paul's perfect happiness with his pig leaves him dead in another way: a depressed drunk. In his small failed life, Paul learns that Dionysus may be the god of transgression, but he is also, as Eagleton puts it, 'an unbearable horror'.[39]

The central story in *A Mouthful of Birds* combines the shock of sexual transgression with the discipline of law. Churchill incorporates the memoirs of *Herculine Barbin* (discovered by Michel Foucault), a nineteenth-century hermaphrodite whose twice-sexed body (an echo of the twice-born Dionysus) gave the historical Herculine/Abel both delicious pleasure and unbearable physical suffering. As Foucault states in his introduction to the volume, the law proscribes and disciplines a body possessed by both genders; it demands a 'true sex', namely one sex.[40] Such discipline is experienced as an attack, precipitating despair and ultimately suicide.

Terror, like desire, defies representation. Which is why, throughout *A Mouthful of Birds*, language gives way to choreographed dances that slip the noose of discourse and its rules of logic and causality. In the 'fruit ballet', characters who never speak to one another come together as a chorus and each chews her/his own arm, becoming, in the magical transfer of possession, both the eater and the eaten. In *Mouthful of Birds* interaction happens only through *The Bacchae*. The play's numbered scenes are like pieces ripped from the body of a no longer coherent world, as though the authors were acknowledging that a play possessed by another play is so violently dismembered it needs numerical sequencing to give it order. At the end, the seven characters speak from the timeless space of post-possession and with the intimacy of voices heard in a radio play. Only Derek, ripped apart as Pentheus, is allowed to will his body into a surgical transformation that, unlike Herculine's scarred and tormented body, 'lets the world in' and feels 'comfortable'. Doreen, wracked by anger in a previous scene, learns to focus her rage on objects that she makes fly around the room. Post-possession, however, 'I can find no rest ... It seems that my mouth is full of birds which I crunch between my teeth. Their feathers, their blood and broken bones are choking me. I carry on my work as a secretary.'[41] That extra-social terror *gets into* ordinary minds and lives becomes fundamental to Churchill's terror dramaturgy of the 1990s and a source of limitless inspiration.

We have noted that terror in the mundane, the swings from there to here, the proximal yet noncausal relation of desire and violence, linguistic interruption and disjunctive form, comprise Churchill's method for invoking the affect of terror. Yet her own formal restlessness and her growing rage at transnational corporate greed and ecological ruin, break out in other plays of the 1980s (*Fen, Serious Money*, *Icecream* and *Hot Fudge*). Under global – later 'turbo' – capitalism human beings are socially illegible without market recognition, either as consumers or commodities. Such themes stretch back to *Objections to Sex and Violence*, but a new element is added. In 1990, war broke out over the division of the former Yugoslavia and by 1992 there was international armed conflict in Bosnia Herzegovina. Over morning coffee people in London and throughout the world were treated to images of terrorism's 'new normal': ethnic cleansing. Emaciated male prisoners from teenagers to the aged were shown in concentration camps, soon to be herded away and executed; thousands (perhaps tens of thousands) of mostly Bosnian and Croat women and girls were raped and tortured in their homes or in sequestered locations, and of course children suffered in the middle of it all, wordless, helpless, terrified. During the siege of Sarajevo, snipers regularly picked off people at the market. The global press carried a photo of a middle-aged woman dressed in kerchief and raincoat, like any urban woman doing her shopping, shot in the back, face down on the sidewalk, her shopping bag at her side. How to explain the terrorism – the targeted ruthless violence – of ethnic cleansing and the acts of revenge they wrought? Rationally, we want and were given explanations. Belying decades of peaceful intermingling and intermarrying among Yugoslavia's ethnic populations, the end of totalitarian rule, with the fall of the Soviet Union in 1991, released centuries-old ethno-nationalist grievances, fuelled by the fear-mongering rhetoric of ambitious, charismatic leaders, by unresolved Cold War rivalries and by a geopolitical arms trade that flooded the region with weapons. Somehow from the rational *there* we get to the *here* of egregious acts of violence, indeed a *system* of violence from which only outside force would produce an exit. Seneca's *Thyestes* explores such a system:

> FURY Go on detestable
> ghost ... [l]et's have a wickedness
> competition, swords
> out in every street ... Then let
> rage harden and the long
> wrong go into the
> grandchildren ... Then there'll be nothing
> anger thinks forbidden,
> brother terrifies
> brother, father sons and
> sons fathers, children's
> deaths are vile and their births
> even worse.[42]

Five months before the opening of Churchill's translation of Seneca's *Thyestes* at the Royal Court Theatre Upstairs in June 1994, *The Skriker* opened in the Cottesloe auditorium of the Royal National Theatre, and that theatrical conjuncture deserves a brief mention. (See Chapters 3, 5 and 6 for fuller discussions of *The Skriker*.) In a sense, *The Skriker* stages a familiar collision between the far off or other worldly 'there' – goblins sickened by the polluted earth – and a recognizable if disturbing 'here' – two rootless young women, one pregnant, the other having just killed her baby. But there is something else in this play: the implacable nature of the Skriker itself. With air and water polluted, the goblin, 'ancient and damaged', bounds out of the underworld with long tirades of bidirectional punning that interweave millennial dread, consumer culture and the nightmare logic of ancient folklore ('All is gone with the window cleaner'). By the end of the play the Skriker *has become* the world, engineering calamitous weather, moving and shape-shifting at terrific speed like turbo capital circulating in and out of international markets.[43] The Skriker preys on human blood (joy, innocence), particularly that of women and children. In the last decade of the twentieth century, Churchill unleashes a theatrical vision of soulless terror and suffering, and I close my chapter by considering two plays from that decade.

'The long wrong': *Thyestes*

Churchill's notes to her translation of Seneca's *Thyestes* play are more extensive than to any other play. After the contortions of the Skriker's language she perhaps relished the discipline of translation. The play's topicality also pleased her: 'I don't think it's just because I've been translating *Thyestes* that the news seems full of revenge stories.'[44] In effect Seneca (4BC–AD64) provides Churchill with a total vision of merciless intergenerational violence, not unlike the 'long wrong' that fuels ethnic violence. Thyestes and Atreus are of course brothers, indeed twin brothers, not ethnic rivals, but the Latin *ethnicus*, from the Greek *ethnikos*, means 'a nation or people classed according to common racial, national, tribal, linguistic or cultural origin'. It is the extended tribe of Atreus, from Tantalus to Orestes, who are cursed with the patriarch's 'burning hunger' and due to whose acts '[f]ortune totter[s] back and forth ... power follow[s] misery and misery power and waves of disaster batter the kingdom'.[45] Only the intervention of an outside authority (Athena's tribunal at the end of the *Oresteia*) brings the revenge killings in the House of Atreus to an end. 'Seneca', Churchill notes, 'lived in dangerous times, and Greek stories must have given him a way of writing about its horrors without seeming too direct'.[46] In turn, Seneca's play allows Churchill a way of writing about the terrorism in 1990s. Seneca anatomizes terror – its local acts and wide effects. As his translator, Churchill claims her living author's right to choose words as 'typical of me and my time', by implication inserting her time, as well as her words, into the ancient Roman play.[47]

On the surface the story is ghoulish and remote: Tantalus, friend to the gods, decides to test them by slaughtering his son Pelops and serving him as a banquet meal. The gods punish Tantalus, tormenting him with hunger and thirst in the underworld; they resurrect Pelops who, through treachery, becomes King of Olympia and fathers twin sons Atreus and Thyestes, then exiles them when they kill their half-brother. Arriving in Mycenae, Atreus takes the throne but Thyestes seduces his wife, throwing into doubt the paternity of Atreus' sons Agamemnon and Menelaus. With the errant wife, Thyestes steals the ram with the golden fleece, takes power, but Atreus retakes the throne, banishing Thyestes and his sons. Seneca's *Thyestes* begins here. Atreus, hungry for revenge, invites Thyestes to return to share the throne, kills and cooks his three sons and serves them up to their father, who senses wrongdoing but eats and drinks their blood (disguised by wine) anyway. Atreus shows Thyestes the hands and heads of his children and then explains the contents of the meal. By the time Seneca took up this well-known story, eight Greek dramatists (including Euripides and Sophocles) and six other

Roman dramatists had written about Atreus and Thyestes but their plays have been lost.[48]

Despite Seneca's reputation for scenery-chewing rhetoric, Churchill discovers that his Latin was 'far blunter, faster and subtler than I'd thought'. She quotes her Renaissance predecessors, inviting a smile at *their*, not Seneca's, grandiloquence. She, on the other hand 'stayed so close to the Latin that I could feel the knobbly foreign constructions just under the English skin, and liked that'.[49] Lacking Latin, I am unable to feel those knobbly constructions, but some English contrasts are revealing. Here is Tantalus' opening line from the Loeb 1912 translation of *Thyestes* that Churchill consulted: 'Who from the accursed regions of the dead haleth me forth...';[50] here is the new Loeb 2004 translation by John G. Fitch: 'From the accursed abode of the underworld, who drags forth the one that catches at vanishing food with his avid mouth?'[51] And this is Churchill's: 'Who's dragging me / grabbing avidly / up / from the unlucky underworld?'[52] Fitch's translation eschews the antiquated 'haleth' but the English of his line is barely speakable, the adjectival clause so complicated ('that catches at vanishing food with his avid mouth') that we may forget it modifies the 'one'. In Churchill's translation 'grabbing avidly', in modifying and rhyming with 'me', may not evoke the specifics of Tantalus' torture, but it draws the eye to 'up', the sole word in line three, and tells the actor to emphasize the act of moving, rapidly *up* (echoing the Skriker's entrance from the underworld).

In line with her perception of Senecan Latin, Churchill's English verse, with its word-combining contractions and short syllabic lines, is considerably faster than that of other translations, hurtling us into the messenger's account of Atreus' butchery and Thyestes' gruesome discovery. Atreus too is hurtled, his hunger for revenge driving him on: 'There's an uproar beating / my heart and turning / things over deep inside. / I'm rushed away and / where to I don't know but / I am being rushed / away'.[53] Churchill might have heard echoes of words she gave to *Mad Forest*'s Vampire, responding to revolution's, and his own, monstrous tempo: 'You begin to want blood. Your limbs ache, your head burns, you have to keep moving faster and faster.'[54] Even as Seneca physicalizes craving, the cosmology of tragedy gives Churchill rein to explore the spatial simultaneity of contemporary terrorism, of there to here. Rather than large acts writ small, penetrating the psyches of ordinary lives, as we have seen in *The Ants*, *Objections to Sex and Violence* and *A Mouthful of Birds* and noted in *Top Girls*, *Fen* and *The Skriker*, tragedy gives us large acts writ large. Tantalus' mere presence pushes the earth into drought: 'The sad land can't bear / you walking on it. / Do you see how the water's / driven in away / from the springs, river beds / are empty...?'[55] And in the Chorus' speech, Atreus' horrendous murders alter the course of the cosmos: 'Sun, where have you gone? / how could you get lost / half way through the sky?... I'm struck with terror... The zodiac's falling. / The ram's in the sea... / the archer's bow's broken, the cold goat / breaks the urn, there go the fish'.[56] Perhaps even more influential for Churchill's writing is the agency given to the natural world in response to human terrorism. As Atreus attempts to cook the flesh, 'Fire jumps over the feast / and two or three times / it's carried back to the / hearth and forced to burn. / The liver's hissing – it's / hard to say if fire / or flesh protested most.'[57] Revenge is a human obsession but, as in *The Skriker*, the non-human world is suffering and responding.

Here, there and *Far Away*

Closing her notes to *Thyestes* Churchill observes that no gods speak to bring relief, not even in the ironic tones of a Dionysus. The reader/spectator has only the memory of the Chorus who 'hoped for something better'. *Far Away* recalibrates this simple dialectic – that within horror and suffering is, somehow, hope. In the Hobbesian world limned in *Far Away*, we pass through the looking glass that once reflected a recognizable, if crumbling, social structure and enter a war of all against all with no sign of resistance or memory of an ethical alternative. In this grotesque topography, 'everything's been recruited' and in the last scene, the play's three characters provide a droll roll call of combatants: birds, cats, children under five, Portuguese car salesmen, Venezuelans, mosquitoes, crocodiles, deer, Latvian dentists – all locked in opposing but shifting camps and fighting to the death. The there-to-here structure, the terrifying in the ordinary, the docile body, so crucial to Churchill's dramaturgy of terror are here not recycled but remade: far away terror is distilled into a parable play designed to deliver a moral jolt, in fact several. Unlike *Thyestes* where power and horror are contrasted to an ordinary existence 'without clatter', in *Far Away* horror *is* the day-to-day, and familial mechanisms of normalization, supported by threatening lies, are deployed to keep that normalization in place. In Scene 1, the child Joan cannot sleep; she has seen her uncle beat prisoners carried by lorry to the shed behind the house; she's seen blood, heard crying. Each of the child's observations is parried by her aunt's lies, until no longer able to lie the aunt inveigles the child by playing on her innocent desire to be helpful: the crying beaten people in the shed were 'traitors' and 'you're part of a big movement now to make things better'.[58]

Once the lie is learned, accommodation follows. With Joan, now grown, and Todd, Churchill chooses, ironically and for the first time, her own scene of committed artists who work for an apparatus (professional theatre) that burdens them with 'contracts' while they worry the finer points of aesthetic fashion (figuration or abstraction?), all the while labouring to beautify a brutality that no longer shocks them. Instead, Churchill gives the privilege of moral outrage to the audience: we see manacled prisoners in ostentatiously individualized hats shuffle in 'parade' towards extermination. State terrorism, no longer far away in refugee camps or military prisons, is not only here, it's normalized, a central feature of cultural production.

In Scene 3, parades are over, hat-making is over; 'everyone is recruited', including Joan and Todd, now married, and Harper who, having colluded in terrorism, is terrified to be seen housing them. But her lies and terror are the artefacts of an older generation. Like Joan as a child, Harper cannot sleep, but Todd and Joan are new social actors for a new world order. Joan no longer fears her aunt's disapproval, but does fear 'the weather [because] the weather here's on the side of the Japanese'.[59] Now a plethora of familiar commodities are murder weapons: '... one killed by coffee or one killed by pins [or by] heroin, petrol, chainsaws, hairspray, bleach, foxgloves...'[60] But 'foxgloves' doesn't fit. The formal brilliance of Scene 3 lies in how characters adhere to familiar thought structures (us versus them), and how the death-dealing mindlessness of those structures is foregrounded (in Brechtian terms 'alienated') through zanily mismatched categories ('Mallards...commit rape, and they're on the side of the elephants and the Koreans'),[61] which in turn satirize our own destructive categories (the 'welfare mother'; Bush's 'axis of evil'). It is easy to be shocked by the sight of the manacled prisoners herded off to death – surely *that* is state terrorism. It is far harder to write terror's language, to invite audiences to feel something like 'the knobbly foreign constructions just under the English skin' – in this case, the shards of broken bodies and a destroyed nature poking through the skin of a well-formed English sentence. Joan calmly states, 'we were burning the grass that wouldn't serve', then asks rhetorically. 'Who's going to mobilize darkness and silence?'[62] Like a true performative, and in affectless tones, the language in Scene 3 does what it says: it brings into being a world of perpetual war in which terrorist acts are indistinguishable from the actions of a young woman journeying to see her husband ('... I killed two cats and a child under five so it wasn't that different from a mission').[63] Of course audiences grasp the sad joke – that our reality, too, is one of continuous war, with nightmare sites like Bosnia and Rwanda in the 1990s and Darfur at present, different in quantity of deaths and agony but not in kind. Joan's actions are hardly far away but, with a small adjustment to our lens, already here and right now. Terrorism has been normalized into manageable terror.

Thematic statements never do justice to the 'knobbly' effects of Churchill's writing on terror precisely because she is never writing *on* terror, as though it were a far-away unchanging object, but rather within it, as in Tim's laughing shriek in *The Ants*, or *near* it, as in terror's intimate relation to desire – a condition, ubiquitous in Churchill, that makes all human contact perilous, sometimes comically so (*Objections to Sex and Violence*). Foucaultian 'mechanisms of normalisation', noted in the discussion of *Softcops*, have traction in Churchill's work but long before she read *Discipline and Punish* she had explored gender normalization in *Vinegar Tom*, *Cloud Nine* and *Top Girls*. Rather it is Foucault's notion of 'the carceral', an omnipresent system of discipline to which everyone submits, that, in the 1990s, matches her own growing horror at unleashed global marketeering, ubiquitous war-mongering and actual war. From *A Mouthful of Birds* through *Thyestes* and *Far Away*, Churchill has given us shocking theatrical images of ordinary life in a state of terror.

Yet, as Joan notes at the end of *Far Away*, river water 'laps round your ankles *in any case*' – whether it's mobilized, and your enemy, or not (italics mine). In that slight equivocation, in Joan's inability or refusal to sort out the river's allegiances, we may hear echoes of the old Heraclitian adage about change and mutability (we never step into the same river twice). Or perhaps Churchill is offering something simpler and more elemental: Joan's capacity still to feel the water subverts her own numb acceptance of terror's ubiquity. This small moment of sentient resistance must also be counted in Caryl Churchill's dramaturgy of terror.

NOTES

1. Daniel Gerould, 'Terror, the Modern State and the Dramatic Imagination', in John Orr and Dragan Klaić (eds.), *Terrorism and Modern Drama* (Edinburgh: Edinburgh University Press, 1990), p. 22. See also, among others, Walter Laqueur, *The Age of Terrorism* (Boston: Little Brown and Company, 1987); Walter Reich (ed.), *Origins of Terrorism* (Washington, DC: Woodrow Wilson Center Press, 1990, 1998); Bruce Hoffman, *Inside Terrorism* (New York: Columbia University Press, 2006).
2. Gerould, 'Terror, Modern State', p. 22.
3. Terry Eagleton, *Holy Terror* (Oxford: Oxford University Press, 2005), p. 1.
4. See Caryl Churchill's note appended to publication of *Objections to Sex and Violence*, Michelene Wandor (ed.), *Plays By Women: Volume IV* (London: Methuen, 1985), p. 52.
5. Hoffman, *Inside Terrorism*, pp. 61–2.
6. Churchill, *Top Girls* in *Plays: Two* (London: Methuen, 1990) p. 141.
7. Churchill, *The Ants* in *New English Dramatists*, vol. XII (Harmondsworth: Penguin, 1969), pp. 91, 95.
8. *Ibid.*, p. 100.
9. *Ibid.*, p. 101.
10. *Ibid.*, p. 103.
11. Michael Bakewell, letter to Elin Diamond, 29 September 2008.

12. Churchill, note, *Objections to Sex and Violence*, p. 52.
13. See Elizabeth Grosz, *Jacques Lacan: A Feminist Introduction* (London and New York: Routledge), 1990, pp. 58–67. Grosz notes that while desire 'can support social laws and values, it is also able to subvert or betray them' (p. 65).
14. Churchill, *Objections*, p. 33.
15. *Ibid.*, p. 26.
16. *Ibid.*, pp. 29, 44.
17. *Ibid.*, pp. 40–1.
18. Jean Baudrillard, *The Spirit of Terrorism*, trans. Chris Turner (London: Verso, 2003), p. 9.
19. Churchill, *Objections*, p. 29.
20. Cited in Hannah Arendt, *On Violence* (New York: Harcourt, Brace & World, 1969), p. 82.
21. Churchill, *Softcops* (London: Methuen, 1984), p. 6.
22. *Ibid.*
23. Churchill, *Softcops* in *Plays: Two* (London: Methuen 1990), p. 6.
24. Michel Foucault, *Discipline and Punish* (New York: Vintage Books, 1979), pp. 113–14.
25. Churchill, *Softcops*, *Plays: Two*, p. 5.
26. *Ibid.* See Foucault, *Discipline*: 'Around each of these moral "representations", schoolchildren will gather with their masters and adults will learn what lessons to teach their offspring.' p. 113.
27. Churchill, *Softcops*, p. 14.
28. Foucault, *Discipline*, p. 283.
29. *Ibid.*, p. 200.
30. *Ibid.*, p. 308.
31. *Ibid.*, p. 25.
32. Churchill and David Lan, *A Mouthful of Birds* (London: Methuen, 1986), p. 5.
33. Churchill and Lan, *Mouthful*, p. 6.
34. Jan Kott, *The Eating of the Gods; An Interpretation of Greek Tragedy*, trans. Boleslaw Taborski and Edward J. Czerwinski (New York: Random House, 1973), p. 222.
35. Eagleton, *Holy Terror*, p. 2.
36. Churchill, *A Mouthful of Birds* in *Plays: Three* (London: Nick Hern Books, 1998), p. 33.
37. Baudrillard, *The Spirit of Terrorism*, p. 9.
38. Churchill and Lan, *Mouthful*, p. 23.
39. Eagleton, *Holy Terror*, p. 3.
40. Michel Foucault (Intro.), *Herculine Barbin*, trans. Richard McDougall (New York: Pantheon Books, 1980), pp. vii–xiii.
41. Churchill and Lan, *Mouthful*, p. 53.
42. Churchill, *Thyestes* in *Plays: Three*, p. 304.
43. See Elin Diamond, 'Feeling Global', in Mary Luckhurst (ed.), *A Companion to Modern British and Irish Drama, 1880–2005* (Oxford: Blackwell Publishing, 2006), pp. 476–87.
44. Churchill, *Thyestes*, p. 301.
45. *Ibid.*, p. 304.
46. *Ibid.*, pp. 299–300.

47. *Ibid.*, p. 296.
48. See R. J. Tarrant (ed.), *Seneca's Thyestes* (Atlanta, GA: Scholars Press, 1985) pp. 40–3.
49. Churchill, *Thyestes*, p. 296.
50. Quoted in *ibid.*, p. 295.
51. John G. Fitch (ed. and trans.), *Thyestes* (Cambridge, MA: Harvard University Press, 2004), p. 231.
52. *Ibid.*, p. 303.
53. *Ibid.*, pp. 312–13.
54. Churchill, *Mad Forest, Plays: Three*, p. 181.
55. *Ibid.*, p. 307.
56. *Ibid.*, p. 334.
57. *Ibid.*, p. 333.
58. Churchill, *Far Away* in *Plays: Four* (London: Nick Hern Books, 2008), p. 141.
59. *Ibid.*, p. 158.
60. *Ibid.*, p. 159.
61. *Ibid.*, p. 155.
62. *Ibid.*, p. 159.
63. *Ibid.*, p. 158.

9

ELAINE ASTON

On collaboration: 'not ordinary, not safe'

One of the defining characteristics of Caryl Churchill's theatre is her desire to work in collaboration with other artists. This is not to say – and it is important to note this at the outset of this collaboration-focused contribution to the *Companion* – that Churchill does not also write by herself. Nevertheless, her reputation for working with practitioners from theatre and other arts-related media is second to none among contemporary British dramatists.[1] In this chapter I aim to detail some of the many ways in which collaboration is important to Churchill's writing: exploring the collaborative choices she has made, the practitioners and contexts this has involved her working with and in over the years, and how these relate to her dramaturgy, aesthetics and politics. To this end, I am adopting a different strategy to the academic's customary outside-in view of plays analysed for their critical, cultural, theatrical or social significance (as evidenced in other of our *Companion* chapters). Instead, given my focus, I am approaching her work from the inside-out: taking collaborative process as a route through to an understanding of Churchill's theatre as 'not ordinary, not safe'.[2]

Finding an artistic community

As both our Chronology and Introduction record, Churchill spent her early writing years working mainly on radio drama which she was drawn to as the medium she enjoyed and grew up with; one which she acknowledges as being more important to her than television which was around at the end of her childhood.[3] Also the relatively fewer theatre opportunities or openings for dramatists in the 1960s, when compared, for example, to the fringe theatre explosion of the 1970s (see below), made radio a viable option, as well as it being a medium which suited her personal, domestic situation at that time: she could combine radio writing with looking after her young children. In contrast to theatre, writing radio drama generally requires little input from the writer in terms of the production process where the director/producer takes charge of the script, casting and actors at the point of broadcast production. As Churchill observes, her writer's involvement was limited to 'just going in for a couple of days and then the thing was finished' and that '[a]ll the time that I was doing radio plays, I don't think I met any writers, or anyone else just connected with the theatre'.[4] This solitary situation changed dramatically in 1972 with *Owners*, Churchill's professional theatre debut and the beginning of her long association with the Royal Court.

Thereafter, Churchill describes 1976 as 'almost as much of a watershed' as 1972[5] as this was the year when she met and worked with the new writing collective Joint Stock on *Light Shining in Buckinghamshire* and the socialist–feminist company Monstrous Regiment on *Vinegar Tom*.[6] Both of these companies figured prominently in the outcrop of 'alternative' theatre groups in the 1970s consequent upon a relatively benign moment in terms of state (Arts Council) funding. Encounters with both groups in 1976 presented Churchill with seminal opportunities for collaborative theatre-making.[7] Churchill was the only playwright to enter into an enduring relationship with Joint Stock with and for whom she also wrote *Cloud Nine* (1979), *Fen* (1983) and *A Mouthful of Birds* (1986). As theatre critic Claire Armitstead observed, '[c]ontemporaries like David Hare had a go, in the days when it was fashionable, but Churchill was the only writer who went back for more'.[8] Joint Stock archivist Rob Ritchie argues that '[f]or some, perhaps, the pressures of the workshop, the obligation to write under the constant gaze of the actors, is too public an exposure of a craft more easily controlled in private'.[9] This explains why writers might not be so keen on this process, but in turn begs the question of why Churchill is the exception who proves the rule. Why did she go 'back for more'?

Commenting on her first encounter with Joint Stock, Churchill explains how this 'attracted me as a method of working, but I'd no idea what it was going to be like, and I'd never worked in a co-operative way. I'd always been shy about showing anyone my work before it was finished, but I liked being more open, and learnt enormously from it.'[10] Her comments about meeting Monstrous Regiment, how they talked through and shared ideas, also reveal Churchill eschewing the solitary habit of not discussing her ideas or sharing her work: 'I felt briefly shy and daunted, wondering if I would be acceptable, then happy and stimulated by the discovery of shared ideas and the enormous energy and feeling of possibilities in the still new company.'[11] Moreover, both instances reflect a willingness on Churchill's part to embrace a new way of working; an attraction to a creative experience *outside* of her own, which is, as Armitstead argues, 'one of the qualities that has enabled her to keep on developing long after most of her contemporaries have either dried up, moved out or become set in their ways'.[12] Churchill's capacity to renew rather than to repeat herself, for which she receives much critical interest and acclaim, is one then which stems partly from her attraction to new ways of working.

Common to these formative experiences of collaboration with Joint Stock and Monstrous Regiment was a shared reading, thinking and researching of ideas. Although many playwrights do not necessarily engage with research as a part of their writing process, Churchill figures prominently among those who do. As Janelle Reinelt writes, Churchill 'is a socialist-feminist intellectual; serious historical and philosophical reading forms the background of her work and often enters the workshops'.[13] Working with the companies meant that Churchill now had the opportunity to belong to an artistic community where sharing reading and researching ideas was an important part of the making process, albeit differently in each case. With Monstrous Regiment it was being in a community of shared feminist ideas and activism (the company first met Churchill on an abortion rally) which made for such a successful collaboration between the writer and the company: '[h]er ideas fitted with ours, and we commissioned her to write it [*Vinegar Tom*]. In terms of our relationship with a writer, it was one of the happiest we ever had.'[14]

In the case of Joint Stock, although tempting to address the mutual attraction of writer and company as a political match-making between Churchill's own left-wing views and those of Joint Stock, whose 1974 *Fanshen* production with David Hare on Chinese communism earned the company a reputation as a political company, this would be something of an oversimplification. This is not least because as Ritchie argues a 'shared political view' for Joint Stock was much harder to identify than their aim of creating new work 'to the highest artistic standards'.[15] If there was a 'shared political view' it was arrived at not through a consensus about a political ideology but through the politicizing processes of the company's democratized, collaborative and creative labour.[16] Becoming involved as a writer in this anti-authoritarian structure – which also characterized the socialist–feminist organization of Monstrous Regiment – had an important influence on Churchill's writing at this time: was seminal to defining and evolving the political fabric of her theatre; informing and shaping her socialist and/or feminist dramaturgy.

Two things are important here. The first is that in terms of finding herself in a community where she could share ideas meant that as a writer Churchill was no longer self-contained in terms of her thinking process. Working with Joint Stock especially, whose pattern of work was to have a period of workshopping, a break for the writer to go away to work on a script and then a final rehearsal phase, introduced a different economy of ideas 'ownership' in which a writer is involved with and has a responsibility for ideas that are not just her own. To take account of and to be accountable to others is exemplified in the case of the Joint Stock production of *Cloud Nine* where the play's exploration of sexual politics, which, unlike the remote historical subject of *Light Shining* to which the actors then had to make their own present-day connections, was workshopped out of the immediate and intimate experiences of those involved:

> It is, of course, the writer's task to make sense of the lives encountered in this way [through the Joint Stock process]. But the initial workshop is always group work and what typically evolves is a sense of responsibility to the people whose experience is to be dramatised. In some cases, as in *Cloud Nine*, the experience is the actors' own personal lives and the writer is then under pressure to give back to the actors a play that does justice to the intimate feelings and anxieties revealed in the workshop ... it is the constant effort to be truthful to the people who are to be presented that characterises the workshop and carries forward into rehearsal.[17]

The responsibility to others is also one which Churchill observes pushes a writer towards a greater recognition of the 'situations' which others have experienced and which as a writer you can then connect to: 'If you're working by yourself, then you're not accountable to anyone but yourself while you're doing it. You don't get forced in quite the same way into seeing how your own inner feelings connect up with larger things that happen to other people.'[18] Churchill's comment is significant in terms of thinking about how the process of being 'forced' to make those larger connections is one that resonates with the political impulse behind and in her plays: often to see how the personal, marginalized lives of ordinary men and especially women are situated in an epic damaged and damaging economy of (an increasingly globalized) capitalism.

Secondly, while talking and sharing ideas played to Churchill's research interests as a writer, her exposure to exercises and improvisations in the group's workshops taught her a lot about creating ideas through practical explorations. This too was something entirely new to her. Before the *Light Shining* workshop she had 'never seen an exercise or improvisation before and was as thrilled as a child at a pantomime'.[19] Creating ideas in a theatre workshop is not a question of working to a strict intellectual or political agenda, but of mixing up (even messing up) ideas through collective, creative labour. While this might, as Ritchie observes, mean 'proceed[ing] in a random, superficial way that would appal any self-respecting historian or sociologist', it is nevertheless the case that 'the benefit of the research is that it complicates received ideas about the subject'.[20] In particular, Joint Stock director Max Stafford-Clark had a 'stock' of games and exercises the performers could use and adapt to the subjects they were exploring; activating ideas, developing characters. For example, a favourite game was to use playing cards to improvise or to act out scenes exploring power relations (where power assigned to a performer in a scene was determined by the number on a playing card).[21] So in *Light Shining* Churchill recollects how the performers 'drew cards, one of which meant you were eccentric to the power of that number, and then improvised a public place – a department store, a doctor's waiting room – till it gradually became clear who it was, how they were breaking conventions, how the others reacted'.[22]

It is important to clarify that in the *Light Shining* workshop the actors were exploring ideas through creative play, rather than improvising Churchill's playscript which was written by Churchill *after* the workshop in the (solitary) writing break (see also Rebellato, Chapter 10). 'The purpose of any workshop', Stafford-Clark argues, 'is to stimulate the writer: a by-product is that it invariably begins to stimulate and enthuse the actors too'.[23] Accounts of *Light Shining* and other Churchill plays workshopped by Joint Stock, or involving a workshop period,[24] give many examples of how this process worked 'to stimulate and enthuse' the performers. It is much harder to identify how this works on the writer, or on the writing. Joint Stock actress Linda Bassett, for example, describes how 'Caryl is creating the work, you are producing the material but the creative process is going on inside her.' Talking specifically of her experience of workshopping in the East Anglian village of Upwell for *Fen*, Bassett gives an account of the actors' work: how they talked to the villagers and brought back their stories to narrate to the company, with 'Caryl drink[ing] it in ... doing research but in a very condensed way'.[25] Of *Light Shining* Churchill writes that she 'could give endless examples of how something said or done by one of the actors is directly connected to something in the text', though finds it 'harder to define ... the effect on the writing of the way the actors worked, their accuracy and commitment'.[26] Other of her comments point to how moments from the workshop helped her to find the 'before–during–after' structure of the play and also record the pleasure of her first-time encounter of creative response: the pleasure as a writer of not just sourcing ideas from the group's work, but of offering something (a speech) directly back to a performer.[27]

Working with Max Stafford-Clark

This collaborative approach to theatre opened up new possibilities for Churchill's playwriting, while at the same time it also meant that, unlike her radio years, she was making contact with theatre practitioners, several of whom would come to figure as some of her most long-standing collaborators. Of particular importance in this regard, is that *Light Shining* was Churchill's first production with Max Stafford-Clark and as Philip Roberts writes marked the start of 'one of the most fruitful partnerships of modern theatre'.[28] Their 'fruitful partnership' was consolidated by Stafford-Clark's subsequent direction of *Cloud Nine, Top Girls* (credited by Stafford-Clark as the '[b]est play I've ever directed'),[29] *Serious Money* (1987), *Icecream* (1989) and *Blue Heart* (1997). To account for the success of this writer–director relationship, which for a majority of modern playwrights is the most significant point of collaboration, requires some understanding of the synergies between Stafford-Clark's rigorous and meticulous approach to directing, and the textual fabric and precision of Churchill's writing.

As a director attracted to working on new plays and with new writers, Stafford-Clark is particularly drawn to Churchill's work on account of her 'incisiveness and a political astuteness and an ability to analyse combined with a theatrical inventiveness' which means that her theatre is 'always exciting'.[30] Churchill's willingness to collaborate is also an important factor in their partnership, given Stafford-Clark's views of 'the writer as a collaborator' and theatre 'as a real collaborative art form', which in turn account for why he regards the writer's presence as 'essential' to the rehearsal process[31] and why he seeks a high level of commitment, thinking and creating from the performers he works with. Hence, the 'accuracy and commitment' of the actors involved in *Light Shining* that Churchill observed, is in some ways attributable to Stafford-Clark's directorial facilitation of a shared thinking and creating process (as described earlier), as well as his adoption of a method which encourages attention to detail and 'accuracy' in the 'larger things that happen to people' which *Light Shining* dramatized.

More specifically, Stafford-Clark's method is to work closely on a script by adopting a particular method of 'actioning'. This involves breaking scenes down into sections to understand the 'action' of a section and then further working on and breaking down a script so that the 'actioning' process for the performer means that they have to think about each and every line, or half line, or indeed any point where one character has a purpose in affecting another. In practical terms this is done by inviting performers to come up with a transitive verb for each 'actioned' moment, as in this example from *Cloud Nine* which shows how the actor, Anthony Sher, breaks down a speech for the character of Clive:

> *Clive educates Harry*: There is the necessity of reproduction. The family is all important. *Clive charms Harry*: And there is there pleasure. But what we put ourselves through to get that pleasure, Harry. *Clive worships Harry*: When I heard about our fine fellows last night fighting those savages to protect us I thought yes, that is what I aspire to.[32]

This is a detailed and lengthy process, but as Stafford-Clark explains it means that it is possible to analyse what each actor is doing and to be clear about what she/he is attempting to do to another actor/character.[33] From the performer's point of view, as actress Leslie Sharp (Dull Gret / Angie in *Top Girls* 1991 revival) explains this 'is a very good way of being totally accurate about what you're doing as an actor'.[34] From the point of view of the political 'action' of Churchill's text it is a method that encourages an attention to the social and political affects arising out of the individual relationships between characters and the connections of these to the larger social scripts that 'write' and determine them. This and other techniques such as Stafford-Clark's card-playing technique in relation to power relations means that the small and detailed work of the actors on the effects and affects of power and powerlessness, rehearses and provides a framework for the realization of Churchill's socialist and/or feminist dramaturgy in performance.

It is not just, however, the way in which Stafford-Clark's 'actioning' method brings out the political 'play' in Churchill's text that is important, but also how this process lends itself to the poetics of Churchill's text; to finding ways, with the actors, of activating the very precise, finely turned language, rhythm and structure of her writing. A case in point is the opening dinner scene of *Top Girls*, which Stafford-Clark directed for the Royal Court, and its use of overlapping dialogue which Churchill pioneered (though had essayed in her earlier short play, *Three More Sleepless Nights*, Soho Poly, 1980). Originally this presented a challenge to Stafford-Clark ('the first scene was a mystery to him')[35] and the actresses who between them all had to figure out not only what it was all about and how it related to the rest of the play, but how they might set about realizing an aural choreography of the lines, rhythms and silences at the same time as making the individual stories into a meaningful, purposeful whole. As actress Deborah Findlay (Isabella Bird / Joyce / Mrs Kidd, in *Top Girls*, 1982 and 1991) explains, the dinner scene could not just be about a group of women telling their stories but needed to be about these women making relationships, and in this respect 'actioning' was again useful, indeed Findlay argues 'crucial to the production'; to the business of establishing who was 'actually trying to affect somebody', and this in turn helped to orchestrate the choreographic rise and fall of the women's voices.[36]

The formative moment of collaboration with Joint Stock and Monstrous Regiment clearly had a bearing thereafter on Churchill's willingness to remain involved with productions of her work; to fulfil the role of 'writer as collaborator'. As Churchill observes, 'I think it's true that once you have done that [worked with the companies], and also if you're used to being at rehearsals a lot and being prepared to make changes if necessary – then I think you are prepared to be fairly open and respond to particular situations.'[37] In the case of *Top Girls*, for example, which had evolved over a long period of solitary thinking and writing time, she was receptive to making small changes to the script she brought unworkshopped to the rehearsal process, while *Serious Money*, which she researched *after* a two-week workshop period, she substantially redrafted and restructured during rehearsals.[38]

Working with actors, Churchill is open to the possibilities of meaning; is willing to 'journey' with an actor on what a line might mean, for example, rather than impose meaning[39] (which might in turn, I would add, be a reflection of her general reluctance to talk about what her plays mean). However, this is balanced by her own 'precise verbal sense' and by her own admission she can be 'very uncompromising' about any suggested changes if there is a risk to the rhythm or point of a line.[40] Bassett, giving the actor's point of view, articulates this differently, observing that while Churchill herself is 'flexible' about the delivery of lines and prefers to leave this task to the actor, it is the lines themselves which are not flexible. 'It is like doing Shakespeare', she says, explaining how Churchill's writing presents the actor with the challenge of hitting the right rhythm in order to get the line right.[41]

Interdisciplinary collaborations

For Churchill it is not just working with actors that she enjoys, but her theatrical inventiveness has also attracted her to collaborations with practitioners from other disciplines: to experimenting with dancers, musicians and singers. This is not theatrical inventiveness enjoyed for its own sake, however, but in Churchill's view this is necessary if theatre is to maximize its power as a medium. In her early essay, 'Not Ordinary, Not Safe',[42] Churchill spelt out that content, form and the means of expression are all vital to theatre. In terms of content she argued that '[s]ubjects change not because the problems are solved but because they become irrelevant', and that form changes as the world changes in order to give adequate expression to life. 'Whenever conventions of subject and form outlast the impetus that formed them they are felt to be inadequate to expressing life', she observes, and 'new conventions' are 'true' to a 'changed view of the world, until in turn they harden into an artificial system'.[43] Churchill's own theatre provides hard evidence of this view: for example, the evolutionary shifts of both form and content; her move into and out of a Brechtian/feminist inflected dramaturgy, reaching for other formal means of giving expression to a world changed, damaged by the flow of global capital. Significantly, to consolidate her point, Churchill also argues that '[g]reater technical range and greater subject range go together, since *one of the ways to increase what we have to say is to increase the range of means of expression*' (my emphasis).[44] To be inventive, to be re-inventive, for Churchill is not to work within the limits of the known and the doable, but to test those limits by exploring different means of technical and artistic expression in order to say what demands to be said about the world we have, or, perhaps, might like to have.

This early statement by Churchill begins to explain why she chose not just to work collaboratively in straight theatre contexts, but also to work outside her comfort zone of text-based theatre. An early endeavour in this regard was her 1984 collaboration *Midday Sun* at the ICA, working with ICA director John Ashford,[45] Pete Brooks (Impact Theatre), Geraldine Pilgrim and Sally Owen (Second Stride) on a 'visual theatre' production for which she contributed 'a cracking short centre-piece script'.[46] More significant in terms of interdisciplinary collaboration was the last of Churchill's Joint Stock projects, *A Mouthful of Birds* (1986), which brought together Joint Stock's collaborative research and acting method with a physical 'text' directed by choreographer Ian Spink. At that time, it was the most collaborative of Churchill's ventures, involving two writers (Churchill and David Lan) and two directors (Spink and Waters) and pushed the collaborative ethos of Joint Stock to an unprecedented level in terms of 'authoring' a performance 'text' between writers, directors and performers who had a mix of dance and actor training and skills.

To write with another writer was in itself a new experience for Churchill. *Light Shining* had started out as a project with two writers, Churchill and Colin Bennett, and both were working independently (but with a shared structure) in the writing break when two weeks in Bennett dropped out.[47] So working with Lan renewed and fulfilled a missed collaborative writing opportunity on *Light Shining* and gave Churchill the chance of 'exchanging ideas' with another writer, 'batting things off each other, something I hadn't really done before. It was very enjoyable.'[48] Moreover, it involved a different writing and working process: a continuous twelve-week period of shared researching, writing and rehearsing, rather than there being discrete periods of workshopped research, solitary writing time and rehearsals.

Underpinning this working process was the commitment of the performers and the experience and vision of the directors. Waters had worked with Stafford-Clark at the Court, assisted with *Cloud Nine* (co-directed the Court revival), directed *Three More Sleepless Nights* and *Fen*, and was therefore fully conversant with Churchill's theatre and committed to the Joint Stock method. One of the founding members in 1982 of the new dance company Second Stride,[49] Spink was a choreographer Churchill was keen to work with – indeed she had hoped he would work with her on *Fen*. Coming from a dance rather than theatre field, Spink shared Churchill's interest in formal experimentation. Specifically, Spink was keen to explore ways of breaking down preconceptions about theatre and dance; of fusing dance with text and music in compositions resistant to the narrative structures of, for example, classical ballet in which he had originally trained, and of looking for a basis on which to build what he describes as 'movement theatre'.[50] As a 'movement theatre' piece, *Mouthful*'s fusion of dance and theatre found a means of communicating the ideas of possession and violence behind the show; of working the language of text and body to 'say' more about the darker depths of possession, abandonment or ecstasy than could be said in words alone. Such a fusion was highly dependent on a mutual exchange of performance vocabularies and skills, and in that sense Joint Stock's collaborative method under Waters' direction, was an appropriate partner for Spink's choreographic principle of a shared ownership of creative material among dancers. At the same time it is important not to underplay the creative tensions this level of collaboration produces, given the interdisciplinary mix of work for the performers, who irrespective of their discipline were required to work on *both* text and dance, and the simultaneous mapping of writing and rehearsing without a full script or physical score. Although the writers found a way of sharing their work (taking a seven-story structure in which they could work on scenes independently of each other), lighting designer Rick Fisher recalls that there was more difficulty for the two directors,[51] while Ritchie also records that '[s]uch [collaborative] departures are not without their hazards. Les Waters' introduction to dance work earned him two cracked ribs and a punctured lung.'[52]

Churchill's collaboration with Spink continued with *Fugue* (Channel 4, Dancelines, 1988), which experimented with the interaction of different media – specifically, starting out with a soap opera, television-styled play that 'danced' into a more abstract world; working off repeated gestures in the way that a fugue uses repeated phrases.[53] Moreover, a brief overview of Churchill's production history more broadly evidences the continuities of interdisciplinary performance collaborations arising out of Second Stride connections. For example, along with Spink, *Fugue* also involved the designer Antony McDonald (then associate director of Second Stride)[54] who went on to design *Mad Forest* (1990). Among composers, Second Stride notably collaborated with Orlando Gough and Judith Weir. Gough, McDonald and Spink all came together with Churchill for *Lives of the Great Poisoners* (1991). Weir joined Spink and Waters for *The Skriker* in 1994, while Spink and Gough renewed their dance–music–text collaboration with Churchill on *Hotel* (1997). More recently Churchill provided words on global warming and climate change for Gough's BBC Proms *We Turned on the Light* (2006), while in 2002, for choreographer Siobhan Davies (formerly of Second Stride), who back in 1979 had originally inspired Churchill's interdisciplinary performance interests, Churchill wrote 'She Bit her Tongue' (a monologue for the Siobhan Davies Dance company's *Plants and Ghosts*). Such continuities of collaboration reflect how the pool of contacts and connections made by Churchill through Second Stride put her in touch with a community of like-minded collaborators: with those open to the possibilities of exploring what can be created through a fusion of disciplines. Further, this also signals how advantageous it is to know about a practitioner's work, the ideas and aspirations which underpin it, and *how* a practitioner works given the complexities of interdisciplinary collaboration in process and practice.

Although the complexities of interdisciplinary work are necessarily different for each of Churchill's projects, the various notes and reflections from those principally involved are insightful in terms of gathering together a few further general observations on collaborative process and some specific insights into how Churchill's writing informs and is informed by these contexts. In terms of process and in contrast to a theatre devising culture which might typically, for example, start with a company of performers all generating 'text' together, Churchill's performance collaborations have tended first to be shaped by those principally involved at the ideas stage – between writer, choreographer, composer, designer, or combinations thereof. From an agreed idea, it has then, as *A Mouthful of Birds* illustrates, been important to find a scenario or structure for each collaborative part to develop in its own right and to come together with all other artistic elements to form an integrated whole. Spink offers this insightful overview:

> It is important that people within the collaborative situation can engage with each other, engage with different viewpoints. Structure is a very important part of the process – talking about structure and making structure (even if it eventually gets thrown away). There is always a point when people have to take control of their particular territory. There has to be a situation of trust and that can only be developed through people fighting everything out right to the bitter end, through knowing and being clear about what they want, and through being very honest about what they want and why. Sometimes the situation does feel very dangerous.[55]

Together, the notes and reflections by Churchill, Gough, Spink and McDonald published with the 'text' of *Poisoners* variously attest to the matters and issues of structure, control and territory Spink describes.[56] A narrative structure woven out of three poison stories, and agreed through lengthy discussions formed a scenario which Gough and Churchill could write to and compose for, which in turn provided a 'constant point of reference' for the movement work after the 'text' was in place. Practicalities (of budget, rehearsal period, etc.) had a bearing on how the work came together, as did certain 'rules' of artistic engagement that had been agreed upon: that performers would work within their own disciplines (unlike *A Mouthful of Birds*) and that the singing would be *a capella*. To make a decision in one art form necessarily had implications for another (*a capella* initiated the need for 'text' before movement), while the discipline-based 'ruling' had consequences (constraints, possibly) for the performers.[57] Moreover, approaches in general to 'rules' could also produce creative tensions. For example, Spink observes that Churchill prefers to work with an idea and to stick to that idea, while he favours more flexibility: working to 'rules' but also being willing to change them.[58] If at times this made the collaborative experience artistically 'dangerous' it was the degree of self-reflexivity and the respect for the 'territories' of all those involved which offset this. As Richard Cave's discussion of the collaboration of *Poisoners* concludes, if there were 'amicably combative approaches' among the key collaborators it was 'respect' for the 'different principles' each brought to the work which prevented it from unravelling.[59]

Although tempting to speculate as Cave does on 'who might have influenced whom' in this kind of collaboration,[60] it becomes a limited or redundant line of enquiry insofar as it does not necessarily serve to illuminate the creativity it produces. More productive (and relevant to discussion here) is an understanding of how Churchill's writing was informed by and was informing her collaborations. The former is again hard to fathom but it is clear that, like her early encounters with Joint Stock, the opportunities for discussing and working out ideas with others in these interdisciplinary contexts is something which also stimulates her work and gets absorbed into her writing. The workshop for *A Mouthful of Birds*, for example, enabled both Lan and Churchill to write scenes 'devised out of their responses to the improvisations'.[61] Working on *Fugue* Churchill saw and seized 'the potential of writing dialogue that was fugal',[62] while Spink explains how earlier work with Second Stride 'influenced the way that she came to see *The Skriker*',[63] a play she had been working on for many years and completed (unworkshopped) before the collaborative performance process. This chimes with Churchill's own explanations of how, writing the play by herself, for the first time she ended up writing movement into the script in the form of stage directions for dancers.[64]

On the other hand, it is relatively easier to grasp how Churchill's work serves as an inspiration to those working in other artistic 'territories' in any given project. 'She gives you a starting point which is potentially very rich and has a number of possibilities,' explains Spink, '[s]he is very generous; she will continue to follow you, as you search out the way of visualising or realising what the material could yield and become.'[65] Important too is the way in which her writing has its own sense of (dance) movement and (music) rhythm. Contributing to an interview at the time of *The Skriker*, dance critic Judith Mackrell argues that 'the way Churchill uses language makes her peculiarly sympathetic to dance. In a lot of her works the language itself has a kind of surface rhythm and music', while theatre critic Benedict Nightingale similarly acknowledges Churchill's use of 'words expanding to embrace music and dance'.[66] Echoing both critics are Gough's notes on 'Eight Rooms' (the first part of *Hotel*) which suggest that Churchill's 'fragmentary libretto' is '[a]lready a move away from naturalism. Allows me to compose the music, i.e. make the text into music, rather than being dragged along by the words.'[67]

Ultimately, 'writing' for all of those involved in these collaborations is less about 'text' than texture: the layering of words, music, dance and design; the combination of these performance vocabularies, in which Churchill's 'text' is an integral element; one which lends itself to a non-hierarchical, interdependent play of art forms in both process and performance. This is about creating collaborative work that pursues Churchill's early vision of theatre as 'not ordinary, not safe'; of performance which gives expression to the nightmare worlds of other realities which, whether imagined out of the desolate hotel room or the damaged underworld of the Skriker, are always, Churchill suggests, those of our own (selfish) making.

New directions

Asked about her attraction to dance–drama collaborations at the time of *The Skriker*, as opposed to straight theatre, Churchill replied '[b]ecause I have found the theatre a bit boring for a while, and during the time I've been tired of it, the things that have stayed with me have been from dance companies like Second Stride and DV8'.[68] That said, she was also at pains to point out in another *Skriker*-focused interview that she had no intention of 'abandoning words altogether' and was just as likely to return to writing 'complicated text' without dance.[69] Recent years have shown her doing precisely that. Alongside her burgeoning list of interdisciplinary collaborations to date (see earlier) are plays that principally renew her connections to the Royal Court, albeit with an expanding range of theatre directors.

For Churchill there is a distinction to be made between her relationship with Stafford-Clark and with the Court: 'I don't actually identify them with each other. I assume I will continue to work with both', she explained in the context of Stafford-Clark's departure from his position of artistic director at the Royal Court in 1993.[70] Working with 'both' translated into the 1997 production of *Blue Heart* for Out of Joint, the new company set up by Stafford-Clark after his departure, and Court productions directed by Stephen Daldry (Stafford Clark's successor), James Macdonald, Ian Rickson and Dominic Cooke. Specifically, Daldry directed *This is a Chair* (1997), *Far Away* (2000) and *A Number* (2002). Macdonald, who had already collaborated with Churchill on *Poisoners* and directed her translation of *Thyestes* (Royal Court, 1994), directed *Drunk Enough to Say I Love You* (2006). In 2002 Rickson and Cooke both directed short works in a series of 'Caryl Churchill Events' (see Churchill Chronology for details). In addition to this, Churchill returned to the National Theatre with a new version of Strindberg's *A Dream Play* (2005) directed by Katie Mitchell, the first woman director for a Churchill production since Pam Brighton directed *Vinegar Tom* in 1976.

This is not, however, to pretend that opening up to this most recent phase of Court collaborations did not put a strain on the working relationship with Stafford-Clark. Around the time of *Blue Heart*, Churchill was finding it hard to write and hard to deliver the play promised for Out of Joint – a play originally envisioned as a satirical and epic treatment of 'freedom'.[71] Prior to this, there had already been some upset between Stafford-Clark and Churchill over *The Skriker* – specifically arising out of Churchill's feeling that Stafford-Clark did not fully 'appreciate' a play that was so important to her.[72] More difficult for Stafford-Clark, however, was when Churchill chose Daldry for *Far Away*.

Stafford-Clark and Daldry are highly respected and mutually respectful opposites: Daldry's open, speculative and playful ways into a text contrast with the close attention to the (affective) detail of Stafford-Clark's approach. Daldry prefers what might be described as physical-actioning: rather than work on lines in terms of 'actioned' moments, he encourages actors to explore gesture and movement to highlight or counterpoint dialogue so that a line, a moment or a scene embody meaning.[73] This process is a route to the 'visual' and the 'experiential' qualities that characterize his style of production.[74] Choosing Daldry, Churchill may well have been exhibiting her attraction to new ways of working. As Stafford-Clark observed, it is perhaps not surprising that 'someone as unremittingly inventive as Caryl needs to be reinvented by her director as well'.[75] 'To be reinvented by her director' on the trio of Daldry-directed plays meant looking to the potential synergies between this new directorial approach and the changed political and theatrical form of her theatre. Gone is the dialectical, affective choreography played out between characters in plays such as *Top Girls* or *Fen*, and in its stead is the elliptical–political *Far Away* fabric out of which are woven the 'frightening' threads of a world increasingly lost to global capitalism.[76] As Stafford-Clark so insightfully describes, 'I say she's [Churchill] developed her own response to a political agenda which she has discovered she cannot effectively address directly any more. The play [*Far Away*] is compressed and surreal but epic, and also functions like an installation.'[77] Daldry's 'experiential' and 'visual' qualities as a director were, therefore, a productive artistic choice for the realization of *Far Away* as an epic visual theatre experience.

At the level of script work, the condensed writing of *Far Away*, or other of Churchill's recent elliptical–political plays like *This is a Chair* or *Drunk Enough to Say I Love You?*, charges director and performers with the task, as Bassett (who played Harper in *Far Away*) explains, of having 'to find your way to every line'.[78] Over her many years of working with Churchill, Bassett has learnt to expect the unexpected from a Churchill script; knows at the first stage of script work to trust to the writing and not to get hung up on meaning, all of which was helpful to early discussions of *Far Away* with Daldry and others.[79] Also beneficial to the rehearsal process was Daldry's interest in encouraging performers to find physical ways to 'unlock' the emotion of a scene – particularly in the third and final scene of *Far Away*, where Churchill's lines cease to mean in any literal sense as they come to embody the 'non-sense' of a global, ecological war zone.[80] In some ways, the more elliptical–political Churchill's writing, the more textured and expansive the challenge is for performers and director to get to the emotional–political heart of the dramatic matter. James Macdonald, discussing the rehearsal process for *Drunk Enough to Say I Love You?*, observes: 'I love the fact that Caryl has moved such a long way stylistically, from the total precision of her work, with its trademark pattern of interruptions, to the much freer shape of her more recent work, where it's really up to the director to excavate the right rhythm for the text.'[81] Political and elliptical necessitates a process of work for director and performers that involves an understanding of the political terrain, but then a figuring out of how to *create* this along with all of the condensed layers of meaning-making possibilities, and experimenting to find a form of 'language for the production'.[82]

Of course, the challenge for any one of Churchill's many theatre and performance collaborators lies in them never being able to second guess what her next play or performance text will be. Guaranteed, however, is that any new work by Churchill will be one richly veined in theatrical, social and political possibilities, which means that the journey she invites potential collaborators to join her on is one which each and every one of them is keen to make.[83] For Churchill, however, there is no final theatre destination. As she concludes when writing on ideas for theatre in the twentieth century, so richly taken up in her own work: 'Life so short, the craft so long to learn'.[84]

NOTES

1. For further discussion listen to 'Reputations: Caryl Churchill', *Theatre Voice*, 8 April 2005, www.theatrevoice.com/the_archive/, discussion chaired by David Benedict, with Linda Bassett, Graham Cowley, Deborah Findlay and Rick Fisher.
2. This is the title of an early essay by Churchill, 'Not Ordinary, Not Safe: A Direction for Drama?', *The Twentieth Century* (November 1960), 443–51.
3. Caryl Churchill interview, 'The Common Imagination and the Individual Voice', *New Theatre Quarterly*, 13 (February 1988), 1–16, 4.
4. Churchill, 'The Common Imagination', 4.
5. Caryl Churchill, Introduction, *Plays: One* (London: Methuen, 1985), pp. xi–xiii, p. xii.
6. For details of Monstrous Regiment see *Companion*, Chapter 1, p. 4 and Chapter 2, p. 20.
7. See Dan Rebellato (Chapter 10) for details of Churchill's experience of working on *Strange Days*, a workshop project in a London junior school that pre-dates her 1976 workshops with Joint Stock and Monstrous Regiment.
8. Claire Armitstead, 'Tale of the Unexpected', *Guardian* (12 January 1994), Arts Section, 4–5, p. 4.
9. Rob Ritchie (ed.), *The Joint Stock Book: The Making of a Theatre Collective* (London: Methuen, 1987), p. 30.
10. Caryl Churchill, interview with Ronald Hayman, 'Partners: Caryl Churchill and Max Stafford-Clark', *Sunday Times Magazine* (2 March 1980), 25–7, 27.
11. Churchill, *Plays: One*, p. 129.
12. Armitstead, 'Tale of the Unexpected', 4.
13. Janelle Reinelt, 'Caryl Churchill and the Politics of Style', in Elaine Aston and Janelle Reinelt (eds.), *The Cambridge Companion to Modern British Women Playwrights* (Cambridge: Cambridge University Press, 2000), pp. 174–93, p. 175.
14. Gillian Hanna, *Monstrous Regiment: A Collective Celebration* (London: Nick Hern Books, 1991), p. xxxvii.
15. Ritchie, *The Joint Stock Book*, pp. 12–13.
16. See comments from Bill Gaskill, co-founder of Joint Stock with Max Stafford-Clark, in 'Joint Stock Theatre Group', in Catherine Itzin, *Stages in the Revolution: Political Theatre in Britain Since 1968* (London: Methuen, 1980), pp. 220–7.
17. Ritchie, *The Joint Stock Book*, pp. 31–2.
18. Churchill, 'Common Imagination', 4.
19. Churchill in Ritchie, *The Joint Stock Book*, p. 119.
20. Ritchie, *The Joint Stock Book*, p. 31.
21. The point of influence and inspiration for this came originally from Keith Johnstone at the Royal Court. See Philip Roberts and Max Stafford-Clark, *Taking Stock: The Theatre of Max Stafford-Clark* (London: Nick Hern Books, 2007), p. 14.
22. Churchill in Ritchie, *The Joint Stock Book*, p. 119.
23. Stafford-Clark, *Taking Stock*, p. 150.
24. *Serious Money*, for instance, was a Royal Court production which involved a shorter, two-week workshop period.
25. Linda Bassett, 'Reputations: Caryl Churchill', *Theatre Voice*, 8 April 2005.
26. Caryl Churchill, *Plays: One*, p. 184.

27. Specific details of these can be found in Ritchie's *The Joint Stock Book*, pp. 119–20.
28. Philip Roberts, *Taking Stock*, p. 24.
29. Stafford-Clark, *Taking Stock*, p. 102.
30. Stafford-Clark in *Omnibus: On Caryl Churchill*, BBC1, November 1988.
31. Stafford-Clark quoted in Lizbeth Goodman, 'Overlapping Dialogue in Overlapping Media: Behind the Scenes of *Top Girls*', in Sheila Rabillard (ed.), *Essays on Caryl Churchill: Contemporary Representations* (Winnipeg: Blizzard Publishing, 1998), pp. 69–101, p. 73.
32. Sher in *Omnibus: On Caryl Churchill*. Clive's speech is quoted from Act I, Scene 4 of *Cloud Nine*.
33. Stafford-Clark in *Omnibus: On Caryl Churchill*.
34. Sharp quoted in Lizbeth Goodman, 'Overlapping Dialogue', p. 84.
35. Observation made by *Top Girls* performer Lesley Manville, quoted in Lizbeth Goodman, 'Overlapping Dialogue', p. 73.
36. Findlay, quoted in Lizbeth Goodman, 'Overlapping Dialogue', p. 85.
37. Churchill, interview with Lynne Truss, 'A Fair Cop', *Plays and Players* (January 1984), 8–10, 9.
38. Churchill explains: 'The workshop was in September, and we started rehearsals in mid-February. I'd gone into the workshop straight from *A Mouthful of Birds*, so I hadn't been able to do the research I'd normally do before a workshop. I spent nearly all the autumn on research. I don't think I could have possibly written a play after the two weeks.' ('Common Imagination', 12.)
39. Discussed by the panel in 'Reputations: Caryl Churchill', *Theatre Voice* and exemplified through taking Pinter's absolute insistence on what a line means as a point of contrast to Churchill's approach.
40. Churchill, 'A Fair Cop', 9.
41. Bassett, 'Reputations: Caryl Churchill', *Theatre Voice*.
42. See note 2.
43. Churchill, 'Not Ordinary, Not Safe', 445.
44. Churchill, 'Not Ordinary, Not Safe', 450.
45. Ashford had directed *Traps* for the Royal Court Theatre Upstairs, 1977.
46. Rob La Frenais, 'Midday Sun', *Performance*, June/July 1984, p. 7. This review is critical of the visual elements of the piece, but singles out Churchill's text as the high point of the production.
47. See Churchill's comments in Ritchie, *The Joint Stock Book*, pp. 119–20.
48. Churchill, 'The Common Imagination', 8.
49. This was along with Richard Alston and Siobhan Davies.
50. For comments and further details on these points see Spink in 'Siobhan Davies, Lloyd Newson and Ian Spink', video (N.R.C.D., University of Surrey, 1989). Full discussion and analysis of Spink's 'text and dance' work with Churchill can be found in Chapter 5 (Libby Worth).
51. Fisher, 'Reputations: Caryl Churchill', *Theatre Voice*.
52. Ritchie, *The Joint Stock Book*, p. 30.
53. This and further explanations are offered by Spink in 'Siobhan Davies, Lloyd Newson and Ian Spink'. Full discussion of *Fugue* can be found in Worth, Chapter 5.

54. The departures of directors Richard Alston and Siobhan Davies left Spink as sole artistic director of Second Stride in 1988, at which point McDonald became an associate director.
55. Spink, 'Collaborations', Interview with Richard Cave, in *Border Tensions: Dance and Discourse: Proceedings of the Fifth Study of Dance Conference* (Department of Dance Studies: University of Surrey, 1995), pp. 293–303, p. 301.
56. See individual introductions by Churchill, Gough, Spink and McDonald in *Lives of the Great Poisoners: A Production Dossier* (London: Methuen, 1993).
57. For example Spink explains, 'It proved quite a difficult process keeping people working strictly within their own original territory. Feedback I subsequently got from some of the dancers suggested that they felt unhappy about being restricted and not being able to use their voices either to sing or express their characters by using text' ('Collaborations', p. 298).
58. Spink, 'Collaborations', p. 299.
59. Richard Cave, 'Ian Spink: Texts and Contexts', *Contemporary Theatre Review*, 14.3 (2004), 63–72, 67.
60. Cave, 'Ian Spink: Texts and Contexts', 69.
61. Spink, 'Collaborations' p. 296. On the other hand, Spink regrets that for the performers this meant that they were working off the writers' responses to the improvisations, rather than it being possible 'to translate more of the improvisatory work directly into the final piece' (p. 296).
62. Spink, 'Collaborations', p. 297.
63. *Ibid.*, p. 299.
64. Churchill, Interview on *The Skriker*, *Late Theatre*, BBC2, January 1994.
65. Spink, 'Collaborations', p. 299.
66. Churchill, Interview on *The Skriker*, *Late Theatre*.
67. Gough, 'Eight Rooms', in *Churchill: Plays Four* (London: Nick Hern Books, 2008), p. 4.
68. Churchill quoted in Armitstead, 'Tale of the Unexpected', 4.
69. Churchill, 'Interview on *The Skriker*', *Late Theatre*.
70. Churchill quoted in Armitstead 'Tale of the Unexpected', 5.
71. See Stafford-Clark, *Taking Stock*, pp. 175–6.
72. Stafford-Clark, *Taking Stock*, p. 108.
73. For a full discussion of Daldry's directing see Wendy Lesser, 'Anatomy of a Rehearsal', in *A Director Calls: Stephen Daldry and the Theatre* (London: Faber & Faber, 1997), pp. 141–80.
74. Lesser, *A Director Calls*, p. 220.
75. Stafford-Clark, *Taking Stock*, p. 178.
76. It is important to note, however, that Churchill's departure into a more elliptical style of writing comes much earlier. Graham Cowley (erstwhile general manager for both Joint Stock and the Royal Court), for example, signals *Icecream* in 1989 as a departure into the elliptical which, moreover, he recalls Stafford-Clark having to wrestle with in rehearsals; being baffled by the script and worried about whether audiences would 'get' the play (Cowley, 'Reputations: Caryl Churchill', *Theatre Voice*).
77. Stafford-Clark, *Taking Stock*, p. 178.
78. Bassett, 'Reputations: Caryl Churchill', *Theatre Voice*.
79. Discussed by Fisher and Bassett in 'Reputations: Caryl Churchill', *Theatre Voice*.

80. Note this rehearsal description from Nina Raine, 'Whose Line is it Anyway?', *Guardian*, (9 December 2006), http://arts.guardian.co.uk/features/story/0,,1967664,00.html:

> On Caryl Churchill's *Far Away*, I learned from Stephen Daldry how physical action can unlock a scene. One of Daldry's great talents is props. The final scene took us to an unspecified war zone. Daldry gave Linda Bassett a series of different props for the same scene. Each one illuminated a different section of the text. Cleaning a gun, she became ruthless and purposeful. When she sorted manically through piles of military documents, it was a graphic illustration of her dilemma – who was on which side in this war? A hip-flask of whisky transformed a passage about allies into maudlin nostalgia. I saw how many stories can be told around the text.

81. James Macdonald in Philip Roberts, *About Churchill: The Playwright and the Work* (London: Faber & Faber, 2008), p. 270.
82. *Ibid.*
83. Stafford-Clark records, for example, that there was fierce competition over *Far Away*, that he himself, Daldry, Rickson and Mitchell, who apparently said she 'would kill to direct it', all wanted this play; *Taking Stock*, p. 178.
84. Churchill, 'Not Ordinary, Not Safe', 451.

10

DAN REBELLATO

On Churchill's influences

In an article published to coincide with Caryl Churchill's seventieth birthday, playwright Mark Ravenhill remarked, 'of all the major forces in British playwriting, I can think of no one else who is regarded with such affection and respect by her peers'.[1] A decade earlier, in an article attempting to discover 'The Playwrights' Playwright', four of the nine writers surveyed chose Churchill as the playwright who most inspired them.[2] Theatre critic David Benedict places her only behind Harold Pinter and David Hare in the public's affections, while Benedict Nightingale considers her 'the most gloriously original, preposterously gifted of all British dramatists'.[3] In 1999, novelist Margaret Forster chose *Top Girls* as her 'play of the millennium' and more recently actress Sophie Okonedo when asked which living person she most admired chose Caryl Churchill.[4]

A sign of the esteem in which she is held may be found in the fact that the Royal Court Theatre, with which she has been associated since 1972, held not one but two seasons of her work in the 2000s. In 2002, to accompany *A Number* in the main house, *Identical Twins, Not Not Not Not Not Enough Oxygen*, and *This is a Chair* were performed in the Theatre Upstairs, alongside readings of *Seagulls, Three More Sleepless Nights, Moving Clocks Go Slow* and *Owners*. In 2008, to mark her seventieth birthday, ten playwrights directed staged readings of ten of her plays: *Owners, Light Shining in Buckinghamshire, Vinegar Tom, Top Girls, Three More Sleepless Nights, Ice Cream, The Skriker, Blue Heart, Far Away* and *A Number*.

Max Stafford-Clark has remarked somewhat sardonically that 'for a lot of people in the theatre, she is Saint Caryl. Drama students gasp at being in the same room as her, near enough to touch the hem of her garment.'[5] Indeed, Caryl Churchill is so widely admired that the risk is to uncritically canonize her plays, to treat her as disconnected from the theatre culture around her.

In this chapter, I want to situate Churchill in the broader historical context of British playwriting, tracing the influences *on* her work and the influence *of* her work. Starting from a consideration of Churchill's standing among contemporary playwrights, actors and directors, I want to argue that there are apparent contradictions in the ways she is discussed and admired but that paying close attention to the way her work has developed, the ambiguity and polyvalence of her work can be better understood, and with it her precise influence on contemporary playwriting.

Churchill's reputation

In preparation for this essay, I contacted a large number of playwrights for their opinion of Caryl Churchill and was overwhelmed by responses, unanimously in praise, often in awe of Churchill's work. Taken together with various tributes published elsewhere, they offer a map of the esteem in which Churchill is currently held by her peers.

The first aspect of her work that is widely admired is her refusal to repeat herself. Dennis Kelly notes the pressure on writers to find a form and a voice and to endlessly reproduce oneself: 'Caryl Churchill seemed to represent the exact opposite, someone who reinvented herself at will and looked at what theatre could be and what she wanted it to be.'[6] For Anthony Neilson, Churchill inspires 'by never ceasing to enquire, to confound, to keep challenging herself and her medium. She has the skills that only age can bring but she's never lost the bravery of youth.'[7]

Just as frequently commented on is Churchill's continual engagement with form, finding new structures and shapes to address her concerns. What her example taught David Eldridge was 'that an expressive, thoughtful exploration of form is always as meaningful as the content it shapes'.[8] April de Angelis notes that in the 1980s when it was still common to hear the view that women playwrights were unable to master the structuring of plays, 'you could point to plays like *Cloud Nine* and *Top Girls* and say, "Rubbish, Caryl Churchill's doing the most incredible things with structure."'[9]

The emphasis on form often goes hand-in-hand with applause for Churchill's determination not to be drawn into turning theatre into reportage. In Martin Crimp's words, 'she always dares to imagine. She is never guilty of what Beckett once called "that dismal conservatism of form and fatal journalism of content" that is still frequently found masquerading as theatre.'[10] Or as Nick Dear trenchantly put it 'the great thing about Caryl Churchill is that there was never of this "write what you know" nonsense'.[11] Colin Teevan compares her favourably with 'all those humourless social realists from the Royal Court [...]: worthy, whingy, not very exciting either formally or politically'.[12] Every play finds a new structure, many of which, as Moira Buffini writes, are 'like sculptures' in their freestanding beauty.[13] Sarah Daniels once suggested that because of her ability to strike out and create fully workable non-naturalistic forms Caryl Churchill is to the contemporary theatre what Picasso was to modern art.[14]

At the same time, many people admire Churchill's ability to address herself to contemporary political and social issues. Daniel Craig notes that 'With *A Number*, cloning was a subject that deeply affected her, it just came gushing out of her [...] It's not that she's looking to discover the next new thing to write about, it's that she fully understands what's already happening.'[15] Similar prescience is identified by Nicholas Wright who has said that 'Caryl's plays say things that we're all thinking but haven't yet expressed.'[16]

Several writers comment on her elegant minimalism, the pleasurable engagement she demands of her audiences. Lucy Prebble, writing about *Icecream* (1989), considers the play 'flamboyantly courageous in what it leaves out'.[17] Both Moira Buffini and Joe Penhall note the way her dialogue allows audiences to 'listen for the first time to how people really speak'.[18] And almost everyone marvels that she can do all of these things and write so comically too.

Churchill is also admired because, quietly, she has worked in support of many other writers. From the moment she was announced as resident dramatist at the Royal Court in 1975, she declared an interest in working with the Young People's Theatre Scheme and has continued, through all the scheme's various incarnations, to do so.[19] She made important interventions in defence of embattled plays like Sarah Kane's *Blasted* (1995) and Gurpreet Kaur Bhatti's *Bezhti* (2004),[20] and gave her name to campaigns against the Thatcherite subsidy cuts and in favour of subsidized theatres programming more new plays.[21]

Admiration for Churchill's work spans the generations. She is admired equally by writers like David Hare and Nicholas Wright whose careers began in the 1970s, Sarah Daniels and Martin Crimp whose work emerged in the 1980s, Mark Ravenhill and Anthony Neilson from the 1990s, and a new generation of twenty-first-century writers like Simon Stephens, Lucy Prebble and Polly Stenham. Her appeal also crosses the Atlantic. Sam Shepard regards *A Number* (2002) as the greatest play since Beckett's *Endgame* (1957).[22] Tony Kushner was reputedly embarrassed when Churchill went to see *Angels in America* (1991) because he considered himself so deeply in her dramaturgical debt.[23] Wallace Shawn, whose play *Our Late Night* (1975) Churchill directed in the late 1990s, declared himself with tongue in cheek a member of the cult of Churchill: 'we fans have a special handshake'.[24]

The appreciation for Churchill's work is not only remarkable for its warmth, then, but also for its breadth. After all, David Hare and Martin Crimp are in many respects at opposite ends of contemporary British playwriting, one a proponent of theatre as a forum for topical debate, the other a cryptic experimenter with language and form. She is admired by proponents of collaborative and devised theatre and by advocates of the single-authored play. While Churchill is still perhaps best-known for the socialist–feminist plays of the 1970s and early 1980s, she is, as we have seen, equally admired for the intensity of her formal experimentation as for the strength of her political commitments.

This is unusual. British theatre has tended to divide between its social realist and formally experimental traditions. I have argued elsewhere that the battle lines were drawn in the late 1950s, when European theatre was expelled from the Royal Court.[25] European theatre has often functioned as a metonym for theatrical experiment and writers and theatre companies have tended to side with what is inaccurately seen as a native English tradition of social realism or a European tradition of formal experiment. On one side is the tradition of Osborne, Wesker, Hare, Edgar and verbatim theatre; on the other is Pinter, Rudkin, Barker, Crimp, Kane and performance art. These lines are by no means impermeable and several writers – Mark Ravenhill, for example – pass between the camps for different projects. The Royal Court has tended to slip between both traditions. Churchill, unusually, seems to be widely claimed for both.

Some theatremakers have located this apparent paradox within her work. Director Richard Eyre detects a 'very fierce, analytical intelligence' and also 'a sense of genuine mystery about human behaviour'.[26] Peter Brook notes that '*la vie intime*' coexists with 'universal chaos' in her work.[27] Benedict Nightingale finds a paradox in her ability to deal with 'the urgent topics of the day' and 'the most basic and timeless of issues' in the same play.[28] Mark Ravenhill is also struck that the plays 'perfectly expressed the anxieties and possibilities of the moment in which they were first performed, and yet have managed to seem new in subsequent revivals'.[29]

I will argue in this essay that attending to the way in which Churchill has situated herself in relation to other theatrical traditions tells us a great deal about her own identity as a writer and the reason she has managed to inspire four decades of playwrights across the world.

Influences on Churchill

Most playwrights of any importance develop a distinctive style of their own, but often they do so after an initial period in which they bear the traces of other writers whom they admire. (One might think of Ayckbourn, Orton or Bond's early indebtedness to Pinter.) Churchill is unusual in the relative lack of clear influence in her writing. She has very occasionally acknowledged a direct debt: she re-read Orton before writing *Owners* (1972)[30] and, for inspiration on weaving multiple stories together, listened to Bob Dylan's 'Lily, Rosemary, and the Jack of Hearts' when writing *Light Shining in Buckinghamshire* (1976).[31] In writing *The After-Dinner Joke* (1978), she allied herself with the kind of television represented by *Monty Python's Flying Circus*.[32] She has credited work by Siobhan Davies, Trisha Brown, Pina Bausch and Second Stride for inspiring her explorations in dance theatre in the 1980s and 1990s while performance art companies The People Show, IOU, Welfare State, and Hesitate and Demonstrate contributed to experiments with form and style through the 1980s.[33] The working practices of Joint Stock involved the productive doubling up of parts that became an important theatrical feature of *Light Shining...*, *Cloud Nine* and *Top Girls* and it is hard to imagine that British alternative theatre's mid-1970s interest in Brecht had no impact on the use of song in *Vinegar Tom* (1976).

Elsewhere we are forced back on guesswork and association. In her early plays of the 1960s, I detect a faint resemblance to the British absurdists like N. F. Simpson, James Saunders and David Campton. Her radio play *You've No Need to Be Frightened* (1961) is centred on a couple and a silent guest and so in outline resembles Pinter's radio play *A Slight Ache* (1959).[34] Meanwhile, *Easy Death* (1962), with its climactic scene in the town square where demagogic orators mix rough poetry with Biblical resonances, may have John Arden's *Serjeant Musgrave's Dance* (1959) lurking behind it. Much later, in its deliberately broken structure and its move from the domestic to the global, *Far Away* perhaps owes a small debt to Sarah Kane's *Blasted*.

A stronger connection between Churchill and her theatrical contemporaries is visible towards the end of the decade. The title alone of her unperformed stage play *The Marriage of Toby's Idea of Angela and Toby's Idea of Angela's Idea of Toby* (written in 1968) has an affinity with similarly sprawling titles coming out of the new theatrical counter-culture, such as *K. D. Dufford Hears K. D. Dufford Ask K. D. Dufford How K. D. Dufford'll Make K. D. Dufford* (1969) by David Halliwell or Naftali Yavin's *Precious Moments From the Family Album to Provide You with Comfort in the Long Years to Come* (1967). In its collision of different styles and theatrical devices it has some connections with similar experiments found in the work of the People Show or the early plays of Howard Brenton, where a literary verbal intensity is mixed with scabrous popular energy in a dizzying succession of theatrical forms.

Her thematic concerns were also beginning to overlap with those of the counter-culture in one important respect. In plays like *The Marriage of Toby's Idea...*, *Lovesick* (1967), *The Hospital at the Time of the Revolution* (written 1972), and *Schreber's Nervous Illness* (1972), Churchill was exploring the nature of madness and mental illness, in a way that coincided with the period's interest in anti-psychiatry. Associated with thinkers like R. D. Laing and David Cooper, the anti-psychiatry movement rejected the normative assumptions of the psychiatric profession and the brutality of some of its treatments, particularly electro-convulsive therapy and lobotomy. In these plays, Churchill characteristically counterpoints the authoritarian certainty of psychiatrists – like Hodge in *Lovesick* and Dr Weber in *Schreber's Nervous Illness* – with the fluid, imaginative riches experienced by their patients. In *The Hospital at the Time of the Revolution*, the argument about psychiatry is widened to encompass the mental mind-set of the colonial relationship, in a way that prefigures some aspects of *Cloud Nine* (see Luckhurst's discussion in Chapter 4). The kind of institutional critique embodied in anti-psychiatry is extended in *Softcops* (1984), inspired by Churchill's reading of Michel Foucault's *Discipline and Punish*.

Churchill once declared that what she writes about is 'power, powerlessness, exploitation, people's longings, obsessions, dreams'.[35] The terms at either end of that list represent the opposed forces brought together in many of her plays: the authoritarian, rational, repressive form of power and the playful, non-rational, irruptive force of dreaming. It is worth emphasizing the significance of dreaming for Churchill, because I want to suggest that this mode of thought has been the one continuous thread guiding us right through her writing life. In its turn, it will, I believe, clarify why her work has been so important to so many writers.

In many of Churchill's plays, characters awake from nightmares. 'I woke in the night and the room was suddenly lit up', recalls the wife in *You've No Need to be Frightened*, 'and I reached out to him and I said, John are you there? And he said of course I'm here. You're not frightened are you? And I said, yes, I am frightened.'[36] Roz in *Abortive* (1971) declares that 'I dream of something violent every night [...] I do find I'm afraid to go to sleep. Just as I am going off I get that feeling like in a nightmare but with no content. I'm frightened something is going to happen.'[37] In the nightmarish *Not Not Not Not Enough Oxygen* (1971), Vivian and Mick admit to feeling 'frightened'.[38] Dawn in bed in *Three More Sleepless Nights* twice declares herself to be frightened.[39] *Top Girls* ends as *Far Away* (2000) begins: with frightened girls coming downstairs in the night having, perhaps, had nightmares.[40] In each case, the dream or the affect of fear suggests a non-rational intuition of something terrible to come.

More loosely but still, I think identifiably, we can find scenes and moments in her plays that seem to operate with a kind of dream-logic: characters superimposed on one another in *Cloud Nine* and *A Number*, impossible encounters in *Top Girls*, figures of fairytale and nightmare walking the earth in the last scene of *Fen* (1983) and through the whole of *The Skriker* (1994), the chaotic iterations of *Traps* (1977) and *Heart's Desire* (1997), all of them suggest oneiric fluidity.

The same period that displayed the emergence of this concern with psychiatry and madness is also the era that sees the emergence of Churchill's distinctive style, a style that remains more or less recognizable across the range of her subsequent plays. Particularly in *Identical Twins* (1968), the dialogue is newly taut and exact, the formal experimentation clearer and more spare than before. The precision and simplicity in the language stylistically links the late 1960s to the early 2000s: compare Teddy's narration in *Identical Twins* with Joan's speech in *Far Away*:

> Clive takes more pills. This is one of those stupid things you regret later. I go on watching. Then I get up without a word and go straight out for a walk, the night is quite mild as the day has been and I feel better for some fresh air.[41]

> I stood on the bank a long time. But I knew it was my only way of getting here so at last I put one foot in the river. It was very cold but so far that was all. When you've just stepped in you can't tell what's going to happen. The water laps round your ankles in any case.[42]

In both cases, this same tone comes through: simple, modest, declarative sentences, embodied in active-voice constructions and unflashy vocabulary choices. It is a style that is both plain and mysterious, pared down but multiplying questions.

The moment when writers find their own style and begin to learn how to inhabit and control it is, on a certain level, a moment of withdrawal from their peers, a process, one might say, of individualization. This would seem to follow from Churchill's ongoing fascination with certain private mental experiences, like dreams. The simultaneity of her arrival at a distinctive style and the emergence of a theme of madness might encourage one to speculate that Churchill's inhabitation of a style was for her a kind of release into a private creative madness; or at least, an inward exploration that set her apart from the world and political engagement. However, it is important to understand that the anti-psychiatry model sees madness not as delusion but an alternative mode of apprehending the world, one that confronts and contests dominant views. For the anti-psychiatrists, like Laing and Reich, the repression of the 'insane' was intimately connected with maintaining the oppressive logic of capitalism and patriarchy. Madness was, in a sense, an oppositional mode of thought that threatened the oppressive distributions of sexual and economic power. Churchill's stylistic maturity is bound up with a particular fascination with how the purely private – dreams, madness – might also be a vision of society.

The workshop phase

Churchill's emergence as a playwright was through the socialist–feminist plays of the mid-1970s, mostly through collaborative workshops organized by political theatre groups, but it is important to note that the development of her distinctive style pre-dates that 'workshop' phase. It is tempting to think that in the mid-1970s Churchill was turning away from the non-rational and from the individualism of the solo playwright in favour of the collectivism of political engagement and of collaborative creation. Instead I want to argue that the workshop phase of her work was in fact an extension of her explorations of creative madness.

This repeated engagement with dreams and the interest in anti-psychiatry seems to have unlocked in Churchill a personal style and attitude to her own writing. This developed as a motif in the early plays, before emerging as a coherent thematic concern in the plays of the late 1960s and early 1970s. It would now develop into a kind of collaborative methodology in her work with the Young People's Theatre Scheme. Churchill's plan to work with the Scheme, to which I have already referred, came to fruition in April 1975 with the project *Strange Days*, a play co-written with the Scheme's head, Joan Mills.

This was the first experience Churchill had of developing a play through a workshop. A year before the more famous projects with Joint Stock and Monstrous Regiment that produced *Light Shining...* and *Vinegar Tom*, this workshop was with nine- and ten-year-olds in a London junior school. Joan Mills' account of the workshops reveals that initial explorations with the children did not yield very much material: 'at first it seemed the children were not interested in anything but television'.[43] The breakthrough came, however, with a workshop session where Mills and Churchill asked the children to discuss what *frightened* them: 'the room was full of stories, monsters, people you couldn't trust, bullying, overbearing authority figures, the supernatural'.[44] It is striking from this distance to note that the workshop came alive when the children were engaged in the very same intense exploration of affect – fear – that had been a running motif throughout Churchill's work up to that point. The scenes that have been published from the final script show a family repeatedly having their tea together; the ordinariness of the scenario is offset by the repetition and small changes that give each scene a skewed and uncanny quality. It prefigures the repeated family dinner scene in *This is a Chair* (1997) and the endlessly restarting domestic drama of *Heart's Desire*.

The following year, as Churchill began workshops with the actors of Joint Stock and Monstrous Regiment, it is striking to observe the language of

Churchill's own account of these workshops. 'I'd never seen an exercise or improvisation before and was as thrilled as a child at a pantomime', she writes.[45] She remembers emerging from her first meeting with Monstrous Regiment 'exhilarated'.[46] Concluding her thoughts on the first workshop with Joint Stock, she remarks, 'This is a slight account of a great deal, and one thing it can't show enough is my intense pleasure in it all.'[47] Once again, what is evident is less the cool rationality of collective political analysis than the intensity of the affect: an almost childlike excitement at the ideas given public form by the exercises.

Churchill's enthusiasm for involvement in workshops and rehearsals is well-known. 'She was there all through the rehearsal process', said Daniel Craig, of the premiere of *A Number*, 'and she loves being there, in the thick of it, trying to make sense of it all.'[48] Gillian Hanna and Mary McCusker of Monstrous Regiment describe working with her as particularly fruitful and sympathetic.[49] Max Stafford-Clark, who has directed the premieres of several of her plays, remembered: 'Working collaboratively is often quite difficult, but with Caryl it was easy. As a socialist liberal feminist humanist she's absolutely committed to collaboration. She'd always be the first person who'd say: "You could cut those five lines. You don't really need those." And I'd think: "Yes, I'd have realised that three days hence."'[50]

Stafford-Clark is no doubt right to say that Churchill's commitment to collaboration was reinforced by her socialist and feminist politics and Elaine Aston, in Chapter 9 in this volume, offers a detailed account of the connection between political principle and theatrical practice. However, it is easy to misrepresent Churchill's attitude to workshops. She has never been an advocate of collective creation of the Ariane Mnouchkine type, where every decision is made collectively. 'There's a misconception sometimes', she has said, 'that the actual writing process becomes collaborative.'[51] To Lynne Truss, she explained:

> I do have a precise verbal sense that means that, though in some ways I'll be extremely open in rehearsal – if someone says can we move this speech to the end, I'll say oh fine let's try moving the speech to the end and see what happens, or someone will say oh look we could cut from here to here and I say oh great it'll still make sense, let's cut, and feel very free – other times I will find myself being incredibly pernickity and saying, 'Look, you're saying "Well", and there isn't one', or 'you've got a word wrong'. For me it actually throws out the whole rhythm and point of the line. At that point I can be very uncompromising.[52]

Churchill has always engaged in workshops but the writing is generally done away from rehearsal and she has always maintained ultimate responsibility for the text.

From the mid-1970s onwards, several plays by Churchill had a workshop phase during their period of composition: after *Strange Days, Vinegar Tom* and *Light Shining...*, there were workshops for *Cloud Nine*, *Fen*, and *Serious Money* (1987), all with director Max Stafford-Clark. There were also workshop processes involved in the production of her texts for the performance art and dance pieces, *Midday Sun* (1984) and *A Mouthful of Birds* (1986). After *Serious Money*, however, Churchill withdrew from the workshop model. There were discussions that led to the text of *Lives of the Great Poisoners* (1991) and she attended some of the exploratory workshops run by Katie Mitchell in preparing for *A Dream Play* (2005), but otherwise she returned to writing alone.

The move away from workshops also marked a disengagement from her fruitful working partnership with Max Stafford-Clark. They would work together again on *Blue Heart* (1997) but not otherwise. There are no doubt several reasons why: one must be Stafford-Clark's relative lack of response to *The Skriker* which was an important play for Churchill;[53] second, the workshop process with which Stafford-Clark is closely associated requires a certain rational testing of ideas which means that delicate writerly intuitions find it hard to survive. Also, Stafford-Clark's rehearsal process of 'actioning' a text – asking the actor to decide upon and speak the action that is being undertaken with each line – demands that ambiguities are resolved and interrupts the rhythm of the language.[54] In many respects, one can see the workshop method as becoming somewhat inimical to Churchill's continuing interest in forms of thought that escape rationality: if workshops are increasingly characterized by rationality and the disambiguation of the text it is unsurprising to see her move away from that process, the better to explore her creativity alone.

Further support for the idea that Churchill was keen to withdraw from the public nature of the workshop process is given in the publication of her collection of one-act plays, *Shorts*, in 1990. Of particular interest is the play *Seagulls*, in which a woman named Valery, with telekinetic powers, is invited to Harvard so that her abilities can be tested under laboratory conditions. A rather shy person, she is rather overwhelmed by the public attention and then finds, when asked to perform her power in front of a fan, that she can no longer do it. Churchill wrote the play in 1978 but did not publish it for twelve years, remarking that in the late 1970s it 'felt too much as if it was about not being able to write for me to want it done at the time'.[55] Whether the play really does express her anxiety about writing – and writing *in public* which is perhaps what the workshop process signifies – her publication of the play in 1990 is of a piece with her withdrawal from workshop collaboration and her near-simultaneous decision to turn down almost all requests for interviews and other public appearances.

Churchill's introduction to workshops was shot through with emotional intensity and an exploration of unconscious materials. Her exit from workshops is wreathed in the same concerns. One can sense a palpable relief in 1989, when Churchill wrote *Icecream* (and its shorter companion piece *Hot Fudge*) without any workshop period, explaining to an interviewer that when writing alone 'more subconscious things can come in and start connecting up. Your research just comes from your life and what you're thinking about.'[56] Her next play, written in three weeks, was a response to the Romanian revolution that overthrew the Ceauşescus but Churchill is just as keen to explore the subjective experience of a revolution in minds overlaid with almost half a century of suspicion and fear; its dramatis personae includes characters from dreams and fantasies – an angel, a talking dog, a vampire – and tellingly the title of the play is *Mad Forest* (1990).

I argued that Churchill did not enter her workshop phase to turn away from her interest in madness, dreams and the non-rational. In emerging from her workshop phase, she did not turn her back on public concerns. However, Churchill's work since 1990 has shown greater trust in her own private image repertoire and mythology to address matters of political and topical significance. The roots of this lie in her early intuition that the private creative act was not trapped in a prison of solipsism but expressed a vision of the world and one that was oppositional to dominant ideological views of that world. It is for this reason that Churchill is able to combine opposing traditions in British theatre writing – both realist and imaginative, representational and metaphorical – and goes a long way to explaining the breadth of her appeal.

Churchill's influence

Churchill's influence on British theatre is pervasive and manifold. The simplest example of her effect is in the typographic device of a forward slash to indicate a point of overlap in dialogue; first introduced in *Three More Sleepless Nights* (1980) and used to particular effect in *Top Girls* (1982), it has become standard and ubiquitous – though Churchill herself no longer uses it. Some of her particular dramaturgical forms have rippled out into other plays: the huge temporal jump between the two halves of *Cloud Nine* (1979), almost unprecedented in British theatre, has since been seen in plays as diverse as Stoppard's *Arcadia* (1993), Shelagh Stevenson's *An Experiment with an Air Pump* (1998) and Mark Ravenhill's *Mother Clap's Molly House* (2001). The first scene of *Top Girls* finds a strong echo in the opening of Sarah Daniels' *Beside Herself* (1990), in which four Biblical women – Delilah, Jezebel, Lot's Wife and Eve – are brought together. Daniels' *Byrthrite* (1988) is set in the seventeenth century, concerns itself with the demonization of women as witches, intersperses its historical scenes with contemporary satirical songs about patriarchy and owes an evident debt to *Vinegar Tom.*

More broadly but perhaps even more significantly, Churchill's influence has been in being the woman playwright who was, in the words of April de Angelis, 'taken seriously by the establishment and so has "broken through"'.[57] Gone are the days when a male journalist could begin a profile of the playwright by noting that 'with her short grizzled curls, high cheekbones and gracious manners [she would] be the first at a dance I would want as a partner'.[58] Churchill has been a formidable role-model for many other women playwrights, but she is no longer defined and confined by her gender. Not for nothing did the director – and feminist – Annie Castledine insist: 'Let's be clear that when we say [she is] great, we don't just mean a great woman playwright but a great playwright. Full stop.'[59]

In the 1990s, Churchill's influence has been most far-reaching and profound in her renegotiation of what it means to write a political play. During her workshop phase, plays like *Vinegar Tom, Cloud Nine* and *Serious Money* included more or less explicit political comment. This should not be exaggerated, since all three plays contain ambiguities and formal devices that complicate the idea that they are in any sense simple polemics. Yet the decision not to use workshops coincides with a withdrawal from explicit commentary, even as the plays continue to address public concerns. *Far Away* addresses itself to global conflict, *A Number* to human cloning, *Drunk Enough to Say I Love You?* to US foreign policy, and *Seven Jewish Children* (2009) to the history of Israel. In each case, however, Churchill's positions are ambiguous, because the structures of the plays ask questions that they do not themselves answer: the relation between the three parts of *Far Away*, for example, or why the relationship of the US with the rest of the world should be expressed through a homosexual relationship in *Drunk Enough*... (This is not to say that critics did not criticize some of these plays for their one-sided polemics, though in each case such critics tended to ignore the plays' formal devices.)[60]

Churchill's reluctance to impose upon the meanings of her plays is not new. After writing *Owners* and *Objections to Sex and Violence* (1975), she felt she was guilty of 'mocking my characters in the way they talked and defining them too tightly, and I wanted to give them more rope, take them more seriously'; she also regretted the title of the latter play, feeling that it tied it to political debates that were not in fact at its heart.[61] The lack of commentary reflects itself both in her avoidance of guiding the audience to particular interpretations of the work and in her reluctance to supply meta-textual commentary in the form of articles and interviews about her own work.

This distinguishes her from her contemporaries, like Howard Barker, David Hare, Howard Brenton and David Edgar, all of whom have published volumes of their writings on theatre. One would be hard put to fill a pamphlet with Churchill's comments on her own work.

Within the plays themselves, this creates a wholly recognizable style that has been widely influential among younger writers. *Far Away*, in particular, has a claim to being the most influential play of the 2000s. Anthony Neilson comments that 'it's not one of her best-known works but I think it had a great impact on the writing community. It was a really modern piece of theatre, the work of someone who loves and understands the medium and wants to see it progress.'[62] Simon Stephens concurs:

> While I was teaching at the Young Writers Programme [at the Royal Court] I taught a session on dramatic structure using *Far Away*. I always used it and I taught the course maybe twenty times. So its a play I've read more than any other. It never failed to astonish me because, with the juxtaposition of the recognizable and the absurd and the tension between a three act play and a structural explosion, she cut right into the quick of the culture at the turn of the millennium. In the final act she predicted the absurdism of the War on Terror. I think it is the defining play of the last ten years.[63]

Polly Stenham, one of the Royal Court's discoveries of 2007, describes it as one of her favourite plays: 'mad and perfect and tiny and nasty and brilliant'.[64]

The play performs a remarkable balancing act between clarity and obscurity, the specific and the general. The three acts each have somewhat recognizable forms: a detective story, a romance, a war story. Yet the relation between the two stories, and the events that must have taken place between the acts, are left unclear. The dialogue has a kind of children's book simplicity to it ('You've found out something secret. You know that don't you?'),[65] yet we never quite know what has happened outside the rooms that the characters inhabit. Churchill's refusal to impose her ideas and meanings on the scenes extends even to the level of punctuation, which steadfastly refuses to insist on the intonation and force of the lines: 'I've worked in abattoirs stunning pigs and musicians and by the end of the day your back aches and all you can see when you shut your eyes is people hanging upside down by their feet.'[66]

Many of these stylistic motifs have been evident in her work since the late 1960s, though it is only in the 1990s that they become so prominent. One can see it reflected, transformed according to each writer's own style, in such plays as Martin Crimp's *Attempts on Her Life* (1997), Sarah Kane's *Crave* (1998), Alexandra Wood's *The Eleventh Capital* (2007), and Mark Ravenhill's *Shoot/Get Treasure/Repeat* (2008).

For Churchill, this withdrawal from explicit commentary has its roots in personal taste and, I would suggest, political conviction. She has often remarked on her distaste for self-revelatory writing: 'I had a horror of that kind of semi-autobiographical novel writing, where people just spin fantasies about themselves. I wanted my writing to stand apart from whatever happened to me.'[67] She has expanded on that spatial metaphor, explaining:

> Somehow it felt to me that writing stories was like painting and writing plays like sculpture. A play stands there like an object, and you can walk round it and touch it. I wanted to write something that would stand away from me, and happen independently; and to create people that would exist in their own right. Writing plays, there's a certain distance and clarity. I liked being freed from the danger of a certain sort of introspection; I liked there being only dialogue and things actually happening.[68]

This is not to say that the plays are impersonal or objective, but that the form of playwriting imposes a gap between author and text that is productive of plural interpretations and gives room for the complexity of the plays to be felt.

But this is not merely distaste for political commentary. Indeed, Churchill seems far more prepared to engage in political interventions, through letters or public appearances, than in detailed commentary on her own work.[69] Indeed, it would be better to think that Churchill's shift away from political editorializing in the plays is in itself a political response to changing times. Max Stafford-Clark's astute response to *Far Away* was that 'she's developed her own response to a political agenda which she had discovered she cannot effectively address directly any more'.[70] Three years previously, *This is a Chair*, with its tiny domestic dramas and grand overwhelming scene titles, produced a kind of political sublime as the viewer's reason and sensibility struggled to coordinate one with the other; as such, it too reflected an exasperation with the ability of theatre directly to address political topics.

But far from being evidence of despair at the impossibility of political theatre, I would suggest it represents something much more affirmative: a valediction to one form of theatrical politics and an embrace of a politics rooted in the dynamics of theatricality itself. The kind of theatre, heavy with political commentary, armoured with analysis, is the kind of rationalist discourse to which her discovery of style in the late 1960s was opposed. Each phase of her career – the early radio plays, the first stage plays, the workshop plays, the dance theatre texts, the plays of the 1990s and beyond – has been motivated by this profound exploration of those forms of apprehension that escape from rationality. Like Adorno, Churchill sees in the totalizing rationality of advanced capitalism a form of oppression that rationalist political theatre only mimics and cannot fundamentally resist.

This is perhaps the explanation for the near-universal regard in which she is held by her peers. Her work shows a determination to insist on the value of the playwright and her or his particular creativity to offer a vision of the world that eludes and goes beyond power. Ironically, then, we are all dependent on Churchill because she is so independent. Churchill's work reminds us, in the words of the political slogan, that another world is possible, and continues to offer models for a political theatre of the twenty-first century.

NOTES

1. Mark Ravenhill, 'She Made Us Raise Our Game', *Guardian*, 3 September 2008, Arts Section, 23.
2. Caroline Egan, 'The Playwright's Playwright', *Guardian*, 21 September 1998, G2, 13. The writers were Ravenhill, Martin Crimp, Shelagh Stevenson and Phyllis Nagy.
3. David Benedict, 'The Mother of Reinvention', *Independent*, 19 April 1997, Arts Section, 4; Benedict Nightingale, 'Chairwoman of the Boards', *The Times*, 13 November 2006, Arts Section, 14.
4. 'Those Essential Items', *Observer*, 26 December 1999, 10; Rosanna Greenstreet, 'Q&A Sophie Okonedo', *Guardian*, 22 July 2006, 8.
5. Lisa O'Kelly, 'Top Girl', *Guardian*, 12 March 1991.
6. Dennis Kelly, email to the author, 26 October 2008.
7. Anthony Neilson, email to the author, 26 October 2008.
8. David Eldridge, email to the author, 26 October 2008.
9. Ravenhill, 'She Made Us', 23.
10. Egan, 'The Playwrights' Playwright', 13.
11. Nick Dear, email to the author, 25 October 2008.
12. Colin Teevan, email to the author, 28 October 2008.
13. Moira Buffini, email to the author, 29 October 2008.
14. Heidi Stephenson and Natasha Langridge, *Rage and Reason: Women Playwrights on Playwriting* (London: Methuen, 1997), p. 6. The comparison is endorsed by April de Angelis and David Eldridge in their emails to me.
15. Lucy Powell, 'Why She's Top Girl', *The Times*, 1 September 2008, Times2, 14–15.
16. Ravenhill, 'She Made Us', 23.
17. Mark Ravenhill, Joe Penhall, Lucy Prebble and April De Angelis, 'Life, Death and Estate Agents', *Guardian*, 16 June 2004.
18. Ravenhill, 'She Made Us', 23.
19. Nancy Mills, 'Courting Violence', *Guardian*, 2 January 1975; Powell 'Why She's Top Girl', 14.
20. 'A Bold Imagination for Action', Letter, *Guardian*, 25 January 1995, 19; 'We Must Defend Free Expression', Letter, *Guardian*, 23 December 2004, 21.
21. Andy Lavender, 'Theatre in Crisis: Conference Report, December 1988', *New Theatre Quarterly*, 5 (1989), 210–16.
22. Paul Taylor, 'One of a Kind', *Independent*, 16 November 2006, Extra, 11.
23. C. W. E. Bigsby, *Contemporary American Playwrights* (Cambridge: Cambridge University Press, 1999), p. 109.
24. Ravenhill 'She Made Us', 23.

25. Dan Rebellato, *1956 and All That: The Making of Modern British Drama* (London: Routledge, 1999), Chapter 5.
26. Lucy Powell, 'Why She's Top Girl', 14.
27. Taylor, 'One of a Kind', 11.
28. Nightingale, 'Chairwoman', 14
29. Ravenhill, 'She Made Us', 23.
30. Caryl Churchill, *Plays: One* (London: Methuen, 1985), p. 4.
31. Rob Ritchie (ed.), *The Joint Stock Book: The Making of a Theatre Collective* (London: Methuen, 1987), p. 20.
32. Caryl Churchill, *Shorts* (London: Nick Hern, 1990), Introduction.
33. Caryl Churchill, *Plays: Three* (London: Nick Hern, 1998), p. 184; Philip Roberts, *About Churchill: The Playwright and the Work* (London: Faber & Faber, 2008), p. 93.
34. Churchill saw a production of Pinter's play at university: Dan Rebellato *et al.*, 'In Memoriam: Harold Pinter (1930–2008)', *Contemporary Theatre Review*, 19.2 (May 2009), p. 247.
35. Nightingale, 'Chairwoman', 14.
36. Roberts, *About Churchill*, p. 9.
37. Churchill, *Shorts*, p. 36.
38. *Ibid.*, pp. 51, 52.
39. *Ibid.*, p. 264.
40. I am grateful to Elaine Aston for suggesting the dovetailing of these two plays.
41. Roberts, *About Churchill*, p. 27.
42. Caryl Churchill, *Plays: Four* (London: Nick Hern, 2008), p. 159.
43. Roberts, *About Churchill*, p. 166.
44. *Ibid.*, p. 167.
45. Ritchie, *The Joint Stock Book*, p. 119.
46. Churchill, *Plays: One*, p. 129.
47. Ritchie, *The Joint Stock Book*, p. 121.
48. Powell, 'Why She's Top Girl', 13.
49. Roberts, *About Churchill*, pp. 185–7.
50. *Ibid.*, p. 14.
51. Benedict, 'The Mother of Reinvention', 4.
52. Lynne Truss, 'A Fair Cop', *Plays & Players*, January 1983, p. 9.
53. Roberts, *About Churchill*, p. 247.
54. For further details of Stafford-Clark's 'actioning' method and partnership with Churchill, see Aston, Chapter 9.
55. Churchill, *Shorts*, Introduction.
56. Roberts, *About Churchill*, p. 115.
57. April de Angelis, email to the author, 29 October 2008.
58. John Barber, 'Feminist You'd Ask to Dance', *Daily Telegraph*, 21 February 1983.
59. Claire Armitstead, 'Tale of the Unexpected', *Guardian*, 12 January 1994, 5.
60. Dan Rebellato, 'The Personal is not Political: Caryl Churchill's *Drunk Enough to Say I Love You?*', *Western European Stages*, 19.1 (Winter 2007), 33–6. Churchill has regretted naming her characters Sam and Jack, since they were too amenable to 'decoding' as Uncle Sam and Union Jack, only the first of which was intentional, and Jack has since been renamed Guy (Churchill, *Plays: Four*, pp. ix–x).
61. Roberts, *About Churchill*, pp. 49–50.

62. Neilson, email to the author, 26 October 2008.
63. Stephens, email to the author, 27 October 2008.
64. Powell, 'Why She's Top Girl', 14.
65. Churchill, *Plays: Four*, p. 139.
66. *Ibid.*, p. 157.
67. Nancy Mills, 'Courting Violence'.
68. Janet Watts, 'Declaration of Independence', *Guardian*, 3 February 1977.
69. E.g. Caryl Churchill, 'Theatre, West Bank-Style', *Guardian*, 21 February 2001, p. 17 and her contribution to a panel at the Royal Court of scientists and theatre-makers debating the cultural impact of climate change in Spring 2006.
70. Roberts, *About Churchill*, p. 146.

SELECT BIBLIOGRAPHY

Collections of plays

Plays: One – Owners, Traps, Vinegar Tom, Light Shining in Buckinghamshire, Cloud Nine. London: Methuen, 1985.

Plays: Two – Softcops, Top Girls, Fen, Serious Money. London: Methuen, 1990.

Churchill Shorts: Short Plays by Caryl Churchill – Three More Sleepless Nights, Lovesick, The After-Dinner Joke, Abortive, Schreber's Nervous Illness, The Judge's Wife, The Hospital at the Time of the Revolution, Hot Fudge, Not Not Not Not Not Enough Oxygen, Seagulls. London: Nick Hern Books, 1990.

Plays: Three – Icecream, Mad Forest, Thyestes, The Skriker, Lives of the Great Poisoners, A Mouthful of Birds, with David Lan. London: Nick Hern Books, 1998.

Plays: Four – Hotel, This is a Chair, Blue Heart, Far Away, A Number, A Dream Play, Drunk Enough to Say I Love You?. London: Nick Hern Books, 2008.

Plays in other editions

The After-Dinner Joke and Three More Sleepless Nights. Cambridge Literature Series, Cambridge: Cambridge University Press, 1995.

The Ants. *New English Dramatists*, Vol. XII. Harmondsworth: Penguin, 1969, pp. 89–103.

Bliss. [O. Choinière] Translation. London: Nick Hern Books, 2008.

Blue Heart. London: Nick Hern Books, 1997.

Cloud Nine. London: Pluto Press, 1979. (Subsequent editions include Nick Hern Books, 1990; Samuel French, acting edition, 1989).

A Dream Play. [A. Strindberg] A new version. London: Nick Hern Books, 2005.

Drunk Enough to Say I Love You?. London: Nick Hern Books, 2006.

Far Away. London: Nick Hern Books, 2000.

Fen. London: Methuen, 1983.

Hotel. London: Nick Hern Books, 1997.

Icecream. London: Nick Hern Books, 1989.

Light Shining in Buckinghamshire. London: Nick Hern Books, 1996.

Lives of the Great Poisoners: A Production Dossier, with O. Gough and I. Spink. London: Methuen, 1993.

Mad Forest: A Play From Romania. London: Nick Hern Books, 1991.

A Mouthful of Birds. London: Methuen, 1986.

A Number. London: Nick Hern Books, 2002.

Objections to Sex and Violence. In M. Wandor, ed. *Plays By Women: Volume IV*. London: Methuen, 1985, 11–53.

Owners. London: Methuen, 1973.

Serious Money. London: Methuen, 1987. (Subsequent editions include Methuen Modern Plays, 1990; Samuel French, Acting Edition, 1990; Methuen Student Edition, 2002.)

Seven Jewish Children – A Play for Gaza. London: Nick Hern Books, 2009 (also downloadable free of charge from Casarotto Ramsay, Nick Hern Books and Royal Court Theatre websites.)

The Skriker. London: Nick Hern Books, 1994.

Softcops and *Fen*. London: Methuen 1986.

This is a Chair. London: Nick Hern Books, 1999.

Top Girls. London: Methuen, 1982. (Subsequent editions include Samuel French, Acting Edition, 1990; Methuen Student Edition, 1991; Methuen Modern Plays, 2001.)

Traps. London: Pluto Press, 1979. Subsequent edition, London: Nick Hern Books, 1989.

Vinegar Tom. In M. Wandor, ed., *Plays By Women: Volume One*. London: Methuen, 1982, 15–43.

Thyestes. [Seneca] Translation. London: Nick Hern Books, 1995.

Interviews

Armitstead, C. 'Tale of the Unexpected' [on *Skriker*]. *Guardian*, Arts Section (12 January 1994), 4–5.

Benedict, D. 'The Mother of Reinvention' [on revivals of *Light Shining* and *Cloud Nine*]. *Independent*, Arts Section (19 April 1997), 4.

Betsko, K. and R. Koenig, eds. 'Caryl Churchill' [on *Top Girls*, *Fen* and *Cloud Nine*]. *Interviews with Contemporary Women Playwrights*. New York: Beech Tree Books, 1987, 75–84.

Cousin, G. 'The Common Imagination and the Individual Voice' [on early writing years, *A Mouthful of Birds* and *Serious Money*]. *New Theatre Quarterly*, 13 (February 1988), 1–16.

Gooch, S. 'Caryl Churchill, Author of this Month's Playtext, Talks to P & P' [on *Owners*]. *Plays and Players* (January 1973), 40 and 1 of playtext insert of *Owners*.

Gussow, M. 'Caryl Churchill: a Genteel Playwright, Angry Voice' [overview of career to *Serious Money*]. *New York Times* (22 November 1987), 1, 26.

Hayman, R. 'Partners: Caryl Churchill and Max Stafford-Clark' [on working with Joint Stock]. *Sunday Times Magazine* (2 March 1980), 25–7.

Hiley, J. 'Revolution in Miniature' [on *Mad Forest*]. *The Times* (10 October 1990), 25.

Jackson, K. 'Incompatible Flavours' [on *Icecream*]. *Independent* (12 April 1989), 15.

Kay, J. 'Interview with Caryl Churchill' [on *Cloud Nine, Serious Money* and *Icecream*]. *New Statesman and Society* (21 April 1989), 41–2.

McFerran, A. 'The Theatre's (Somewhat)Angry Young Women' [interview with eight women playwrights, including Churchill, on the Women's Movement and women's playwriting]. *Time Out* (28 October–3 November 1977), 13–15.

Mackrell, J. 'Flights of Fancy' [on *Skriker*]. *Independent* (20 January 1994), 25.

Simon, J. 'Sex, Politics, and Other Play Things' [on *Top Girls, Fen* and *Cloud Nine*]. *Vogue* (August 1983), 126, 130.

Thurman, J. 'The Playwright Who Makes you Laugh about Orgasm, Racism, Class Struggle, Homophobia, Woman-Hating, the British Empire, and the Irrepressible Strangeness of the Human Heart' [on *Cloud Nine*]. *Ms.* (May 1982), 51–7.

Truss, L. 'A Fair Cop' [overview of career to *Softcops*]. *Plays and Players* (January 1984), 8–10.

Vidal, J. 'Legend of a Woman Possessed' [on *A Mouthful of Birds*]. *Guardian* (21 November 1986), 17.

Winer, L. 'Caryl Churchill, Ex-Ideologue, Trusts to Luck' [on Churchill's dislike of interviews and *Icecream*]. *New York Times* (29 April 1990).

Books

Aston, E. *Caryl Churchill* [1997]. Second edition, Plymouth: Northcote House, 2001.

Cousin, G. *Churchill the Playwright*. London: Methuen, 1989.

Fitzsimmons, L. *File on Churchill*. London: Methuen, 1989.

Kritzer, A. H. *The Plays of Caryl Churchill: Theatre of Empowerment*. Basingstoke: Macmillan, 1991.

Rabillard, S., ed. *Essays on Caryl Churchill: Contemporary Representations*. Winnipeg: Blizzard Publishing, 1998.

Randall, P. R., ed. *Caryl Churchill: A Casebook*. London: Garland, 1988.

Roberts, P. *About Churchill: The Playwright and the Work*. London: Faber & Faber, 2008.

Tycer, A. *Caryl Churchill's Top Girls*. London and New York: Continuum, 2008.

Essays and articles

Amich, C. 'Bringing the Global Home: The Commitment of Caryl Churchill's *The Skriker*'. *Modern Drama* 50:3 (Fall 2007), 394–413.

Amoko, A. 'Casting Aside Colonial Occupation: Intersections of Race, Sex, and Gender in *Cloud Nine* and *Cloud Nine* Criticism'. *Modern Drama* 42:1 (1999), 45–58.

Aston, E. 'Telling Feminist Tales: Caryl Churchill'. In *Feminist Views on the English Stage*. Cambridge: Cambridge University Press, 2003, 18–36.

'"A Licence to Kill": Caryl Churchill's Socialist–Feminist "Ideas of Nature"'. In Gabriella Giannachi and Nigel Stewart, eds., *Performing Nature: Explorations in Ecology and the Arts*. Bern, Peter Lang, 2005, 165–78.

Barnett, C. '"Revengeance is Gold Mine, Sweet": Alchemy and Archetypes in Caryl Churchill's *The Skriker*'. *Essays in Theatre/Etudes Théâtrales* 19:1 (2000), 45–57.

Bazin, V. '"[Not] Talking 'Bout My Generation": Historicizing Feminisms in Caryl Churchill's *Top Girls*'. *Studies in the Literary Imagination* 39:2 (Fall 2006), 115–34.

Brewer, M. 'Colonial Metaphors of Blackness and the Reality of White Racial Oppression: Caryl Churchill's *Cloud Nine*'. In *Staging Whiteness*. Middletown, CT: Wesleyan University Press, 2005, 136–142.

Burke, J. T. '*Top Girls* and the Politics of Representation'. In E. Donkin and S. Clement, eds., *Upstaging Big Daddy: Directing Theater as if Gender and Race Matter*. Ann Arbor: University of Michigan Press, 1993, 67–78.

Churchill, C. 'Not Ordinary, Not Safe: A Direction for Drama?' *The Twentieth Century* (November 1960), 443–51.

'Driven by Greed and Fear'. [on the City and *Serious Money*] *New Statesman* (17 July 1987), 10–11.

[on *Light Shining*]. In R. Ritchie, ed., *The Joint Stock Book: The Making of a Theatre Collective*. London: Methuen, 1987, 118–21.

Clum, J. M. 'The Plays of Caryl Churchill'. *Modern Drama* 38:1 (1995): 131–3.

Devlin, J. 'Joint Stock: From Colorless Company to Company of Color'. *Theater Topics* 2 (1992), 63–76.

Diamond, E. 'Refusing the Romanticism of Identity: Narrative Interventions in Churchill, Benmussa, Duras'. *Theatre Journal* 37:3 (October 1985), 273–86.

'Caryl Churchill's Plays: The *Gestus* of Invisibility'. In Elin Diamond, *Unmaking Mimesis: Essays on Feminism and Theater*, London: Routledge, 1997, 83–100.

'Caryl Churchill: Feeling Global'. In Mary Luckhurst, ed., *A Companion to Modern British and Irish Drama 1880–2005*. Oxford: Blackwell, 2006, 476–87.

Domvros, P. '"Alice Doesn't": Refusing the Seduction of the Narrative in Caryl Churchill's *Vinegar Tom*'. *Gramma: Journal of Theory and Criticism* 2 (1994), 47–60.

Dymkowski, C. 'Caryl Churchill: *Far Away* ... but Close to Home'. *European Journal of English Studies* 7:1 (2003), 55–68.

Edwardes, J. 'Celebrating Caryl Churchill'. With April de Angelis, Stella Feehily and Laura Wade. *Time Out* (14 November 2006). www.timeout.com/london/theatre/features/2259.html.

Evan, R. 'Women and Violence in *A Mouthful of Birds*'. *Theatre Journal* 54:2 (May 2002), 263–84.

Evenden, M. '"No Future without Marx": Dramaturgies of "The End of History" in Churchill, Brenton, and Barker'. *Theater* 29:3 (1999), 100–13.

Fitzsimmons, L. 'I Won't Turn Back for You or Anyone: Caryl Churchill's Socialist–Feminist Theatre'. *Essays in Theatre* 6:1 (November 1987), 19–29.

Gardner, J. E. 'Caryl Churchill's *Top Girls:* Defining and Reclaiming Feminism in Thatcher's Britain', *New England Theatre Journal* 10 (1999), 89–110.

Gray, F. 'Mirrors of Utopia: Caryl Churchill and Joint Stock'. In J. Acheson, ed., *British and Irish Drama Since 1960*. Basingstoke: Macmillan, 1993, 47–59.

'Caryl Churchill'. In J. Bull, ed., *British and Irish Dramatists since World War II*. Detroit, MI: Thomson Gale, 2005, 51–65.

Hammond, B. S. '"Is Everything History": Churchill, Barker and the Modern History Play'. *Comparative Drama*, 41:1 (2007), 1–23.

Hanna, G. ed. [for details of *Vinegar Tom* and *Floorshow*] in *Monstrous Regiment: A Collective Celebration*. London: Nick Hern Books, 1991.

Harding, J. M. 'Cloud Cover: (Re)Dressing Desire and Comfortable Subversions in Caryl Churchill's *Cloud Nine*'. *PMLA* 113:2 (March 1998), 258–72.

Innes, C. 'Caryl Churchill: Theatre as a Model for Change'. In *Modern British Drama 1890–1990*. Cambridge: Cambridge University Press, 1992, 460–72.

Itzin, C. 'Caryl Churchill'. In *Stages in the Revolution: Political Theatre in Britain Since 1968*. London: Methuen, 1980, 279–87.

Jernigan, D. '*Serious Money* Becomes "Business by Other Means": Caryl Churchill's Metatheatrical Subject'. *Comparative Drama* 38:2–3 (2004), 291–313.

'*Traps, Softcops, Blue Heart* and *This is a Chair*: Tracking Epistemological Upheaval in Caryl Churchill's Shorter Plays'. *Modern Drama* 47:1 (2004), 21–43.

Jung, W. 'Reading of a Post-Modern Feministic Body in *The Skriker*'. *Journal of Modern British and American Drama* 17:3 (2004), 181–208.

Keyssar, H. 'The Dramas of Caryl Churchill: The Politics of Possibility'. In *Feminist Theatre*. Basingstoke: Macmillan, 1984, 77–101.

Kintz, L. 'Performing Capital in Caryl Churchill's *Serious Money*'. *Theatre Journal* 51:3 (1999), 251–65.

Kritzer, A. H. 'Madness and Political Change in the Plays of Caryl Churchill'. In J. Redmond, *Madness in Drama*. Cambridge: Cambridge University Press, 1993, 203–16.

'Dionysus in Bucharest: Caryl Churchill's *Mad Forest*'. *In-Between: Essays and Studies in Literary Criticism* 4:2 (1995), 151–61.

'Caryl Churchill (1938–)'. In W. W. Demastes, ed., *British Playwrights, 1956–1995: A Research and Production Sourcebook*. Westport, CT: Greenwood, 1996, 107–18.

'Political Currents in Caryl Churchill's Plays at the Turn of the Millennium'. In M. Maufort and F. Bellarsi, eds., *Crucible of Cultures: Anglophone Drama at the Dawn of a New Millennium*. Brussels: Peter Lang, 2002, 57–68.

La Frenais, R. 'Midday Sun', *Performance* (June/July 1984), 7.

Lavell, I. 'Caryl Churchill's *The Hospital at the Time of the Revolution*'. *Modern Drama* 45:1 (Spring 2002), 76–94.

Lee, H-W. '"Playing a Role": Caryl Churchill's Theatrical Art and Political Art in *Cloud Nine*'. *The Journal of English Language and Literature* 40:4 (1994), 755–78.

Light, A. '*Mad Forest* (Royal Court Theatre, London)'. *Feminist Review* 39 (1991), 204–10.

Marohl, J. 'De-realised Women: Performance and Identity in *Top Girls*'. *Modern Drama* 30:3 (September 1987), 376–88.

Mitchell, T. 'Caryl Churchill's *Mad Forest:* Polyphonic Representations of Southeastern Europe'. *Modern Drama* 36:4 (December 1993), 499–511.

Müller, K. P. 'A Serious City Comedy: Fe-/Male History and Value Judgments in Caryl Churchill's *Serious Money*'. *Modern Drama* 33:3 (1990), 347–62.

Neblett, R. L. '"Nobody Sings About It": In Defense of the Songs in Caryl Churchill's *Vinegar Tom*'. *New England Theatre Journal* 14 (2003), 101–22.

Pocock, S. '"God's in this Apple": Eating and Spirituality in Churchill's *Light Shining in Buckinghamshire*'. *Modern Drama* 50:1 (Spring 2007), 60–76.

Quigley, A. E. 'Stereotype and Prototype: Character in the Plays of Caryl Churchill'. In E. Brater, ed., *Feminine Focus: The New Women Playwrights*. Oxford: Oxford University Press, 1989, 25–52.

Rabey, D. I. '*Mad Forest*'. *Theatre Research International* 17:1 (1992), 74–8.

Rabillard, S. 'Churchill's *Fen* and the Production of a Feminist Ecotheatre'. *Theater* 25:1 (1994), 62–71.

Ravenhill, M. 'She Made Us Raise Our Game'. *Guardian*, Arts Section (3 September 2008), 23.

Rebellato, D. 'The Personal Is Not Political: Caryl Churchill's *Drunk Enough to Say I Love You?*'. *Western European Stages* 19:1 (Winter 2007), 33–6.

Reinelt, J. 'Caryl Churchill: Socialist Feminism and Brechtian Dramaturgy'. In *After Brecht: British Epic Theater*. Ann Arbor: University of Michigan Press, 1994, 81–107.

'Caryl Churchill and the Politics of Style'. In E. Aston and J. Reinelt, eds., *The Cambridge Companion to Modern British Women Playwrights*. Cambridge: Cambridge University Press, 2000, 174–93.

Roberts, P. and M. Stafford-Clark. 'Case Study of *Cloud Nine*' and 'Case Study of *Serious Money*'. In *Taking Stock: The Theatre of Max Stafford-Clark*. London: Nick Hern Books, 2007, 68–96; 124–46.

Silverstein, M. '"Make Us the Women We Can't Be": *Cloud Nine* and the Female Imaginary'. *Journal of Dramatic Theory and Criticism* 8:2 (1994), 7–22.

'"My Skin Used to Wrap Me Up": Staging the Body in *A Mouthful of Birds*'. *Essays in Theatre/Etudes Théâtrales* 15:2 (1997), 177–90.

Solomon, A. 'Witches, Ranters and the Middle Class: The Plays of Caryl Churchill'. *Theater* 12:2 (1981), 49–55.

Soto-Morettini, D. 'Revolution and the Fatally Clever Smile: Caryl Churchill's *Mad Forest*'. *Journal of Dramatic Theory and Criticism* 9:1 (1994), 105–18.

Spink, I. 'Collaborations'. In *Border Tensions: Dance and Discourse, Proceedings of the Fifth Study of Dance Conference*. Department of Dance Studies: University of Surrey, 293–302.

Swanson, M. 'Mother/Daughter Relationships in Three Plays by Caryl Churchill'. *Theatre Studies* 31 (1986), 49–66.

Thomas, J. 'The Plays of Caryl Churchill: Essays in Refusal'. In A. Page, ed., *The Death of the Playwright?* Basingstoke: Macmillan, 1992, 160–85.

Wandor, M. 'Free Collective Bargaining' [on *Cloud Nine*]. *Time Out* (30 March–5 April 1979), 14–16.

'Existential Women: *Owners* and *Top Girls*'. In *Look Back in Gender: Sexuality and the Family in Post-War British Drama*. London: Methuen, 1987, 119–25.

'Biology and Property Values: *Owners*' and 'Utopias: *Cloud Nine*'. In *Post-War British Drama: Looking Back in Gender*. London: Routledge, 2001, 170–2; 181–5.

Waterman, D. 'Caryl Churchill's *Cloud Nine*: The Fiction of Race and Gender in a System of Power'. *Forum Modernes Theater* 14:1 (1999), 86–92.

Wilson, A. 'Hauntings: Ghosts and the Limits of Realism in *Cloud Nine* and *Fen* by Caryl Churchill'. In N. Boireau, ed., *Drama on Drama: Dimensions of Theatricality on the Contemporary British Stage*. New York: St Martin's, 1997, 152–67.

Yan, H. 'Staging Modern Vagrancy: Female Figures of Border-crossing in Ama Ata Aidoo and Caryl Churchill'. *Theatre Journal* 54:2 (May 2002), 245–62.

Yi, J. 'Envisioning Identities: Political and Theatrical Innovations in Caryl Churchill's *Top Girls*'. *Journal of Modern British and American Drama* 18:1 (2005), 141–68.

Web and media sources

Benedict, D. with L. Bassett, G. Cowley, D. Findlay and R. Fisher. 'Reputations: Caryl Churchill'. *Theatre Voice* (8 April 2005), www.theatrevoice.com/the_archive/.

Churchill, C. *The Legion Hall Bombing* [clips, 1978]. *BFI Screenonline* www.screenonline.org.uk/tv/id/557937/.

Interview [on *The Skriker*] *Late Theatre*, BBC2, January 1994.

The Skriker [video recording, 1994]. National Theatre Archive.

Top Girls. VHS video, Approaching Literature Series. Milton Keynes: Open University, 1996.

We Turned on the Light (synopsis), The Ashden Directory, www.ashdendirectory.org.uk.

Churchill, C. and I. Spink. *Fugue*. Channel 4, Dance-Lines, June 1988.

Omnibus: On Caryl Churchill. BBC1, November 1988.

Royal Court Theatre. *A Number*. Education Resources. http://www.royalcourttheatre.com/files/downloads/a_number_edupack.pdf.

INDEX

Cambridge Companions to...

AUTHORS

Edward Albee edited by Stephen J. Bottoms
Margaret Atwood edited by Coral Ann Howells
W. H. Auden edited by Stan Smith
Jane Austen edited by Edward Copeland and Juliet McMaster
Beckett edited by John Pilling
Aphra Behn edited by Derek Hughes and Janet Todd
Walter Benjamin edited by David S. Ferris
William Blake edited by Morris Eaves
Brecht edited by Peter Thomson and Glendyr Sacks (second edition)
The Brontës edited by Heather Glen
Frances Burney edited by Peter Sabor
Byron edited by Drummond Bone
Albert Camus edited by Edward J. Hughes
Willa Cather edited by Marilee Lindemann
Cervantes edited by Anthony J. Cascardi
Chaucer, second edition edited by Piero Boitani and Jill Mann
Chekhov edited by Vera Gottlieb and Paul Allain
Kate Chopin edited by Janet Beer
Caryl Churchill edited by Elaine Aston and Elin Diamond
Coleridge edited by Lucy Newlyn
Wilkie Collins edited by Jenny Bourne Taylor
Joseph Conrad edited by J. H. Stape
Dante edited by Rachel Jacoff (second edition)
Daniel Defoe edited by John Richetti
Don DeLillo edited by John N. Duvall
Charles Dickens edited by John O. Jordan
Emily Dickinson edited by Wendy Martin
John Donne edited by Achsah Guibbory
Dostoevskii edited by W. J. Leatherbarrow
Theodore Dreiser edited by Leonard Cassuto and Claire Virginia Eby
John Dryden edited by Steven N. Zwicker
W. E. B. Du Bois edited by Shamoon Zamir
George Eliot edited by George Levine
T. S. Eliot edited by A. David Moody
Ralph Ellison edited by Ross Posnock
Ralph Waldo Emerson edited by Joel Porte and Saundra Morris
William Faulkner edited by Philip M. Weinstein
Henry Fielding edited by Claude Rawson
F. Scott Fitzgerald edited by Ruth Prigozy
Flaubert edited by Timothy Unwin
E. M. Forster edited by David Bradshaw
Benjamin Franklin edited by Carla Mulford
Brian Friel edited by Anthony Roche
Robert Frost edited by Robert Faggen
Elizabeth Gaskell edited by Jill L. Matus
Goethe edited by Lesley Sharpe
Günter Grass edited by Stuart Taberner
Thomas Hardy edited by Dale Kramer
David Hare edited by Richard Boon
Nathaniel Hawthorne edited by Richard Millington
Seamus Heaney edited by Bernard O'Donoghue
Ernest Hemingway edited by Scott Donaldson
Homer edited by Robert Fowler
Horace edited by Stephen Harrison
Ibsen edited by James McFarlane
Henry James edited by Jonathan Freedman
Samuel Johnson edited by Greg Clingham
Ben Jonson edited by Richard Harp and Stanley Stewart
James Joyce edited by Derek Attridge (second edition)
Kafka edited by Julian Preece
Keats edited by Susan J. Wolfson
Lacan edited by Jean-Michel Rabaté
D. H. Lawrence edited by Anne Fernihough
Primo Levi edited by Robert Gordon
Lucretius edited by Stuart Gillespie and Philip Hardie
David Mamet edited by Christopher Bigsby
Thomas Mann edited by Ritchie Robertson
Christopher Marlowe edited by Patrick Cheney
Herman Melville edited by Robert S. Levine
Arthur Miller edited by Christopher Bigsby (second edition)
Milton edited by Dennis Danielson (second edition)
Molière edited by David Bradby and Andrew Calder
Toni Morrison edited by Justine Tally
Nabokov edited by Julian W. Connolly

Children's Literature edited by M. O. Grenby and Andrea Immel

The Classic Russian Novel edited by Malcolm V. Jones and Robin Feuer Miller

Contemporary Irish Poetry edited by Matthew Campbell

Crime Fiction edited by Martin Priestman

Early Modern Women's Writing edited by Laura Lunger Knoppers

The Eighteenth-Century Novel edited by John Richetti

Eighteenth-Century Poetry edited by John Sitter

English Literature, 1500–1600 edited by Arthur F. Kinney

English Literature, 1650–1740 edited by Steven N. Zwicker

English Literature, 1740–1830 edited by Thomas Keymer and Jon Mee

English Literature, 1830–1914 edited by Joanne Shattock

English Novelists edited by Adrian Poole

English Poets edited by Claude Rawson

English Poetry, Donne to Marvell edited by Thomas N. Corns

English Renaissance Drama, second edition edited by A. R. Braunmuller and Michael Hattaway

English Restoration Theatre edited by Deborah C. Payne Fisk

Feminist Literary Theory edited by Ellen Rooney

Fiction in the Romantic Period edited by Richard Maxwell and Katie Trumpener

The Fin de Siècle edited by Gail Marshall

The French Novel: from 1800 to the Present edited by Timothy Unwin

German Romanticism edited by Nicholas Saul

Gothic Fiction edited by Jerrold E. Hogle

The Greek and Roman Novel edited by Tim Whitmarsh

Greek and Roman Theatre edited by Marianne McDonald and J. Michael Walton

Greek Lyric edited by Felix Budelmann

Greek Mythology edited by Roger D. Woodard

Greek Tragedy edited by P. E. Easterling

The Harlem Renaissance edited by George Hutchinson

The Irish Novel edited by John Wilson Foster

The Italian Novel edited by Peter Bondanella and Andrea Ciccarelli

Jewish American Literature edited by Hana Wirth-Nesher and Michael P. Kramer

The Latin American Novel edited by Efraín Kristal

The Literature of the First World War edited by Vincent Sherry

The Literature of World War II edited by Marina MacKay

Literature on Screen edited by Deborah Cartmell and Imelda Whelehan

Medieval English Literature edited by Larry Scanlon

Medieval English Theatre edited by Richard Beadle and Alan J. Fletcher (second edition)

Medieval French Literature edited by Simon Gaunt and Sarah Kay

Medieval Romance edited by Roberta L. Krueger

Medieval Women's Writing edited by Carolyn Dinshaw and David Wallace

Modern American Culture edited by Christopher Bigsby

Modern British Women Playwrights edited by Elaine Aston and Janelle Reinelt

Modern French Culture edited by Nicholas Hewitt

Modern German Culture edited by Eva Kolinsky and Wilfried van der Will

The Modern German Novel edited by Graham Bartram

Modern Irish Culture edited by Joe Cleary and Claire Connolly

Modernism edited by Michael Levenson

The Modernist Novel edited by Morag Shiach

Modernist Poetry edited by Alex Davis and Lee M. Jenkins

Modern Italian Culture edited by Zygmunt G. Baranski and Rebecca J. West

Modern Latin American Culture edited by John King

Modern Russian Culture edited by Nicholas Rzhevsky

Modern Spanish Culture edited by David T. Gies

Narrative edited by David Herman

Native American Literature edited by Joy Porter and Kenneth M. Roemer

Nineteenth-Century American Women's Writing edited by Dale M. Bauer and Philip Gould

Old English Literature edited by Malcolm Godden and Michael Lapidge

Performance Studies edited by Tracy C. Davis

Postcolonial Literary Studies edited by Neil Lazarus

Postmodernism edited by Steven Connor

Renaissance Humanism edited by Jill Kraye

The Roman Historians edited by Andrew Feldherr

Roman Satire edited by Kirk Freudenburg

The Spanish Novel: from 1600 to the Present edited by Harriet Turner and Adelaida López de Martínez

Travel Writing edited by Peter Hulme and Tim Youngs

Twentieth-Century Irish Drama edited by Shaun Richards

The Twentieth-Century English Novel edited by Robert L. Caserio

Twentieth-Century English Poetry edited by Neil Corcoran

Victorian and Edwardian Theatre edited by Kerry Powell

The Victorian Novel edited by Deirdre David

Victorian Poetry edited by Joseph Bristow

War Writing edited by Kate McLoughlin

Writing of the English Revolution edited by N. H. Keeble